Praise for *Neither Snow nor Rain*

"Answers every question you've ever had ... Postal Service ... Surprises abound ... some early-20th-century families se ... ust to save on train fares?" —*Week*

"A good, quirky history book ... Lively, fu... Leonard delivers a lot here, and moves fast as he entertains ... Remember how exciting it was to get birthday cards in the mail? *Neither Snow nor Rain* is that much fun, and I think you'll enjoy it. If you're stamping around for something different to read, you'll love every letter." —*Journal Record*

"Surprisingly fascinating." —*Gist*

"A lively examination of America's most ubiquitous public institution ... Captivating and thoughtful." —*Washington Independent Review of Books*

"Leonard doesn't shrink from discussing the issues facing one of the nation's oldest services. He tosses in a fair amount of postal lore, and one doesn't have to be a history buff or a stamp collector to appreciate his tales ... A compelling [story] worth reading." —*Deseret News*

"Lively ... brisk [and] informative ... A spirited look at the business and impact of delivering mail." —*Kirkus Reviews*

"An engrossing account of a once-vital service that may soon be nothing more than a memory." —*Mental Floss* (25 Amazing New Books for Spring)

"[Leonard] has a zesty prose style, a great sense of humor, a fine eye for the telling anecdote and a lucid way of unraveling some of the controversies and challenges our postal service has faced in its 224 years of existence." —*Chicago Tribune*

"Devin Leonard's marvelous history of the United States Post Office recounts the American experience from a singular and highly entertaining angle. Along the way, you'll encounter a visionary founding father, glad-handing rogue politicians, terrified biplane pilots, firebrand union bosses, and children with postage attached to their overcoats mailed cross-country as parcel post. I dare you to put it down." —William J. Bernstein, author of *A Splendid Exchange* and *Masters of the Word*

"Devin Leonard has achieved something astonishing. He has taken the Post Office—too often disparaged as the carrier of 'snail mail' in this age of instant communication—and delivered a vivid and surprising story filled with indelibly drawn personalities including a founding father, an obsessive nineteenth-century smut-hunter, the swashbuckling pilots of the earliest, nearly suicidal airmail service, and many others. With crisp prose and unflagging narrative drive, Leonard reveals the forgotten history of the institution, and makes abundantly clear, the story of the Post Office is also the story of America." —Fergus M. Bordewich, author of *The First Congress: How James Madison, George Washington, and a Group of Extraordinary Men Invented the Government*

"Devin Leonard has given us a fast-moving, richly detailed portrait of the U.S. Postal Service—a system far more important to the country than is generally understood. Any devout fans of Cliff Clavin will be both proud and horrified by what Leonard unearths, but ultimately readers will be cautiously optimistic about this institution's future." —Brad Stone, author of *The Everything Store: Jeff Bezos and the Age of Amazon*

"A wonderfully written and insightful history of a great but beleaguered American institution. Devin Leonard brings the story of the Postal Service to life with memorable characters, from Benjamin

Franklin to Franklin Roosevelt and many others, with cameos from the likes of William Faulkner and Ethel Merman. Who knew that the Postal Service had such a colorful history? Luckily, Devin Leonard knew it, and now so do we."

—Terry Golway, author of *Machine Made: Tammany Hall and the Creation of Modern American Politics*

"In *Neither Snow nor Rain*, Devin Leonard tells the fascinating (yes, fascinating!) story of an endangered species, the US Postal Service. Leonard's well-told story, which shows that mail delivery is a critical part of a functioning civilization, will be eye-opening to those who think the USPS should go the way of the buggy whip."

—Bethany McLean, coauthor of *The Smartest Guys in the Room* and *All the Devils Are Here*

NEITHER
SNOW
NOR RAIN

A History of the
United States Postal Service

DEVIN LEONARD

Grove Press
New York

To Eileen, Colin, and Faith

"The postal establishment of the United States is the greatest business concern in the world. It handles more pieces, employs more men, spends more money, brings more revenue, uses more agencies, reaches more homes, involves more details and touches more interests than any other human organization, public or private, governmental or corporate . . . There are other nations that number more people. But there is none whose intercommunications, in area of sweep and magnitude of proportions, approaches the United States."

—Charles Emory Smith, U.S. Postmaster General, 1899

"No one really runs the Post Office."

—Winton Blount, U.S. Postmaster General, 1968

Contents

Prologue

Growing up in Queens, Evan Kalish didn't go to the post office very often. When he needed to send somebody something, he used his computer and later his iPhone. But everything changed after Kalish graduated from Brown University in 2008. He wanted to see the whole country and set off on a three-month road trip to Minnesota in his Toyota Camry. He took pictures of himself in front of post offices in every town he visited so he had proof that he had actually been to these out-of-the-way places, and he started sending letters to his friends while he was on the road. "I really got into it," he says.

The more post offices he visited, the more fascinated Kalish became. They were everywhere, and each one was different. When he returned to New York, Kalish was so inspired that he decided to visit every post office in America. It would take years, of course. There were 36,723 post offices in the United States. So what? Kalish would see the whole nation by the time he was through.

Kalish created a blog cheerfully entitled "Going Postal" and began to chronicle his travels on the Internet. He visited every post office in New York City and Long Island and most of the ones in northern New Jersey. He traveled I-95, snapping pictures of himself in front of post offices from Baltimore to Boston. Kalish swooned over the one in Nashville, the walls of which were decorated with hundreds of autographed photos of country music stars. He was charmed by a purple post office in Phillipsville, California, near the

Oregon border. He cultivated a palate for the stylish post offices constructed during the New Deal era, which often had splendid murals, some of them painted by famous American artists like Ben Shahn and Milton Avery. The murals turned Kalish's journey into a treasure hunt. "It's almost like the institution is a giant museum," Kalish says. "It's fun to try to see if you can find all the galleries."

Sometimes postmasters tried to chase Kalish away, saying that he had no right to take pictures of their buildings. What if he was a terrorist? Kalish responded that they couldn't hassle him as long as he was outside on public property. Others recognized Kalish from his blog and gave him tours, pulling old photographs from their filing cabinets to show him. Kalish made a lot of friends this way, which was nice for someone who could be rather shy.

By the end of 2010, Kalish had visited 1,561 post offices and had made an unexpected discovery: he wasn't alone. He met a man who had been to 20,000 post offices over the course of 40 years. He befriended two others who had each been to more than 10,000. Kalish went on a summer excursion with his fellow enthusiasts to visit post offices on islands off the coast of Maine. They chartered a boat and went to MacMahan Island. There are no roads on MacMahan Island, just unmarked trails. But there was a post office waiting for them. They took a ferry to Bustins Island to visit another one in a small yellow building along with the public library. "The ferry we happened to take was also the mail ferry!" Kalish wrote on his blog.

Kalish announced on "Going Postal" that he had been to another 1,253 post offices in 2011. But the more Kalish immersed himself in the infrastructure of the U.S. Postal Service, the more there was to see. He now understood that behind all of those post offices, there was a network of 461 processing plants, some with floors big enough to hold several football fields, through which millions of letters and packages flowed. He couldn't just walk into these places; they weren't public buildings. But with the help of his postal connections, he found people who let him in. Everywhere Kalish looked, he saw mail trucks and mailboxes. To think that he had spent most of his life oblivious of them all.

But Kalish needed to move quickly. The U.S. Postal Service was awash in red ink. In 2011, it revealed that it had lost $8.5 billion the year before. As people abandoned the mail, it wanted to close post offices, shutter processing plants, and shed employees. Kalish was working on a graduate degree in geospatial analysis at the University of Pennsylvania. He hung a map on the wall of his apartment showing Pennsylvania's endangered post offices in concentric circles. He didn't have classes from Friday until Monday evening. "I would take my car every weekend and visit clusters of them," Kalish says. "It was a race against the clock."

The U.S. Postal Service is a wondrous American creation. Six days a week, its 300,000 letter carriers deliver 513 million pieces of mail, more than 40 percent of the world's total volume. In parts of America that it can't reach by truck, the USPS finds other means to get people their letters and packages. It transports them by mule train to the Havasupai Indian Reservation at the bottom of the Grand Canyon. Bush pilots fly letters to the edges of Alaska. In thinly populated parts of Montana and North Dakota, the postal service has what it refers to as "shirt pocket" routes, which means that postal workers literally carry all their letters for the day in their shirt pockets. At a time when the USPS is losing several billion letters a year to the Internet, it still has to do this six days a week because it is legally required to provide universal service to every American home and business. Is it any wonder the USPS struggles to make money, even now that it also delivers packages on Sundays for Amazon?

People often talk about how the postal service is lumbering and inefficient compared with private sector competitors such as UPS and FedEx. But the USPS delivers more items in nine days than UPS does in a year. It transports more in seven days than FedEx brings to its customers in a year. In 2011, Oxford Strategic Consulting, an English firm, studied the postal services in developed countries and found that the USPS was by far the most efficient at handling letters, delivering 268,894 per employee—twice as many as the UK's Royal Mail and five times that of Germany's Deutsche Post. The USPS refers to the study proudly, though being the world's most efficient letter handler doesn't have the same cachet that it did a generation ago.

The USPS seems archaic in the age of Twitter, Facebook, Instagram, and Snapchat. But for much of its history, the American postal service has been at technology's sharpest edge. It developed a system of sorting mail on trains in the nineteenth century that was considered a wonder of the age. The U.S. Post Office Department, as it was once known, pioneered commercial aviation in the early twentieth century. In the 1950s, it created high-speed letter sorting machines with electric eyes that read zip codes and handwritten addresses. Postal services around the world use this technology now, but its slow deployment in America is a story that one long-serving deputy postmaster once confessed made him want to cry.

The USPS seems from the outside like a listless bureaucracy, full of people who have gravitated there for security, not because they are consumed with ambition. "Nobody aims to be a postal worker," says Orlando Gonzalez, a letter carrier and union organizer in New York. "That's not someone's goal. But I know countless people that have come here and stayed." It can be an insular place, suspicious of people and ideas from outside.

But fascinating people have passed through its ranks. Benjamin Franklin, America's first postmaster general, was only one of them. Long before Abraham Lincoln was president of the United States, he was the postmaster of New Salem, Illinois. Harry Truman held the title of postmaster of Grandview, Missouri. Walt Disney was a substitute carrier in Chicago. Bing Crosby was a clerk in Spokane, Washington. Rock Hudson delivered mail in Winnetka, Illinois. The mercurial jazz bassist and composer Charles Mingus toiled anonymously in post offices in Los Angeles and San Francisco before becoming famous in the 1950s. Four decades later, the USPS honored Mingus with his own stamp, but neglected to mention that he was a former employee.

Some famous postal workers didn't care for the job. The novelist William Faulkner, author of classics like *The Sound and the Fury* and *As I Lay Dying*, spent three years as postmaster at the University of Mississippi until he was forced to resign in 1924 for his obvious disinterest. A postal inspector furnished him with a long list of his transgressions, which included treating patrons rudely, failing to forward mail, and writing the greater part of one of his books while he was on duty. "I will be damned if I propose to be at the beck and call of every itinerant scoundrel who has two cents to invest in a postage stamp." Faulkner wrote in his letter of resignation. The scabrous author Charles Bukowski worked for the postal service as a substitute carrier. In his 1971 novel *Post Office*, Bukowski depicted the job in nightmarish terms. "Every route had its traps and only the regular carriers knew of them," he wrote. "Each day it was another god damned thing, and you were always ready for a rape, murder, dogs, or insanity of some sort. The regulars wouldn't tell you their secrets."

Like most large institutions, the USPS has a darker side. It has been plagued by racism and scandal. It has a shameful legacy of censorship, including banning material about birth control and novels like James Joyce's *Ulysses*. In the 1980s and 1990s, postal workers went berserk on the job, murdering their coworkers. For much of its history, postmasters and rural letter carriers were hired primarily because of their political connections, not for their qualifications. It was a system that made many uncomfortable, but it persisted until 1970.

At the same time, however, the postal service has been a beacon for generations of working-class Americans, a place where they could earn a paycheck and rise into the middle class. It was not uncommon for brothers and sisters, fathers and sons, mothers and daughters to spend their entire careers at the USPS. This was especially true for African Americans and Hispanics. They couldn't always find jobs in the private sector. But they knew there was always work for them at the post office. And Bukowski aside, a lot of people like working there. True, clerks who wait on us at the post office can seem perennially disaffected. "Why are they the way they are?" *Washington Post* columnist Mary McGrory asked in 1988. "Why are they so angry at us? Post offices have ropes to keep us in line. The clerks' faces tell us they wish we hadn't come. I wish they could realize that we have not come to cause them harm. All we want to do is send packages and buy commemoratives, which I enjoy—apparently more than I am supposed to."

Letter carriers, on the other hand, talk about how nice it is to leave the post office in the morning and be on their own for most of the day. Who hasn't secretly wanted to trade jobs on a warm spring day when we are stuck inside at our desks? Their mailbags may be much lighter these days, but they still have their junk mail or "job security," as letter carriers call it.

Perhaps more than anything else, the USPS reflects the changing way that Americans see their government. The country's founding fathers, among them Franklin and Washington, envisioned the postal service as a force that would bind Americans together, bringing them not only letters from friends and family members, but newspapers and magazines that would foster a common culture. "We are so diverse that only extraordinary means could have held us together when so many forces seemed designed to tear us apart," Lawrence O'Brien, Lyndon Johnson's postmaster general, said in an eloquent 1966 speech. "There are a number of reasons why the United States did not become the dis-United States and why we did not evolve into the North American Balkans. There are many factors that combined and unified America. The process was carried on silently, almost in secret, underneath the temporary upheavals in our history. It moved by a chain of paper that transported the elements of Americanism through thousands of miles, across mountains and desert, from city to frontier, a chain stretching into every clearing and valley. This link consisted of the postal service and the publications—magazines and newspapers—that provided a common store of images, of heroes, of folklore, of truth, and of inspiration and ideals."

In the late 1970s, American attitudes toward government and toward the USPS began to change. Even before the election of Ronald Reagan and the triumph of a new conservatism, lawmakers and their cheerleaders in the business community began speaking of the postal service as a threat. If left unchecked, they argued, the USPS would extend its tentacles into new forms of communication better handled by the private sector. Therefore, the USPS had to be reined in; but the more the USPS's foes restricted its operations, the more they laid the groundwork for the postal service's current crisis.

Now the USPS is slowly vanishing. It has sold off its historic post offices. It has closed processing plants. A decade and a half ago, the USPS employed 905,766 people; in 2014, it had a workforce of 617,877. But even as the USPS shrinks, its losses continue to swell. By its own calculations, it owed nearly $71 billion in mid-2015. The possibility of that money being repaid seems unlikely.

In other moments of crisis in the postal service's history, Congress has intervened to rescue it. Americans, after all, have depended on the postal service to bring them love letters, messages from family members in distant parts of the country, and newspapers that keep them connected to the rest of the world. Businesses have relied on the postal service to take bills to their customers and return with checks. Strange as this may sound, for most of its history, America could not have functioned without the USPS. "It is one of the biggest businesses in the country," President Harry Truman said in 1951. "And without it, the rest of the country would not be able to do business at all. Without the postal service all our activities would come to a standstill—business, national defense, family life, everything."

Today, nobody in Washington seems to possess the political will to save the U.S. Postal Service. Or perhaps the politicians simply don't care because the issue is no longer as relevant to their constituents. Republicans want the USPS to cut mail service and close more postal facilities. Otherwise, they argue, the postal service will require a taxpayer bailout. Democrats and their allies in the postal workers' unions accuse Republicans of exaggerating the agency's financial troubles because they want to destroy the government mail system. People in the technology industry say that the Internet is killing the USPS and that this is how it was meant to be, but the Internet may be the postal service's best hope.

1

The Founding Father

The placard above the door on Second Street in Philadelphia said "The Sign of the Bible." That was how Benjamin Franklin knew he was in the right place on a cool Monday morning in October 1723. The 17-year-old Franklin was a newcomer to the city. He had arrived the previous day after fleeing Boston, where he had worked as an apprentice in a printing shop run by his older brother, James. Benjamin didn't like taking orders from his sibling, nor did he appreciate it when James beat him for his insubordination. So Benjamin ran away, first to New York and then to Philadelphia, arriving by boat from Burlington, New Jersey. He had spent the night in a waterfront boardinghouse and had only a few coins left in his pocket. Now Benjamin Franklin needed a job.

This is what brought him to the doorstep of Andrew Bradford, Philadelphia's most prominent printer. The Sign of the Bible was his shop. He published the *American Weekly Mercury*, Philadelphia's first newspaper, and one that was circulated throughout the colonies. Bradford also operated a general store on the first floor of his Second Street house where customers could choose from whalebone, pickled sturgeon, silk clothing, and Spanish snuff, along with Bibles and other books that Bradford printed.

Bradford welcomed Franklin and offered him breakfast. He had no work for his visitor at the moment but said there might be an open apprenticeship at another printing shop. Franklin was grateful for the advice and the free meal, but he wasn't impressed with his host. Franklin would later write that he found Bradford "very illiterate." He was even more contemptuous of the *American Weekly Mercury*, which he described as "a paltry thing, wretchedly managed, no way entertaining, and yet was profitable to him." At the time, Franklin was a penniless, teenage runaway, but he thought he could do much better.

After working as an apprentice for five years, Franklin opened his own printing shop in Philadelphia. He ran a general store on the premises that competed with Bradford's, offering a more vast and eccentric selection, which, according to one of his biographers, included at various times soap, slates, pencils, ink, sealing wax, wafers, fountain pens, quills, inkhorns, chocolate, linseed oil, coffee, powdered mustard, compasses, scales, patent medicine, protractors, Rhode Island cheese and cod, white stockings, duck, barrels of mackerel, tea, saffron, spermaceti, and spectacles. In addition, Franklin acquired a paper called the *Pennsylvania Gazette*, which he transformed into a fierce competitor to the *American Weekly Mercury*.

Franklin may have been brighter than Bradford, but his rival was no fool. Bradford printed speeches and proclamations for the Pennsylvania and Maryland assemblies and paper money for New Jersey, and also used his government connections to secure an appointment as the postmaster of Philadelphia. The job didn't pay much; postmasters worked on commission, keeping 10 percent of the postage they collected from their customers. But publishers in colonial America eagerly accepted the position because it gave them a competitive advantage. As master of the local post, Bradford received a steady flow of free out-of-town newspapers, which provided him with material for the *Weekly Mercury*. It was common at the time for publishers to reprint entire articles from other papers without crediting them. The post office itself was a wellspring of news. People gathered there to gossip and trade information, furnishing more items for Bradford's paper. Best of all, postmasters controlled the circulation of newspapers in their regions. Bradford sent the *Weekly Mercury* through the mail at no cost and prohibited his riders from carrying the *Pennsylvania Gazette.*

How Franklin surmounted these obstacles and transformed the *Gazette* into the most widely read paper in the colonies is one of the most celebrated early American success stories. No one tells it with more wit and candor than Franklin himself in his autobiography. He put out a superior paper and ran his business more frugally than his competitor. He also understood that Bradford's postal riders were often in need of extra funds, so Franklin bribed them to carry his paper.

For Franklin, however, the final victory came when he pried the postmastership from his competitor's hands. In 1737, the British government removed Bradford because he had neglected to submit his financial reports for three years in a row, and it named Franklin as his successor. "I accepted it readily," Franklin wrote, "and found it of great advantage for, though the salary was small, it facilitated the correspondence that improved my newspaper, increased the number demanded, as well as the advertisements to be inserted, so that it came to afford me a considerable income. My old competitor's paper declined proportionately."

At first, Franklin allowed Bradford to send the *Weekly Mercury* through the mail, but he wasn't overly disappointed when the British told him to stop because Bradford hadn't paid his debts to the government from his time as postmaster. "He suffered greatly from his neglect in due accounting," Franklin wrote with evident satisfaction. "And I mention it as a lesson to those young men who may be employed in managing affairs for others, that they should always render accounts, and make remittances, with great clearness and punctuality." Franklin, on the other hand, was such a fastidious bookkeeper that in addition to his duties in Philadelphia, the British named him the comptroller of the entire colonial postal system, which meant that he kept track of the finances of 13 American post offices stretching for more than 1,500 miles of dirt roads from Portsmouth, New Hampshire; to Charleston, South Carolina.

In the years that followed, Franklin became famous for his experiments with electricity, his inventions, his political philosophizing, and his best-selling *Poor Richard's Almanack*. He did so well as a publisher that he was able to retire in 1748 from the day-to-day operation of his business and become a gentleman of leisure. But even then, Franklin kept his postal position. The job didn't require that much of his time, and it had its perks. As a postmaster, Franklin was entitled to "frank" letters, meaning he could send and receive them free—the term came from *francus*, the Latin word for free—enabling him to regularly exchange letters with intellectuals in Europe who publicized his achievements, thereby helping to make Franklin one of the world's most admired Americans. He inscribed his mail with his personal franking symbol: "Free. B. Franklin."

The job profoundly influenced Franklin's political thinking. He began to think of the colonies not as individual provinces but as parts of a potential nation bound together by shared institutions like the post office. But for this vision to become a reality, the fledgling postal service needed to be improved. The mail arrived once a week in Philadelphia, New York, and Boston in the summer and every other week in the winter if the weather permitted. The roads were especially bad in the South, making delivery even less predictable there.

In 1751, Franklin learned that Elliott Benger, the crown's deputy postmaster and the official in charge of the colonies, was ill and might die. Franklin began surreptitiously campaigning for his job. He wrote to a friend in London, asking him to lobby British postal officials on his behalf and gave him permission to spend up to £300 on any necessary greasing of palms. Franklin asked him to be discreet: "I would only add that, as I have respect for Mr. Benger, I should be glad the application were so managed as to not give him any offense if he should recover."

Benger held on for two more years, but when he finally died, Franklin got his job. Much to his dismay, he had to share the appointment and its £600 annual salary with William Hunter, another printer-postmaster from Virginia. However, the amiable Hunter generally deferred to Franklin so the arrangement worked well. Now Franklin had his chance to reconceive the colonial post. In doing so, he would lay the foundation for a system that would become the largest hard-copy delivery service the world has ever known.

Almost as soon as the written word appeared, people began sending mail. Archaeologists have determined that by 1900 BC, the ancient Assyrians had established one of the first postal services. Merchants used it to exchange messages written in cuneiform on tablets sealed in clay envelopes, and they trusted it enough to send each other currency. "I provided your agents with three minas of silver for the purchase of lead," one businessman wrote to another. "Now, if you are still my brother, let me have my money by courier."

Typically, however, ancient rulers didn't allow commoners to use their postal services. They reserved the post for their own use as a tool for controlling their subjects and consolidating their power. Two centuries later, the Egyptian pharaohs created a network of postal routes traveled by horsemen who carried messages written in hieroglyphs on papyrus to their princes and military leaders. Only the most highly born Egyptians could send mail through the official post. Merchants had to use slaves to deliver their messages.

King Darius of Persia, who reigned from c. 521 to 486 BC, presided over perhaps the most celebrated ancient postal system and used it to extend his power throughout the Middle East and into Asia. The king copied his orders onto wax-covered tablets using a metal stylus and entrusted them to his postmen, who were legendary for their efficiency. "Nothing mortal travels so fast as these Persian messengers," marveled the Greek historian Herodotus. "These men will not be hindered from accomplishing at their best speed the distance which they have to do, either by snow, or rain, or heat, or by darkness of night. The first rider delivers his dispatch to the second, and the second passes it to the third; and so it is borne from hand to hand along the whole line, like the light of the torch-race."

Do these lines sound familiar? They are nearly identical to those carved in stone above the entrance of the monumental James A. Farley Post Office in New York City designed by McKim, Mead & White and opened in 1914. William Mitchell Kendall, one of the firm's architects, read Greek for pleasure in his off-hours and selected a modified translation by Harvard professor George Herbert Palmer to adorn the building: "Neither snow nor rain nor heat nor gloom of night stays these couriers from the swift completion of their appointed rounds." Many have assumed that this is the motto of the U.S. Postal Service, but the USPS doesn't have one. It was just the world's largest postal service nodding respectfully to one of its most illustrious forbears.

The Romans improved on the Persian system after the founding of their empire in 27 BC, creating an imperial post that delivered letters written on papyrus and animal skins all the way from Britain to Constantinople on the empire's paved roads. The Roman couriers, easily identified by the emblems on their bronze shields, traveled in chariots, helping themselves to food and horses in the towns along the way. They also acted as the emperor's spies, fingering subversives and undesirables. Their targets, many of them early Christians, were sentenced to hard labor in post houses, cleaning the stables and performing other undesirable tasks. An early pope endured such punishment.

The demand for mail slackened in Europe after barbarians invaded Rome in AD 410. The Dark Ages, a time of almost universal illiteracy, engulfed the continent. Kings and queens couldn't read and bragged about it, but Catholic monks kept both the written word and mail delivery from vanishing entirely. They exchanged letters through foot posts, using messengers who strolled, or ran if necessary, from monastery to monastery with sacks of mail over their shoulders. And in the Middle East and China, where the written word flourished and paper was first used as a medium of correspondence, it was a golden age of mail delivery.

The Muslim caliphs established mail routes linking their cities, and in the ninth century, officials published the first written postal manual documenting how letters flowed through their system. "My throne rests on four pillars—a blameless judge, an energetic chief of police, an honest minister of finance, and a faithful postmaster who gives me reliable information on everything," said Caliph Abu Jafar Mansur, ruler of the Arabian Empire in the eighth century. And when Marco Polo visited China in the late thirteenth century, he was amazed by Emperor Kublai Khan's far-reaching postal service. The Chinese post riders carried Kublai Khan's proclamations and the state newspaper, the *Imperial Gazette*, on the nation's highways, stopping to rest and change horses at relay stations so elegantly furnished, it was said, that a prince would feel comfortable staying in one.

Once the Dark Ages ended, postal systems sprang up again in Europe. By 1297, the University of Paris had created one so that teachers and students could stay in touch with their families in distant parts of the continent. Knightly orders delivered letters to their armored members. Butchers who traveled throughout the northern part of the continent bore messages along with their meats. In London, foreign business owners, referred to as "strangers," transported mail over the oceans between London and seaports in other lands. This system was known appropriately as the Strangers' Post.

At the end of the fifteenth century, the Holy Roman Empire named Francis von Taxis of the Thurn and Taxis family as its first imperial postmaster. Francis and his relatives established a network of post houses from Vienna to the Netherlands. Their horn-blowing riders wore a strip of badger skin to identify themselves. At first, the Thurn and Taxis post handled only imperial correspondence, but when the empire complained about the system's cost, Francis persuaded his overlords to let him open it up to the commoners so their fees would cover its costs.

Other European posts went through similar transformations. In 1516, King Henry VIII of England called for the creation of his country's first national mail delivery service with postal stations "in all places most expedient." It would be called "the King's Posts," and Henry and his successors treated it as such. No letters traveled on Britain's postal roads without their approval and they probably knew the contents of every message. In England, as in other European countries, it was customary for postal officials to unseal mail and have a look.

In 1635, King Charles I of England opened the Royal Mail to the public. It charged by the number of sheets used and the distance traveled. It cost twopence to send a single sheet of paper within an 80-mile radius. The price was twice that for a "double letter" and three times as much for a "triple letter," and the charge rose if a letter traveled out of the first postal zone into another. The senders rarely paid for postage; it was the recipients who had to reach for their purses when they collected their mail at the post office. The Royal Mail didn't use stamps; clerks just jotted the fee on the outside of the letter. It was an expensive and cumbersome system, but the Royal Mail generated a surplus for the British government, which it used to help finance its military adventures around the world. As English citizens began to colonize the New World, the British hoped to make more money by starting a postal service there.

It wouldn't happen right away. Only a few thousand settlers lived on the eastern shore of the Atlantic coast in the early seventeenth century, and they were primarily interested in hearing from their friends and relatives in Europe. They entrusted their letters to the ship captains who crossed the ocean and received a penny a letter. The captains left pouches in taverns and coffeehouses in which letters could be deposited. People riffled through the same bags to see if any messages had arrived for them. The British government formalized the system in 1639, designating a tavern owned by Richard Fairbanks as the first colonial post office.

As their numbers increased, colonists needed to communicate with each other and created posts inland. In 1673, New York's governor Francis Lovelace established a monthly post between New York and Boston on a trail known as "the King's Highway." Today, it is part of U.S. Route 1. The same year, William Penn, the governor of Pennsylvania, established a post in his region connecting Philadelphia with cities in Delaware and Maryland. In the south, plantation owners set up their own system, using slaves to relay letters from plantation to plantation. If one of these planters failed to keep the mail moving, he forfeited a hogshead of tobacco.

In 1692, King William III awarded Thomas Neale an exclusive contract to establish a privately operated postal system throughout the colonies. Neale was an odd choice for such a venture. He was a swindler and a carouser who ingratiated himself with the royal family by staging the nightly games of chance for the king and his courtiers. He never set foot in the colonies himself, letting New Jersey governor Andrew Hamilton run it for him.

Hamilton quickly discovered that it wouldn't be easy. In a dispute that foreshadowed future hostilities between the crown and its American subjects, Virginia and Maryland refused to participate, saying it was unfair for the king to make his colonial subjects pay Neale for mail delivery when they could do it themselves. The Neale post ultimately failed, and its namesake died heavily in debt in 1699. After that, the crown assumed control of the system and forced the colonies to go along. In 1729, its users could expect weekly mail delivery at 13 American post offices, the largest of which could be found in Boston, New York, and Philadelphia.

That was progress, but the colonial post was still primitive compared with those in Europe. Riders carried mail on dirt paths through wilderness where there were more wolves and bears than people. Ferrymen made them wait for hours while they filled their boats with other customers before taking the couriers across rivers. Mail carriers didn't make much money and supplemented their incomes by running errands for people. In one instance, a rider in New England brought a herd of oxen to a farmer, which must have meant some of his letters didn't arrive on time. Native Americans sometimes attacked colonial postmen; at other times, indigenous people competed with them. The "savages" knew the territory better than their white counterparts and provided faster service.

Early colonial postmasters endured their own hardships. They typically ran their post offices out of their homes and had to live with customers showing up at all hours seeking mail. Their patrons kept charge accounts, and it could take a while for them to pay up. One indignant New Jersey postmaster took out an advertisement in a local paper, demanding overdue postage from customers, some of whom hadn't paid him in nearly four years: "This is to give notice that all persons in town and country that are indebted to Andrew Hay, postmaster at Perth Amboy, for postage of letters, to pay the same or they may expect trouble."

Future postmaster generals would joke that that Franklin set a bad example for them by dispensing jobs within the colonial post office to many of his relatives. His illegitimate son, William, replaced him as Philadelphia's postmaster. A year later, Franklin promoted William to comptroller of the colonial post and gave the city postmastership to one of his wife Deborah's relatives. Franklin found jobs in other towns for two of his brothers, a nephew, and two more of Deborah's family members. Richard Bache, his daughter Sally's fiancé, pleaded for a postal position, but Franklin refused him at first, believing Bache to be a fortune hunter. Eventually even Bache was hired after marrying into the family.

Despite his weakness for hiring family members, Franklin vastly improved the system. He had little choice if he wanted to get paid. The crown promised Franklin and William Hunter, his fellow deputy, that they could split an annual salary of £600, the equivalent of $182,000 today. But the money was not guaranteed; the two men would have to take it from the colonial post's profits, if there ever were any. It had lost money ever since the days of Thomas Neale.

So, even before their appointments officially went into effect in 1753, Franklin and Hunter embarked on an inspection tour, spending much of the next year visiting post offices and surveying postal routes from Maine to Virginia. They came up with better routes, avoiding river crossings where surly ferrymen impeded the progress of their riders. As a result, the system's users enjoyed faster delivery. They cut the time it took for a letter to travel from Philadelphia to New York to a day and a half. Where once it had taken six weeks for a Philadelphian to send a letter to a Bostonian and receive a response, now the circular exchange took only three weeks. Already, Franklin was drawing Americans more closely together through the post.

Franklin created the Dead Letter Office in Philadelphia, which became a repository for unclaimed messages. He started a penny post in Philadelphia, enabling residents to receive their mail at home for an extra penny if they didn't want to journey to the post office to pick it up themselves. Franklin encouraged his postmasters to circulate all sorts of newspapers. The European posts didn't do that, but Franklin was fashioning a distinctly American one,

Somebody had to pay for these improvements. Franklin and Hunter borrowed £900 to cover their costs, but their investment paid off. In 1760, the colonial post generated its first surplus, and the two deputy postmasters were able to collect their salaries. Franklin thought it would do even better if he lowered postage rates, which he believed would spur people to send more mail. The crown reduced the rates for longer distances but kept the local rates in place.

Franklin now spent most of his time in England, where he lobbied the British government on behalf of the Pennsylvania assembly, trying to win it more control over the state's affairs. He left the daily operations of the colonial postal service to a protégé, James Parker, another publisher turned postmaster. But Franklin stayed in close touch with Parker and kept track of the postal service's finances. The British government didn't seem to have a problem with the long-distance arrangement, reappointing Franklin and Hunter to their positions and praising their stewardship.

Hunter died in 1761 just months after receiving his salary. Franklin wrote fondly of his late partner, saying that they had worked in "perfect harmony," but he longed to run the colonial post by himself and pocket the full £600. Instead, the crown named John Foxcroft, another Virginian, to be his partner. The diplomatic Franklin made the best of it, returning to America and traveling with him from Maine to Virginia, looking for new ways to improve the system. They decided to have riders carry mail at night as well as by day, which meant that a Philadelphian could send a letter to Boston and receive a reply in six days. Philadelphians could send a letter to New York and get a response in 24 hours. When the British took control of Canada in 1763 at the end of the French and Indian War, Franklin and Foxcroft supervised the creation of a postal road from Albany, New York, to Montreal.

Then Franklin returned to London, where he stayed for another ten years, representing a growing number of state assemblies in their increasingly tense dealings with Parliament. Even then, Franklin still audited the financial statements of the colonial post and handled complaints. American postmasters requested a shipment of bugles, certain that their riders would collect more letters if they could announce their arrival with the blast of a shiny horn. Franklin took up the matter with the British authorities, but the Royal Mail said the Americans should buy their own bugles.

As the relationship between England and the colonies deteriorated, Franklin feared he would lose his position. Lord Sandwich, the crown's postmaster general, disapproved of Franklin's pro-American sympathies and asked how Franklin could run the colonial post when he spent all his time in England. Franklin responded that there were plenty of Americans in London with similar appointments who rarely went home. "It is the practice in many other instances to allow the non-residence of American officers who spend their salaries here, provided care is taken that the business be done by a deputy or otherwise," Franklin wrote to his son William.

Franklin had given up his publishing business long ago and needed his postal income more than ever. "If I should lose the post office, which among the many changes here, is far from being unlikely, we should be reduced to our rents and interest of money for subsistence, which will by no means afford the chargeable housekeeping and entertainments we have been used to," Franklin wrote to his wife. "For my own part, I live here as frugally as possible not to be destitute of the comforts of life, making no dinners for anybody, and contenting myself with a single dish when I dine at home and yet such is the dearness of living here in every article, that my expenses amaze me."

Unflattering stories about Franklin appeared in the English press. He was sure that his enemies were planting them to force him to resign as deputy postmaster, but he refused to give them satisfaction. "In this they are not likely to succeed, I being deficient in that Christian Virtue of Resignation," Franklin wrote to his sister, Jane. "If they would have my Office, they must take it. I have heard of some great Man whose Rule it was, with regard to Offices, *never to ask for them, and never to refuse them*; to which I have always added, in my own Practice, *never to resign them.*"

However, Franklin's loyalty to his fellow Americans was too strong. He fought the Stamp Act, a tax on colonial newspapers and legal documents that had nothing to do with the colonial post. He sealed his fate in 1772 when he shared letters written by Thomas Hutchinson, the governor of Massachusetts, with a friend who leaked them to the *Boston Gazette*. In his private correspondence, Hutchinson mocked his subjects and called for the British to send more troops to Massachusetts to punish the more radical ones. The Massachusetts assembly called for Hutchinson's resignation. Franklin confessed to his role in making the letters public, and he was removed from the colonial post.

Franklin was furious. As far as he was concerned, he had transformed the colonial post from a money-losing operation to a steady source of income for the crown, and this was the thanks he received? Now that he had been dismissed, Franklin warned that Americans could expect British postal officials to routinely open and read their letters just as they did with their subjects at home. "How safe the correspondence of your Assembly committees along the continent will be through the hands of such officers may be worth consideration," he wrote, "especially as the post office act of Parliament allows a postmaster to open letters."

Franklin's removal reverberated in the colonies. The insurgent Sons of Liberty accosted postal riders and relieved them of their pouches. William Goddard, a virulently anti-British newspaper publisher, took the postal rebellion further. He had been forced to set up his own private delivery network to distribute his paper, the *Pennsylvania Chronicle*, because it was too incendiary for the official mail. Now Goddard converted it into the Constitutional Post, a competing service that picked up and delivered mail at 30 of its own post offices between Virginia and New Hampshire. He persuaded state assemblies to adopt his operation, promoting it as "the New American Post Office." Tired of the British-controlled colonial post, the states embraced the Constitutional Post. "The people never liked the institution," wrote one of Goddard's supporters, "and only acquiesced in it out of their unbounded affection for the person [Franklin] that held the office and who had taken infinite pains to render it convenient."

The Revolutionary War began on April 19, 1775 with the battles of Lexington and Concord, and the following month, the Second Continental Congress convened in Philadelphia to discuss the creation of an American state. The delegates drew up a plan to convert the Constitutional Post into the official American post office and selected Franklin to be its postmaster general at a salary of $1,000 a year or the equivalent of $30,000 today; Franklin donated the money to wounded American soldiers. His son-in-law Richard Bache became his comptroller, and Goddard accepted an appointment as surveyor of postal roads. On Christmas Day, the British disbanded the old colonial post, and Franklin presided over North America's primary communications channel, headquartered in Philadelphia and reaching from Falmouth, Maine; to Savannah, Georgia. Now, when Franklin franked his mail, he mischievously replaced his familiar "Free, B. Franklin" with the most appropriate "B. free Franklin."

On July 4, 1776, America's founding fathers declared independence from Great Britain. This made Franklin the new nation's first postmaster general. That fall, however, he departed for France to serve as America's ambassador to the court of King Louis XVI. Franklin arranged for his son-in-law to succeed him as postmaster general, much to the disappointment of Goddard, who thought *he* was the father of the American postal service and deserved the job more. After all, what had Richard Bache done to deserve such an honor, other than marrying Franklin's daughter? For his part, Bache blamed Goddard when there was a breakdown in mail delivery between Congress and General George Washington. "As he had frequently threatened to resign his office, I thought this was a proper time to do it," Bache wrote. Goddard departed and bore a grudge against the Franklin family until his death.

In France, Benjamin Franklin became a celebrity, sporting a fur cap in the streets of Paris and cultivating an image for himself as a wise frontiersman, even though he had always been a city dweller. But what was happening with the post office back home in America troubled him. In 1782, the Continental Congress removed Bache as postmaster general, replacing him with Ebenezer Hazard, the former postmaster of New York. Franklin was still annoyed about this when he returned to Philadelphia after the war ended in 1785. As the father of the American post office, he felt that the department was still his and that his son-in-law and chosen successor was entitled to the top job.

The loss of his beloved frank mail privileges exacerbated the insult. Franklin complained that even the British hadn't treated him so shabbily. "When the English ministry formerly thought fit to deprive me of the office," he wrote, "they left me, however, the privilege of receiving and sending my letters free of postage, which is the usage when the postmaster is not displaced for misconduct in the office, but in America, I have ever since had postage demanded of me, which since my return from France, has amounted to above fifty pounds, much of it occasioned by my having acted as a minster there."

Franklin was now an elderly man. Still, at the age of 81, he went to the Constitutional Convention in Philadelphia in 1787. He was the oldest delegate and dozed through many of the debates, but his presence elevated the historic event. "The most single-minded politicians could never long forget that there was a philosopher among them, incomparably able, when he chose, to speak with large wisdom, the pleasantest humor, and a happy grace," his biographer Carl Van Doren writes. The resulting document gave Congress the power to establish post offices and post roads, but it didn't say anything more about the mail.

In 1790, Franklin passed away in his Philadelphia home. He achieved much as an inventor, a writer, a philosopher, and an architect of a new American nation. He was surely proud of the postal service he had nurtured too. It operated 75 post offices and transported 265,545 letters on 1,875 miles of post roads extending in an unbroken line along the Atlantic coast. There was also a western artery: a post road from Philadelphia to Pittsburgh. Waves of settlers were venturing deeper into the American interior in search of cheap land and economic opportunity. Would the General Post Office, as it was now known, follow these pioneers?

George Washington, the Revolutionary War general who was elected America's first president in 1789, believed that the United States needed a far-reaching post office, and needed it immediately. Washington owned 50,000 acres of land in western Virginia and Maryland. As he rode through his property, it troubled him to discover how tenuously the settlers there were connected to the new nation. Washington feared they would fall under the sway of the Spanish, who controlled the territories beyond the Mississippi River, or the English, who still held Canada. "The Western settlers (I speak now from my own observation) stand as it were upon a pivot," Washington wrote. "The touch of a feather, would turn them any way."

Washington was convinced that a strong central government would keep the young nation from fraying. He wanted to create an American university where people from around the country could study and share ideas. He wanted to create a standing military in which Americans could serve together. He also asked Congress to pass legislation creating a strong post office. Like Franklin, Washington wanted the postal service to be a force that promoted enlightenment, circulating newspapers and political documents that would guard the public from tyrants and demagogues spreading misinformation.

Not everybody shared Washington's vision. Secretary of State Thomas Jefferson and his supporters feared that the president was constructing a massive federal system that would be as oppressive as European monarchies. The postal service continued to operate under temporary legislation, but Congress didn't create a lasting operation until 1792. The debate showed how conflicted Americans remained about the nature of the federal government.

In the House of Representatives, some members predicted that the post office would be a dangerous force, spying on the public like the French and British posts and meddling in politics. "It is easy to see what hand could be made of the post offices, if ever they are under the direction of an improper person," argued Alexander White, a congressman from Virginia. "At the time of a general election, for instance, how easy would it be for this man to dictate to particular towns and villages, 'If you do not send such a man to Congress, you should have no post office; but if you elect my friend, you should have a post office and the roads should run agreeably to your wishes.'" Others feared that the postmaster general and his deputies would knock down buildings if they stood in the way of prospective postal roads and would abolish tolls and turnpikes and build new ferry landings beside existing ones that had been operating for decades, putting them out of business. To prevent that, Congress retained the power to select the locations of post offices and postal roads, rather than granting it to the postmaster general. Anyone who opened mail outside the Dead Letter Office would be fined $100, and mail robbers could expect the death penalty.

There was another emotional debate about how much the Post Office should charge for delivering newspapers. Elbridge Gerry, a congressman from Massachusetts, thought that newspapers were so important to the well-being of the young nation that they should be carried for no charge. "Wherever information is freely circulated, there slavery cannot exist," Gerry argued. "Or if it does, it will vanish as soon as information has been generally diffused." The majority of his colleagues disagreed, saying the Post Office needed to charge something to defray its delivery costs. In the end, Congress set a nominal rate of one cent for newspapers traveling less than 100 miles and one and a half cents for those going farther.

The cheap newspaper rates meant that the General Post Office needed to charge much more for letters if it was going to break even. It set a six-cent rate for a letter sent less than 30 miles, and the rates rose steadily after that, reaching 25 cents for letters traveling more than 450 miles. The rates doubled if a sender used two sheets of paper and tripled if he used three. To make sure that citizens didn't try to circumvent the system and send messages more cheaply through private carriers, a persistent problem in Franklin's time, Congress mandated that nobody but government postal workers and the riders and stagecoach drivers they hired could transport letters. Anybody who set up a competing "foot or horse post" would be severely fined.

Six cents was a lot of money at a time when the average daily wage for an American was 50 cents. Like Franklin, most people in the federal government did not want to pay those prices. So Congress permitted a long list of officials to frank their mail, including the president, the vice president, members of the House and Senate, the secretary of state, the secretary of war, the secretary of the treasury, and the postmaster general himself, of course. The list would grow over the years to include ex-presidents and ex-vice presidents and their spouses as well.

Washington signed the landmark postal act in February 1792. Within a few years, the General Post Office was delivering mail in new states like Vermont, Kentucky, and Tennessee. Settlers on the western frontier inundated Congress with petitions pleading for post offices so they, too, could receive mail. By the turn of the century, there were 903 post offices and 20,817 miles of post roads in the United States, a phenomenal increase in less than a decade.

The post offices' rapid growth did little to mollify lawmakers who still feared the government was creating a leviathan in the General Post Office. Vice President Thomas Jefferson lamented to his ally James Madison in 1798 that the federal government had the right to "go to cutting down mountains" if they impeded mail routes. Jefferson warned that politicians would fill the General Post Office with their supporters. "I view it as a source of boundless patronage to the executive, jobbing to members of Congress and their friends, and a boundless abyss of public money," he wrote to Madison. "You will begin by only appropriating the surplus of the post office revenues, but the other revenues will soon be called into their aid, and it will be a scene of eternal scramble among the members, who can get the most money wasted in their State; and they will always get most who are meanest."

Yet Jefferson didn't curtail the Post Office's expansion when he became president in 1801. By the end of his first term, the Post Office extended from Washington to Chicago and employed two men that it described as "faithful, enterprising, hardy young woodsmen" to carry mail from Cleveland to Detroit. Delivery times were improving too. "To write from Portland (Maine) to Savanna and receive an answer back required at the beginning of the century 40 days; now only 27 are necessary," Postmaster General Gideon Granger boasted in a report to Congress. "For the same purpose, between Philadelphia and Lexington (Kentucky) 32 days were formerly needed, now only 16. Between Philadelphia and Nashville formerly 44 days, now only 30."

However, Granger wanted to make sure that the postal service wasn't used for what he considered to be sinister purposes. He urged Congress to pass a law forbidding anyone but a "free white person" to carry mail. He worried that if American blacks—whether enslaved or free—learned to send each other messages, they would rise up against their white masters just as blacks had done a decade before in Santo Domingo, a rebellion that led to the founding of an independent Haiti.

In a letter to the Senate, Granger laid out his vision of what would happen if Congress failed to act. "The most active and intelligent [blacks] are employed as post-riders," he wrote. "These are the most ready to learn, and the most able to execute. By travelling from day to day, and hourly mixing with people they must, they will acquire information. They will learn that a man's rights do not depend on his color. They will, in time, become teachers to their brethren. They will become acquainted with each other on the line. Whenever the body, or portion of them, wish to act, they are an organized corps, circulating our intelligence openly, their own privately. Their traveling creates no suspicion, excites no alarm. One able man among them, perceiving the value of this machine might lay a plan which would be communicated by your post-riders from town to town, and produce a general and united operation against you. It is easier to prevent the evil than to cure it." Congress heeded Granger's warning and banned all blacks from carrying mail. It would take a war between the North and the South to lift it.

2

Interlopers I

In December 1831, two unhappy Frenchmen could be seen trudging through the snow with their luggage on the bank of the Ohio River in Kentucky. The French political philosopher Alexis de Tocqueville and his companion, Gustave de Beaumont, had hoped to travel from Pittsburgh to New Orleans on *The Fourth of July*, a patriotically named steamboat. But the temperature plunged below zero, and *The Fourth of July* became lodged in the ice on the Ohio River outside of Cincinnati and could go no farther. So Tocqueville and Beaumont disembarked and walked 25 miles in cold that Tocqueville described as "Siberian" to Louisville, Kentucky, where they arranged to travel in an open mail cart to Memphis, Tennessee.

Tocqueville recounted the bumpy ride in his *Democracy in America*, still considered one of the most insightful and prescient books about the United States. "Day and night we passed with great rapidity along the roads, which were scarcely marked through immense forests," Tocqueville wrote. "When the gloom of the woods became impenetrable, the driver lighted branches of pine, and we journeyed along by the light they cast. From time to time, we came to a hut in the midst of the forest; this was a post-office. The mail dropped an enormous bundle of letters at the door of this isolated dwelling, and we pursued our way at full gallop, leaving the inhabitants of the neighboring log houses to send for their share of the treasure."

Tocqueville described the American postal service as "the great link between minds." The settlers in these woods, he observed, lived in rude wooden cabins, with a bed, a few chairs, a gun, and often a slave. But they almost always had a freshly published newspaper to read. "It's difficult to imagine the incredible rapidity with which thought circulates in the midst of these deserts," Tocqueville wrote. "I do not think that so much intellectual activity exists in the most enlightened and populous district in France." For Tocqueville, the postal service was a distinctly American phenomenon, something that made the embryonic nation different from its older cousins across the Atlantic.

The General Post Office was indeed a marvel of its time. It now operated 8,686 post offices; this was twice as many as Great Britain, which had roughly the same number of citizens as the United States. It was five times as many as France, which had a larger population than the United States. The American Post Office used private contractors to transport mail by horseback, stagecoach, steamboat, and three-wheeled sulky over 116,000 miles of post roads, and often generated a yearly surplus.

Granted, many things about the General Post Office hadn't changed since Franklin's time. It didn't provide much in the way of home delivery, which meant that people had to visit the post office if they wanted their mail. Americans still didn't use stamps or envelopes. Most postmasters ran their operations out of their homes. This was true even in New York in the 1820s, when Theodorus Bailey, the city's postmaster, padded downstairs every morning in his bathrobe and slippers to say hello to his clerks before eating breakfast with his family.

But whether Tocqueville realized it or not, he was witnessing an institution in the throes of one of the most significant changes in its history. President Andrew Jackson, whom Tocqueville described as "a man of violent temper and very moderate talents," had come to Washington two years earlier determined to cleanse the federal government of Republicans and Federalists and replace them with members of his own party. This was the beginning of the modern patronage-based political party system. Jackson got rid of many people at the General Post Office, which employed 8,764 postmasters whose ranks outnumbered the country's 6,332 soldiers in the early years of his presidency.

At a meeting at the White House, John McLean, the highly regarded sitting postmaster general, who had been appointed by James Monroe, objected to Jackson's demand to fire several of his deputies because they weren't Democrats. Jackson rose from his chair and paced the room with his clay pipe in his mouth. Finally, he turned and said, "Mr. McLean, will you accept a seat upon the bench of the Supreme Court?" McLean went on to distinguish himself on the high court.

With McLean out of his way, Jackson named William Barry, a former lieutenant governor of Kentucky, as the new postmaster general and moved the position from the Treasury Department into his cabinet so he would have more control over what was now known as the U.S. Post Office Department. Jackson also fired a large number of its employees. Not all of them went quietly. One night General Solomon Van Rensselaer, the postmaster of Albany, New York, and a hero of the War of 1812, showed up at the White House after learning that he would be removed from his position because he was a Federalist. Van Rensselaer waited patiently until Jackson finished with a reception. Then he confronted the president. "General Jackson, I have come here to talk to you about my office," Van Rensselaer said. "The politicians want to take it away from me, and they know I have nothing else to live upon."

When Jackson ignored him, Van Rensselaer began to disrobe. That got Jackson's attention. "What in Heaven's name are you going to do?" Jackson asked. "Why do you take off your coat here?"

"Well, sir, I am going to show you my wounds, which I received in fighting for my country against the English!"

"Put it on at once, sir!" Jackson said. "I am surprised that a man of your age should make such an exhibition of himself."

The following day, Jackson told his aides that Van Rensselaer would keep his position. "I take the consequences sir; I take the consequences," Jackson said. "By the Eternal! I will not remove the old man—I cannot remove him. Why . . . did you know that he carries more than a pound of British lead in his body?"

But as the Post Office became most politicized, there were predictably scandals. Barry, the new postmaster general, awarded stagecoach contracts to the administration's allies, and resigned in 1835 to avoid impeachment. Jackson replaced him with Amos Kendall, a former newspaper publisher and one of his chief political advisers. Kendall ran the Post Office more ably, but he too became engulfed in controversy. He will be forever remembered for trying to ban abolitionist literature from the mail. Within months of his appointment, the New York–based American Anti-Slavery Society flooded southern post offices with its newspapers addressed to politicians, businessmen, and ministers, an effort that has been called the first direct mail campaign. A mob broke into the post office in Charleston, South Carolina, seized a sack of the papers, and burned it that night at a rally. In other southern cities, citizens marched in torch-lit parades, protesting the northern mailers.

Rather than jailing the mail robbers, Kendall condemned the American Anti-Slavery Society, accusing it of using the public mails to spark a race war by disseminating "large masses of newspapers, pamphlets, tracts and almanacs, containing exaggerated, and in some instances, false accounts of the treatment of slaves, illustrated with cuts, calculated to operate on the passions of the colored men, and produce discontent, assassination, and servile war." Kendall called for a federal law banning such literature from the mail. Jackson endorsed the idea, calling the abolitionist mailing "a wicked plan of exciting the Negroes to insurrection and to massacre." But Congress rejected the proposal, calling it unconstitutional, and even southern senators, happy to let individual states block such material from the mail, objected to granting the federal government such broad censorship powers.

The Post Office weathered these crises. The greater threat to its survival was the public's dissatisfaction with high postage rates. But in 1837, America was shaken by an economic panic. Banks failed along with many businesses they supported. In such a climate, people went to great lengths to avoid paying to send letters. They often mailed sheets of paper with short coded messages on the outside that recipients could quickly read and return without being charged. They created secret messages by circling words on the front pages of newspapers and mailing them to friends.

An easier way to send a letter cheaply was to bypass the Post Office altogether. It wasn't uncommon to see people at steamboat wharves and train stations asking strangers bound for other cities to take their letters. Some realized that there was money to be made by doing this. When the Post Office discovered what they were up to, it arrested the interlopers. After all, the law forbade anyone to start a competing horse or foot post. But that didn't stop the exodus of mail from the system. The only thing that could save the Post Office Department was a radical reform that it vehemently opposed.

The Tontine Reading Room at the corner of Wall and Water streets in Manhattan had long been a gathering place where bankers, stock-brokers and others in the financial industry traded stock tips over coffee. Alexander Hamilton, the secretary of the treasury, had met there with his Federalist allies. Some said that the New York Stock Exchange was founded at the three-story building in 1792 rather than under a nearby buttonwood tree, as legend has it.

One day in 1838, William Harnden, a frail high-strung 26-year-old with dark hair and extravagant sideburns, wandered into the Reading Room. He seemed out of place among the regulars. He came from a small town north of Boston. Harnden had previously worked as a conductor and ticket salesman on the Boston & Worcester Railroad, one of America's earliest train lines, but the long shifts had become too much for him. Harnden quit and drifted to New York.

One day, Harnden confided to James Hale, the Reading Room's genial proprietor, that he needed to find work. Hale had a suggestion. He sold tickets for the *John W. Richmond*, a steamship that traveled between New York and Providence. His customers frequently asked if Hale could get a passenger to carry their letters to Providence or Boston. "I immediately advised him to travel between the two cities and do errands for the business men," Hale later recalled. "I also suggested that the new enterprise should be called 'The Express,' which gave the idea of speed, promptitude, and fidelity."

Harnden came up with a professional-sounding advertisement that he placed in the *New York Evening Post*: "IMPORTANT TO MERCHANTS, BROKERS, BOOK-SELLERS AND ALL BUSINESS MEN," it declared. "Wm. F. Harnden having made arrangements with the New York and Boston Transportation and Stonington and Providence Rail Road Companies, will run a car through daily from Boston and New York and visa versa, for the purpose of carrying specie, package of goods, small bundles, mail, and be early the following morning in any part of the city, free of charge. Responsible agents will accompany the car for the purpose of collecting drafts, notes and bills, and will transact any other businesses that may be entrusted to his care."

The advertisement, as one period writer put it, was "an elegant fiction." Harnden had no railroad car, just a seat on the train and a carpetbag in which he carried his customers' goods, and not many at first. He showed up one day at the Reading Room ready to give up. "I can't make it go," Harnden said, slamming his fist on the counter. Hale calmed him down and told him that the Cunard steamship company would soon begin carrying passengers between Liverpool and Boston. These well-to-do travelers would arrive in the United States with letters and parcels that they needed delivered to cities like New York and Philadelphia. Perhaps Harnden could be of service?

Harnden promptly negotiated a deal with Curard to handle all the shipping for its customers on the new line. As his business grew, Harnden hired the kind of "responsible agents" that he promised in his advertisements and they carried trunks rather than carpetbags. He moved his office from the back of a stationery store to a proper building on Wall Street and opened branches in Philadelphia and Boston. Top-hatted customers often brought him bundles of letters, which Harnden boxed up and carried for 25 cents, which was what the Post Office would have individually charged for many of them.

Everything seemed to be going Harnden's way until January 13, 1840, when he dispatched his younger brother, Adolphus, to Boston on a steamship known as the *Lexington* with $40,000 in cash and valuables. After boarding, Adolphus, who was slight like his brother but more easygoing, locked up the cash in a portable safe and went belowdecks to relax. Around 7 PM, cinders from the smokestack ignited bales of cotton piled on the deck. The wind fed the flames and soon the *Lexington* was ablaze. So many people crowded into the ship's lifeboats that the vessels sank along with the passengers. Other travelers leaped into the icy Long Island Sound and tried unsuccessfully to swim for the shore. Only four people survived the wreck. Adolphus's body washed up on a Long Island beach. He didn't have the $40,000, but police found a pouch on his corpse containing 146 letters, which they took to a local post office and mailed.

That's when the Post Office Department discovered all the letters that Harnden's company had been carrying, It was one thing for him to transport packages; the Post Office didn't handle those at the time. But in the department's view, Harnden was violating its letter monopoly and it decided to investigate him, along with the other private express operators that he had inspired. Harnden seems to have found out about it. "Receive nothing mailable," he warned one of his associates. "You will have no small number of Post Office spies at your heels. They will watch you very closely. See that they have their trouble for the pains."

It was too late for that. In 1841, President John Tyler appointed Charles Wickliffe, a former speaker of the Kentucky house of representatives, to be his postmaster general. A ruddy-faced man with dark hair that flowed past his collar, Wickliffe released the results of the investigation in his first annual report to Congress. Philadelphia's postmaster lamented in the report that Harnden was "making a deep hole in the coffers of Uncle Sam." The postmaster of New York said he was losing a third of his letter business to Harnden and Harnden's imitators. However, the report also included a remarkable admission by Nathaniel Greene, Boston's postmaster. Greene said he had hired Harnden to transport mail between New York and Boston because he thought it would more problematic to shut him down. "Mr. H. deservedly enjoys the highest confidence of the business community," wrote one of Greene's aides.

Wickliffe vehemently disagreed. He argued that if the private express companies weren't put down, they would destroy the Post Office. "These private expresses will only be found to operate upon the great and profitable thoroughfares between great commercial points, while the extremes are left to depend upon the operations of the United States mail, crippled and broken down for the want of means," Wickliffe wrote. "Between New York and Boston, between Philadelphia and Baltimore, or between New York and Buffalo, individual enterprise might supply the wants of the community in the rapid and cheap transportation of letters and packets. Will the same enterprise penetrate the savannahs and swamps of the south or the wilds of the west and daily or weekly convey to the door of the planter and husbandman the letter of business or friendship, the intelligence of commerce and politics?"

After being singled out by Wickliffe, Harnden started a different kind of delivery service, the Harnden Foreign Passenger Express, which brought European immigrants to the United States. He opened offices in England, Scotland, Ireland, and Germany and promoted the new service fanatically. When one of his agents informed him that he had ordered a thousand advertising cards for the new business line that were "a little smaller than my hand," Harnden became enraged.

"His hand?" Harnden fumed. "Make them a foot square, and the color red. If a thing is worth doing at all, it's worth doing thoroughly."

Harnden made sure the flyers were plastered on the walls of hotels and railroad stations. It is estimated that he brought 100,000 foreigners to the United States by the end of 1844. It wasn't uncommon to see families from Ireland and Germany parked with their luggage in Harnden's American offices to be transported to the Midwest, where they were most likely to find work. Yet for all his human cargo, Harnden lost everything on the new venture, including his health, which had never been good in the first place. In his final days, he rode to work in a carriage because he didn't have the strength to make the trip on foot. In January 1845, the man who would become known as the father of the private express industry died of tuberculosis at age 33. Harnden was buried outside Boston. His friends erected a monument above his grave with the biblical inscription: "Because the king's business required haste."

Unfortunately for the Post Office, Harnden had inspired many other mail-carrying outlaws. One of them was Henry Wells, an apprentice of Harnden's and the future cofounder of Wells Fargo, the delivery company that would later turn itself into a bank that still exists today. Born in the village of Thetford in eastern Vermont in 1805, Wells was broad shouldered and more than six feet tall with a regal beard and curly brown hair. In his early thirties, he became Harnden's agent in Albany because of his close connections to steamboat owners on the Hudson River. Wells tried to persuade Harnden to extend his service to Buffalo, but Harnden laughed at him. "If *you* choose to run an express to the Rocky Mountains, you had better do it on your own account," Harnden said. "*I* choose to run an express where there is business."

Wells thought Harnden was foolish. In 1841, he left Harnden & Company and formed his own company with George Pomeroy, another of Harnden's protégés. They started an express service between Albany and Buffalo. There was no direct train line linking the two cities at the time. Wells would catch a train out of Albany and move his trunks between trains and stagecoaches at all hours for three days until he arrived in Buffalo. In the winter, he could be seen on Buffalo's snowy streets making his deliveries door-to-door in a sleigh.

Later, Wells would boast that he endeared himself to the city's residents by bringing them oysters. "It may amuse you to hear that the oyster was a powerful agent in expediting our progress," he wrote. "That very delicious shell fish was fully appreciated by Buffalonians— and deeply they felt the sad fact that there was on one occasion toward spring no oysters in Buffalo and Mr. Leidly [a restaurant owner] asked me why the Express could not bring them. Bring oysters by coach over such roads? was my astonished exclamation. His answer was the keystone to all success in enterprise: 'If I pay for them—charge just what you will.' They were brought—opened in Albany and brought to Buffalo at the cost of three dollars a hundred—and the arrival of those oysters by Express at Buffalo created a sensation." Presumably, Wells salted the open bivalves before taking them on their final journey, to keep them from spoiling.

Along with oysters, fresh fish, and bank notes Wells started a letter delivery service in 1844 that openly competed with the Post Office Department, despite its monopoly. His firm charged six cents to carry one letter between New York and Buffalo, less than one-fourth of the government's 25-cent price for the same distance. Wells joined forces with other private carriers like Lysander Spooner's American Letter Mail Company and James Hale's Hale and Company (this was the same Hale who owned the Tontine Reading Room) to transport letters inexpensively up and down the East Coast and across the Atlantic to Europe. The insurgents used stamps before the Post Office, selling books of 20 for one dollar. As letters traveled though this alternative postal system, they often bore the postmarks and distinctively designed stamps of multiple companies. Hale's stamps, for instance, were octagonal. Private carriers even provided home delivery, handing letters off to local companies like Boyd's City Despatch in New York and Blood's City Despatch in Philadelphia that had their own mailboxes on the streets of these cities long before the government instituted them.

For Charles Wickliffe, the flourishing private mail network was a nightmare. The Post Office responded by arresting private letter carriers as they boarded trains in cities with their mailbags. There is a painting from this era of postal inspectors on horseback pursuing one of Wells's carriers through the night in upstate New York. But Wells argued that the government had no right to harass his company when it delivered mail more cheaply and efficiently than the Post Office. The public in the region supported Wells. Local businessmen put up bail money for his jailed employees. Town councils passed resolutions calling on citizens to boycott the Post Office.

A federal prosecutor brought the first case against George Pomeroy, Wells's partner, in Utica. The lawyer representing Pomeroy told him to plead guilty. But Wells wouldn't hear of it. Instead, the case went to trial and the jury exonerated Pomeroy. The same thing happened in other cases against other private carriers. Postal laws forbade them to operate horse and foot posts, but the lawyers for the private carriers said there were no rules against carrying mail on trains and steamships, and judges sided with them in many cases.

Reeling from its courtroom defeats, the Post Office tried to buy Wells's company. Wells countered with an audacious proposal of his own. He offered to purchase the U.S. Post Office Department. Selah Hobbie, one of Wickliffe's chief aides, was dumbfounded.

"Zounds, sir," Hobbie replied. "It would throw 16,000 postmasters out of work."

At the same time Wickliffe was trying to fend off Henry Wells and Wells's fellow private express men, he had to contend with another set of critics: northern merchants and liberal activists calling for lower postal rates. Perhaps the staunchest of these advocates of cheap postage was Joshua Leavitt, an evangelical minister turned abolitionist. Born in 1794 and raised in Heath, Massachusetts, Leavitt graduated from Yale College with a divinity degree and preached in Connecticut before moving to New York and becoming the editor of the *New York Evangelist* in 1830. He transformed it into one of America's most influential Presbyterian publications. The tall, gaunt Leavitt worked six days a week in a tiny office in downtown New York City, hounding subscribers to pay their bills so he could keep the paper afloat and support his wife and five sons. He often quarreled with his wealthy financial backers, who found him to be unyielding and irascible. But they had to admit that Leavitt knew how to get people to read the *Evangelist*.

The paper became his pulpit. Leavitt accused the city's theater owners of corrupting the public with their titillating shows. He decried alcohol consumption, saying that it was destroying America. "Intemperance is filling our alms-houses with paupers, our hospitals with patients, our asylums with madmen, our penitentiaries with criminals, and our streets with vagrants," Leavitt wrote. He denounced slavery, calling it "a national sin," and became one of the founders of the American Anti-Slavery Society, which enraged pro-slavery forces in the South with its mass mailing of abolitionist newspapers. Leavitt was spit on and attacked in the streets of New York by hooligans with southern sympathies, but all this only encouraged him.

In 1837, financial crisis followed by a depression brought an end to the *Evangelist*, and Leavitt considered returning to the pulpit. But the same year, the American Anti-Slavery Society named him editor of the *Emancipator*, a once sleepy house organ. Leavitt immediately set out to liven it up, publishing accounts by runaway slaves of the brutalities they had endured on the plantation. He lambasted his own Presbyterian Church for supporting slavery. "So long as the church sanctions and sustains it, slavery is impregnable against all moral influences," he wrote. He excoriated his longtime allies in the American Anti-Slavery Society for refusing to allow women to vote in its elections. "Horrible!" Leavitt wrote facetiously. "What are we coming to? Why, the efforts of the last thirty years to educate and elevate the sex has actually infatuated some of the dear creatures to make them think that women have souls, and intellects, and the capacity of forming opinions, even on such intricate subjects as the right or wrong of slavery."

Leavitt thought that America's progress was also being hobbled by an overpriced postal system that permitted only the wealthy and politically connected to freely exchange ideas through the mail. He became convinced that cheaper rates would not only bring Americans together, but also save the embattled U.S. Post Office Department. Leavitt pointed to England to make his argument. In 1837 British educational reformer Rowland Hill had published a pamphlet entitled *Post Office Reform: Its Importance and Practicality*, arguing that the Royal Mail should abandon its complicated system of high postage and adopt a low, uniform rate for a half-ounce letter. Hill favored a penny, saying it would spur such a boom in letter writing that the Royal Mail would actually make more money. He also called for the Royal Mail to sell stamps, which would encourage people to prepay for their letters and further increase its income.

Lord Lichfield, England's postmaster general, dismissed Hill's proposal as sheer folly. "Of all the wild and visionary schemes which I have ever heard of, this is the most extraordinary," he proclaimed. But the British public wanted cheaper postage, and Parliament ultimately embraced Hill's "visionary scheme." When the new prices went into effect on January 19, 1840, police stood guard outside London's General Post Office to manage the crowd eager to send letters. That year, the Royal Mail handled 169 million letters, more than twice as many as the year before. British letter writers began using envelopes, which people had previously shied away from because they would have counted as a second sheet of paper and doubled postage. There was a greeting card explosion as people started mailing each other Christmas and Valentine's Day cards. Some prolific correspondents even traveled with a portable writing table, which some present-day historians have called "the Victorian laptop."

Leavitt marveled at the British postal system when he visited England in 1843 to attend the World Anti-Slavery Convention. "It is the complete leveler," he wrote. "The poorest peasant, the factory-girl, the match-vender, the beggar, even, enjoy the benefits of the cheap postage, as they do of the vital air, on precisely the same terms with the richest banker, the proudest peer, or royalty itself." He was convinced that cheap postage in America would pay for itself and even eliminate the nation's vilest institution. "Give us the British system of postage, and slavery is dead!" Leavitt wrote.

At the U.S. Post Office Department, Charles Wickliffe was skeptical. He sent one of his assistants to study the English system and decided it wouldn't work in his country. "The mode of managing and conducting the post office in the Kingdom of Great Britain is not only different from, but much less expensive than in the United States," Wickliffe wrote, adding, "I am convinced upon a most thorough examination into the habits, conditions, and business of the people of the two countries—the circumscribed limits and dense population of the one, the extensive boundaries and sparse population of the other—that nothing like the same ratio of increase in correspondence in this country would follow the like reduction of postage as has taken place in England." Cheap postage, Wickliffe concluded, would be as destructive to the U.S. Post Office Department as Henry Wells and his private mail conspiracy.

Finally, in 1844, Congress intervened with a rescue plan. William Merrick, a Whig from Maryland and chairman of the Senate Committee on Post Office and Post Roads, wanted to close the legal loopholes that allowed private couriers to transport mail on steamships and trains, but just as important, he argued, the Post Office, which he referred to as "the most important implement in the hands of civilization," needed to regain the public's support. "The operations of the system, as it exists, have become odious, and the subject of complaint everywhere—particularly in the most populous parts of the country" Merrick lamented on the Senate floor. "And it was found impossible to carry out the extensions called for by the wants of the people, because of the deficiency in the revenues of the Post Office Department produced by private competition in every portion of the populous parts of the country."

Like Joshua Leavitt, Merrick believed the answer was cheaper postage. "Find the proper rate," he urged his colleagues. "Fix it there now, and the institution will grow and spread as the population grows and spreads westward, and in its progress will go on and spread with them, following the march of civilization, till it should have reached the banks of the Columbia river and the shores of the Pacific ocean, and will prosper even there." Merrick advocated five cents for letters traveling less than 300 miles and 10 cents for those going beyond.

Senators from the industrial North who represented big cities with heavy mail users supported Merrick. But their colleagues from the agrarian South vehemently opposed his bill, saying that cheap postage would bankrupt the Post Office and cause the federal government to raise taxes to keep it going. "This is a bill for the benefit of cities, to the injury of the country," protested Congressman William Payne, a Democrat from Alabama. "It is a New York bill; a New England bill." Payne warned that Merrick's bill might even destroy the Post Office altogether at a time when Americans were migrating to the western parts of the country far from their friends and family. "Look at the vast regions now uncultivated, which extend to the setting sun," he said. "These are to be populated. Your children are to inhabit them. Are you prepared, by the adoption of this bill, to annihilate the Post Office Department, and thereby cut off all communication with them?"

Despite the southern opposition, Congress ratified the bill in early 1845 and President John Tyler signed it in his final days in the White House. Now that he could no longer undercut the government's rates, Henry Wells stopped carrying letters, but he declared victory, saying he deserved credit for forcing the Post Office to lower its prices. He and William Fargo, his new partner, began ferrying packages across the Great Lakes from Buffalo to emerging cities like Chicago and Detroit. It wouldn't be long before he would challenge the Post Office again.

As some skeptics predicted, the reduced rate didn't spark an English-style letter boom. In 1847, the Post Office Department's yearly letter volume had risen by only 15 percent to 47 million. But perhaps Congress simply hadn't cut the prices enough. The Post Office was also slow to introduce stamps, so postmasters began creating their own that could be used for local letters within their districts. That year, Cave Johnson, President James Polk's postmaster general, received authorization from Congress to issue a five-cent stamp bearing Benjamin Franklin's portrait, and a 10-cent stamp commemorating George Washington. But Johnson had to persuade some of his own postmasters that the stamps were genuine and should be honored. Even then, most American still sent their letters collect.

It took another campaign by advocates of cheaper postage to get the transformative result that they desired. In New York and Boston, they formed societies that distributed Joshua Leavitt's meticulously argued pamphlets praising the English mail system and condemning what he considered the backward American one. Influential magazines like the *New Englander* and *Harper's* published articles calling for English-style postal reform. The public inundated Congress with petitions calling for lower rates. "No American citizen can hesitate to lend his aid to accomplish a measure which is fraught with so many blessings to every portion of our community," the directors of the New York Cheap Postage Association wrote in 1850. "It benefits alike the post office and the people. And why should Congress delay any longer in complying with the wishes of the people, who have been for seven long years petitioning for *cheap postage*."

In 1851, Congress lowered the postage for a half-ounce letter to three cents. People who didn't use stamps would have to pay the old rate. In the weeks before the new law went into effect on July 1, people held back their letters so they could take advantage of the discount. The New York City postmaster worried about running out of stamps and put a limited number on sale. Even so, New Yorkers mailed five times as many stamped letters on the first day as they had done previously. Philadelphians sent 20,000 stamped letters, double their usual number. Two years later, stamp usage became compulsory.

Americans were exhilarated by the changes. "Maybe the letters will come pouring upon you in such multitudes that you'll wish for the old rate of postage," a woman in Connecticut teased her cousin. Family members encouraged each other to write even if they had nothing to say. "It is a very good plan for you to correspond with your relatives in Wisconsin," a father told his son. "It will do you and them good in several ways. Do not neglect it. Do not fall into the notion that you cannot write, unless you have some *news* to tell. Items of news may be gathered from the newspapers, but a friendly correspondence has, or should have, another purpose—to express sympathy and good feeling, and to keep up with an acquaintance with and a pleasurable remembrance of each other." That may sound quaint in the age of e-mail, but it was an entirely new idea for people who had once avoided writing letters because they were so expensive to send.

These new American letter writers began using envelopes just as the English had done. "The practice of inclosing letters in envelopes is now universal," wrote Eliza Leslie, author of *The Behaviour Book:*

A Manual for Ladies, in 1853. "The postage now is in almost every instance pre-paid, it being but three cents when paid by the writer, and five if left to the receiver. Therefore, none but the very poor send unpaid letters." Leslie told her readers always to keep a little box of stamps on their writing tables. "Be careful not to allow yourself to get entirely out of post-office stamps," she wrote. "Replenish your stock in time. If the gum seems too weak, go over it afresh with that excellent cement, 'Perpetual Paste.'"

Leslie insisted that the ability to craft a proper letter became a sign of good breeding. "To write a legible and handsome hand is an accomplishment not sufficiently valued," she wrote. "And yet of what importance it is! We are always vexed when we hear people of talent making a sort of boast of the illegibility of their writing, and relating anecdotes of the difficulty with which it has been read, and the mistakes made by its decipherers. There are persons who affect bad writing, and boast of it, because the worst signatures extant are those of Shakespeare, Bonaparte, and Byron. These men were great in spite of their autographs, not because of them."

Unlike the Royal Mail, however, which remained profitable after lowering its postage, the American Post Office fell into a pattern of generating deficits, one that would continue well into the next century. By 1854, the number of American post offices had risen to 23,584, and the number of postal roads had increased to 219,935. But the system cost a lot of money—$8.6 million to be precise. The Post Office's revenues that year were only $6.7 million. In other words, Charles Wickliffe was right; the United States wasn't Great Britain. However, Congress was content to subsidize the Post Office as long as people received their mail. The department still talked about how it needed to operate like a business, but Congress regarded it as a public service.

In a country as vast as America, this was inevitable. Gold was discovered in California in 1848, and the state became a mecca for fortune hunters. But the Post Office carried mail only to Missouri's western border. Between St. Joseph, Missouri, and California, there was only wilderness populated largely by Indians who were understandably hostile to settlers and to anybody who tried to deliver mail. So initially, the Post Office loaded mail onto steamships that traveled from New York to the narrow Isthmus of Panama. There, laborers unloaded it, carried it nearly 50 miles to the Pacific Ocean, and reloaded it onto another vessel that went around the western coast of Mexico to Los Angeles and San Francisco. The entire journey could take three months. Bayard Taylor, a travel writer for the *New York Tribune* sent to cover the gold rush, described what happened in 1849 when the steamship *Panama* arrived in San Francisco with 37 bags bursting with 45,000 letters and what he described as "bushels of newspapers."

That evening, Taylor ended up joining the postmaster and his eight clerks and sorting mail with them in the one-story San Francisco post office. People desperate for their mail tried to get in. "There were knocks on the doors, taps on the windows, and beseeching calls at all corners of the house," Taylor wrote. "The interior was well lighted; the bags were emptied on the floor, and ten pairs of hands engaged in the assortment and distribution of their contents. The work went on rapidly and noiselessly as the night passed away, but with the first stream of daylight, the attack commenced again. Every entrance was barricaded; the crowd was told through the eyehole that the office would be opened that day to no one; but it all availed nothing. Somebody yelled, 'Curse such a Post Office and such a Postmaster! I'll write to the Department by the next steamer. *We'll* see whether things go on in this way much longer.'"

When the postmaster finally opened the doors, thousands of people waited for the mail for more than six hours, standing in a line that stretched up and down the city's hills. "Those who were near the goal frequently sold out their places to impatient candidates, for ten and even twenty-five dollars," Taylor wrote. "Indeed, several persons, in want of money, practiced this game daily as a means of living! Vendors of pies, cakes, and newspapers established themselves in front of the office to supply the crowd, while others did a profitable business by carrying cans of coffee up and down the lines."

Henry Wells shrewdly saw an opportunity in California. He and Fargo opened an office in San Francisco in 1852 and hired riders to provide mail service to mining camps in the surrounding hills where there were no post offices. To mollify the Post Office, Wells Fargo put its letters in stamped envelopes purchased from the government, which meant that its customers paid twice for their mail, but in a state with little government delivery, they didn't have a choice. Naturally, the Post Office monitored Wells Fargo closely. "We have to request a more strict observance of stamping letters," Wells Fargo wrote to its agents. "We are called upon by the mail agent, who assures us that fines will be imposed for any infringement of postal laws." But as long as Wells Fargo paid the proper postage, the government didn't interfere. For residents of these California towns, Wells Fargo was the post office. The alternative private delivery service that Congress had largely put out of business on the East Coast had resurfaced in the West.

In 1853, Wells himself made his one and only trip to the West Coast, where he was overwhelmed by the fast pace of San Francisco at the height of the gold rush. "I am called sanguine at home," Wells wrote. "But I am an old fogey here and considered entirely too slow for this market." He preferred life in Aurora, New York, a town in the Finger Lakes region of the state where he built a mansion and later founded a women's college bearing his name. But Wells had the right men in California. His company prospered while the Post Office struggled to get mail to California's shores.

Though it wasn't widely known at the time, Wells Fargo carried mail for the Post Office too. It underwrote the famous Overland Mail Company founded by John Butterfield, who won a $600,000 yearly contract in 1857 to carry mail by stagecoach on a 2,800-mile trail from Memphis through Texas, parts of what is now New Mexico, and Arizona to San Francisco. It took an average of 21 days for Butterfield's stages to make the cross-country journey. "Remember boys," he told his drivers, "nothing on God's earth must stop the United States Mail."

Along the way, Butterfield's men faced Indian attacks, water shortages, and paths so rocky that their passengers feared the coaches would splinter. "Our heavy wagon bounded along crags as if it would be shaken to pieces every minute, and ourselves disemboweled on the spot," wrote Waterman Ormsby, a correspondent for the *New York Herald*. When he finally arrived in San Francisco, he decided to stay awhile. "Had I not just come out over the route, I would be perfectly willing to go back, but I know what Hell is like," Ormsby wrote. "I've just had 24 days of it." Butterfield could withstand bad publicity, but in 1859, the Overland Mail Company nearly failed when Congress adjourned without appropriating funds to pay what it was owed for carrying mail. Wells and his partners chose this moment to oust Butterfield and take control of the company, continuing to carry the mail for the government.

Wells Fargo played a similar role in the Central Overland California & Pike's Peak Express Company, better known as the Pony Express. It would become the most famous story in American postal history, one that would be told over and over again, mythologized by Buffalo Bill Cody's traveling Wild West shows, and later featured in movies, comic books, and television shows. However, the Pony Express was more ephemeral than most people realize. It lasted for a mere 18 months and was really more of a publicity stunt than a business.

The Pony Express was the handiwork of three enterprising deliverymen—William Russell, Alexander Majors, and William Waddell—who desperately wanted to win a contract to move mail by stagecoach on a central route from St. Joseph, Missouri, to Sacramento and then on to San Francisco. The partners were not neophytes. Their firm had shipped supplies to military forts in Utah, where troops protected settlers from Indian attacks. It was a phenomenal business until President James Buchanan declared war on the Mormon Church in 1857. The church's leader Brigham Young ordered his raiders to burn the company's wagons, and this devastated Russell, Majors, and Waddell financially.

The partners were heavily in debt in 1860 when Russell, an extravagant character known for his expensive clothes and deal-making prowess, persuaded the Post Office to allow its riders to speed mail in nine days by horseback between Missouri and California using a relay system similar to the one that had worked so well for the fabled Persian couriers. As cannons fired and onlookers cheered, Johnny Fry, the first Pony Express rider, set off at nightfall on April 3, 1860, from St. Joseph, Missouri, with 49 letters, five telegrams, and copies of eastern newspapers specially printed on tissue paper so they would be less of a burden. Ten days later, William Hamilton arrived at 2 AM in San Francisco where crowds stoking bonfires greeted him. "It took seventy five ponies to make the trip from Missouri to California in 10½ days, but the last one—the little fellow who came down in the Sacramento boat this morning had the vicarious glory of them all," the *San Francisco Bulletin* wrote. "Upon him an enthusiastic crowd was disposed to shower all their compliments. He was the veritable Hippogriff who shoved a continent behind his hoofs so easily; who snuffed up sandy plains, sent lakes and mountains, prairies and forests, whizzing behind him, like one great river rushing westward."

With such florid coverage, the story of the Pony Express was destined to take on mythic qualities. Wild West characters like Buffalo Bill and Wild Bill Hickok would become associated with it. Decades later when both men had become international celebrities, they didn't bother to explain that nether of them had been a Pony Express rider, though they did work for the freight-hauling operation owned by Russell, Majors, and Waddell. Hickok had been too old and heavy at the time; he would have weighed down his steed and slowed the mail.

This is not to say, however, that the Pony Express didn't have heroic riders. Robert "Pony Bob" Haslam covered 360 miles in a single ride while all around him Indians attacked settlers. He didn't plan to be in the saddle that long; when Haslam arrived at the appointed way station, he found that the relief rider was too afraid to travel the route, so Pony Bob continued on with the mail. Haslam didn't encounter any hostile natives himself during that famous ride, but when he carried President Abraham Lincoln's inaugural address in 1861 through Nevada, he narrowly escaped an attack by Indians, one of whom shot him in the jaw with an arrow, knocking out five of his teeth.

The tale of the Pony Express is often told as an allegory for the American West. As Pony Bob and his fellow horsemen raced to deliver mail on time, workers erected telegraph poles along their route that would hold wires running from St. Joseph, Missouri, to San Francisco and ultimately connect the East and West coasts. When the transcontinental telegraph line was completed in October 1861 and people could send electronic messages in the blink of an eye, the Post Office no longer needed the Pony Express and its colorful horsemen to provide urgent delivery. They had been rendered obsolete by the arrival of new technology and the modern world. As for slower mail, the Post Office could send that via stages or steamships until railroads enabled it to transport mail between coasts by the end of the decade.

But the story of the last days of the Pony Express is more nuanced. Russell, Majors, and Waddell charged five dollars a letter, but they never carried enough mail to turn a profit. The Central Overland California & Pike's Peak Express (COC & PPE) became known among riders as the "Clean Out of Cash & Poor Pay Express."

In April 1861, the owners were so strapped that they turned over the final third of the route in California to a competitor. And who might it have been? Wells Fargo could easily handle the extra mail. Ultimately, the Pony Express failed, and its owners lost $200,000, the equivalent of $5 million today. Its legendary riders, Pony Bob among them, became Wells Fargo employees. The glory days of the Old West weren't over yet; Wells Fargo continued to operate pony expresses between Sacramento and places like Virginia City, Nevada. Small wonder that the company's ensuing decades became fodder for movies, such as *Stagecoach* and *The Music Man*; a television show called *Tales of Wells Fargo*; and a comic book series.

The battle between the Post Office and private competitors would continue for decades. It wasn't until 1894, for instance, that the Post Office finally put a stop to Wells Fargo's extensive letter delivery business in California. But who was the villain in this ongoing saga? For the Post Office, the interlopers threatened its ability to serve all Americans. But private companies like Wells Fargo saw themselves at odds with a powerful government agency that was bent on destroying its rivals even when it couldn't provide the same services as efficiently. At various times in the postal service's history, both sides were right.

3

Comstockery

It was a crisis unlike any the postal service had previously experienced. In February 1861, six southern states—South Carolina, Florida, Alabama, Mississippi, Georgia, and Louisiana—declared themselves a new nation and seized 9,000 post offices within their borders. Jefferson Davis, president of the newly formed Confederate States of America, appointed John Henninger Reagan to be his rebel postmaster general. A former Texas congressman with a fiery gaze and a thick, wavy beard, Reagan didn't know much about letter delivery. He appealed to southern postal officials in Washington to join him and bring along copies of the most recent annual report, maps of southern mail routes, and anything else that might be helpful. He hired an English firm to create Confederate stamps with Davis's portrait. Unlike his rivals in the north, Reagan wanted to run a self-supporting southern postal operation, setting a five-cent rate for half-ounce letters and eliminating money-losing routes.

Reagan's northern counterpart was Montgomery Blair, Abraham Lincoln's postmaster general. If Reagan looked like a warrior, Blair resembled a scholar, with clean-shaven face and delicate features. But Blair was just as formidable. He was the son of Francis Blair, a Kentucky newspaperman who befriended Andrew Jackson and became the publisher of the *Congressional Globe* and a member of Jackson's kitchen cabinet in the 1830s. Young Monty Blair grew up in a house across the street from the White House that still stands, where his father received visitors like John Calhoun, Henry Clay, Daniel Webster, and other towering political figures of the antebellum era.

Blair became a prominent lawyer, representing Dred Scott, a slave who sued for his freedom in a landmark case in which the Supreme Court ruled that blacks had no rights under the Constitution. Blair also assisted in the defense of John Brown, who attacked a federal armory in Harpers Ferry, Virginia, in 1859 in hopes of leading an armed slave rebellion. Blair's reedy voice irritated some, but he could make a persuasive argument, bolstering his points with references to the Bible and Greek mythology. The Blairs helped found the Republican Party and supported Abraham Lincoln when he ran for president in 1860. When Lincoln won the election, he rewarded Blair by naming him postmaster general.

Blair found himself besieged by job seekers. "They left him at 2 this morning and commenced at 8 this morning," wrote his brother-in-law Gustavus Fox. Lincoln was consumed with postal appointments too. Charles Francis Adams, his ambassador to England, was surprised when Lincoln spent most of their first meeting discussing a vacancy in the Chicago post office rather than international affairs. "I have troubles enough," Lincoln wrote to a friend. "When I last saw you, I was having little troubles; they filled my mind full; since then, I have big troubles and they can do no more—what do you think has annoyed me more than any one thing? . . . Now I tell you; the fight over two post offices—one at Bloomington [Illinois] and the other in Pennsylvania. That is the thing that is troubling me most."

Of course, Blair also had to operate a wartime postal system. As the Union army moved around the country, small-town post offices with a single postmaster and one or two clerks would be flooded with more mail than they could ever hope to handle. Blair assigned a postmaster to each regiment who made sure the troopers got their letters. He also wanted to punish the Confederates for seizing post offices. Reagan had hoped to negotiate a treaty with the North that would allow for the flow of letters between the two sides, but Blair wasn't in a conciliatory mood. He responded to Reagan's overtures by cutting off mail service to the South on March 31, 1861. Letters sent to the South were forwarded to the Dead Letter Office and returned to their senders. Blair also canceled all existing stamps so southern postmasters couldn't use them as currency (a common practice at the time) and issued new ones.

Southern sympathizers in border states like Missouri had to rely on mail smugglers to get letters to their sons fighting in the Confederate Army. Absalom Grimes, a riverboat captain from St. Louis, posed as a traveling salesman to pass unmolested through enemy lines with a carpetbag full of mail. Sometimes, he made his furtive rounds with several young women who carried dozens of letters in their ruffled skirts. Meanwhile, the line between the North and the South kept changing. Sometimes, residents of Nashville got their mail from the Confederate post office; other times, they received letters via the northern one. It all depended on which army was occupying their town that week.

But secession had its advantages for Blair. Without opposition from conservative southerners in Congress, he was able to introduce sweeping postal reforms. Blair eliminated the long-distance charge for letters, so that northerners could send letters weighing half an ounce anywhere in the Union for three cents. He also introduced the money-order system so that people no longer needed to send currency through the mail, which could be stolen by robbers or sticky-fingered postal workers.

Haunted by the long lines of women who waited at post offices for letters from their husbands and sweethearts in the Union Army, Blair started free home delivery in 1863. For the first time in its history, the Post Office hired a permanent staff of letter carriers—449 in the first year—to walk the streets of 49 northern cities. New York got 137; another 113 delivered letters in Philadelphia. Smaller cities like Pittsburgh got three carriers. Syracuse, New York; and Nashua,

New Hampshire, made do with one carrier each. In many cities residents enjoyed at least two deliveries a day, which meant they could send dinner invitations in the morning and get responses in the afternoon. The system worked even though there were no home mailboxes. If the postman's knock or whistle received no answer, he returned later in the day and tried again. Free home delivery soon spread to other cities, and within three decades only people in rural parts of the country had to go to a post office to get their mail.

Blair radically improved mail transportation, too. For decades, postmasters had wrapped the letters they received with paper and twine and sent them by stagecoach or train to large distribution post offices called the Great Mails. There, clerks unwrapped the bundles and sorted the letters, tossing them into racks of pigeonholes representing different cites and addresses. Then they wrapped them up again and sent them on to the next large post office in the Great Mail chain. Because of all the stops, it could take as long as two weeks for a letter to travel from Maine to Florida.

Now that railroads crisscrossed the country, Blair thought it made more sense for clerks to ride trains and sort mail while it was in transit. In 1864, Blair gave George Armstrong, an assistant postmaster in Chicago, permission to start what has been called the first official railway mail service between his city and Clinton, Iowa, on the Chicago & North Western Railway. Joseph Medill, publisher of the *Chicago Tribune*, told Armstrong it would never work. "It is impractical," Medill said. "Why, the government would have to employ a regiment of men to follow the postal cars for the purpose of picking up letters that would be blown out of the car and left along the track."

Armstrong invited Medill along for the first trip, and the newspaper publisher became an important supporter of the new service, helping Armstrong overcome opposition from powerful postmasters in cities like Philadelphia and Boston as he rolled out the service nationally. These urban postal officials feared that Armstrong would poach some of their clerks to work on his trains and that they would lose a percentage of the commissions they received for every letter, newspaper, or book sorted in their building. That's exactly what happened, but Armstrong had Blair and Medill behind him, so the postmasters had to make the best of it.

The Railway Mail Service became an elite operation within the Post Office Department. Clerks who rode the rails threw bags of letters from speeding trains and grabbed incoming ones with hooks. They memorized as many as 4,000 post office addresses in order to sort mail faster. They practiced at home using portable pigeonhole cases, and they were frequently tested on both their memory skills and their letter-tossing techniques. The men who survived this grueling process developed a uniquely collective sprit. They slept together in dormitories on the upper floors of big city post offices and developed their own slang, referring to letters with wrong addresses as "nixies," registered letters as "reds," and, much later, airmail as "flypaper."

Blair had less success when he tried to do away with franking abuses. It was bad enough that members of Congress used the post office to freely blanket their districts with copies of speeches that no one paid attention to in Washington. Politicians also sent their dirty laundry home to be cleaned without paying, simply by signing the packages with their names. One congressman reportedly sent a piano through the mail without paying. Blair wasn't able to stop senators and congressmen from franking but he was able to rein in postmasters who allowed friends and family members to frank their mail. "The postmaster cannot leave his frank behind him for the use of his family when he is traveling on pleasure or business," Blair wrote. "Therefore, if a person enjoying the privilege of a frank is known not to be in the vicinity, the frank is to be disregarded, the letter rated, and postage marked due."

Blair also vastly expanded the duties of postal inspectors, then known as "special agents." Much of their work was unglamorous. They examined the books at post offices and the department's dealings with stagecoach and steamboat companies to make sure it wasn't overcharged. Early special agents also spied on postmasters to make sure they encouraged customers to vote for the political party in power with sufficient zeal.

But postal inspectors also solved crimes. James Holbrook's *Ten Years Among the Mail Bags; or, Notes from the Diary of a Special Agent of the Post-Office Department*, published in 1855, became a best seller and is thought to have helped inspire the modern detective novel, with its tales of mail robbers and malefactors who tried to use the public mails for nefarious purposes. "A mail bag is an epitome of human life," Holbrook wrote in the opening section of his book. "All the elements which go to form the happiness or misery of individuals—the raw material so to speak, of human hopes and fears—here exist in a chaotic state." Someone had to protect it.

In 1864, Blair noted that the Post Office had only 16 special agents for 29,047 post offices, if he included the "disloyal" post offices in the South, which of course, he did. But as the postal system became cheaper, faster, and more convenient to use, strange items began to flow though it. Thanks to cheaper printing technology and the development of the daguerreotype, publishers could produce inexpensive pornographic books with arresting photographs that they could mail to customers. Blair was shocked to discover that Union troops read such material at their camps. The deeply religious Blair feared indecent literature would weaken the resolve of the Union Army, and he called for legislation barring obscene material from the mail. In 1865, Lincoln signed a new law stating that "no obscene book, pamphlet, picture, print, or other publication of a vulgar and indecent character, shall be admitted into the mails of the United States." By this time, it should be noted that Blair, who resided in the border state of Maryland, had resigned from his position because radical members of his party didn't consider his antislavery position strong enough.

However, the new law didn't eradicate pornography. After the war, young men in search of jobs poured into the cities, where they could buy obscene books openly on outdoor stands. Morris Jesup, a wealthy banker and one of the founders of the Young Men's Christian Association in New York, believed such literature served as a gateway to a debauched existence. He sent Anthony Comstock, his eager 28-year-old protégé—broad shouldered, thick legged, and extravagantly side-whiskered—to Washington in 1873 to lobby Congress for a new law that would make it easier for the federal government to prosecute malefactors who sent sexually explicit material by mail.

At an early age, Comstock felt he was destined for glory. As a child in New Canaan, Connecticut, he was enchanted when his mother read him stories from the Bible about saintly heroes battling satanic foes. Comstock never smoked. He shared a bottle of homemade wine with a friend one night, woke up with a violent hangover, and became a lifelong temperance advocate. Comstock later claimed that as an adolescent, he rid the area of a local saloon keeper, breaking into his establishment late at night, turning on the taps, and warning the barkeep in an anonymous note to leave New Canaan or else. But for all his professed virtue, Comstock's own diaries reveal that he was also a chronic masturbator, which filled him with guilt and may have had much to do with his eventual calling as an anti-pornography crusader.

After his older brother Samuel died at Gettysburg, Comstock enlisted in the Union Army. Stationed in St. Augustine, Florida, Comstock tried to get the other soldiers to attend church with him. They didn't appreciate his nagging and let him know, trashing his room in the barracks one night. Comstock tried to laugh it off, writing in his diary that "the boys" were giving him an initiation, even though he had been in St. Augustine for a year and perhaps it was a little late for that.

After the war, Comstock found a sales job at a dry goods store in New York, bought a house in Brooklyn, and married Margaret Hamilton, a minister's daughter who was 10 years older. They had one child, a daughter who died soon after her birth. Comstock found solace in a new crusade. As Comstock told it, a fellow employee at the dry goods store became afflicted with a sexually transmitted disease after developing an interest in erotic literature. Comstock went to the bookstore where his friend made his purchases, bought some illicit reading material, and returned with a police captain who arrested the dealer.

Newspapers picked up the story of the valiant dry goods salesman. One columnist suggested cheekily that if Comstock wanted to prove himself as a purification agent, he should visit St. Ann's Street, where vendors openly hawked such books. Comstock invited a reporter to join him this time, collaring several more smut dealers and earning more glowing coverage. After that, he grew more ambitious. He figured out that a handful of publishers produced a total of 169 sexually explicit books available in New York. He believed that if he put them out of business, the supply of obscenity would dry up. William Hayes, a Brooklyn surgeon, was the most prolific of them; he took his life when he learned of Comstock's interest. Comstock tried to purchase the late doctor's printing plates from his wife so he could dissolve them in acid at the Brooklyn Polytechnic Institute. The widow wanted $650. Comstock didn't have that kind of money, but he knew where to find it.

He wrote to the New York YMCA asking for the funds. Morris Jesup intercepted the letter and was so moved that he wrote Comstock a check for $650 and installed him as the secretary of the YMCA's newly formed Committee for the Suppression of Vice. Within a year, Comstock seized more than twelve tons of offensive literature, and 200,000 salacious items including photographs, rings, knives, song-lyric sheets, playing cards, and what he referred to as "obscene and immoral rubber articles." He kept his collection at the American Tract Society Building on Nassau Street in lower Manhattan, where it could do no harm. But even with the money and imprimatur of the YMCA, Comstock didn't always succeed in putting smut merchants behind bars. It was the era of Boss Tweed, and the city was a lawless place. Pornographers bribed prosecutors to drop the charges against them. Corrupt state judges tossed out cases against booksellers and rubber goods dealers.

Comstock didn't get very far when he attempted to have his adversaries prosecuted under the federal postal law. He jailed the early suffragette sisters Victoria Woodhull and Tennessee Claflin for publishing details about a prominent minister's liaison with a married woman in their newspaper and mailing it to subscribers. But a federal jury acquitted the two women after the judge explained that the law made no mention of newspapers. The triumphant sisters mocked Comstock in their paper. "From Maine to California, we believe the new order of Protestant Jesuits called the YMCA is dubbed with the well-merited title of the American Inquisition," they wrote. "We do not mean by this to assert that its leaders are like those of the Spanish institution of the same character. We should no more think of comparing Comstock . . . with Torquemada, than of contrasting a living skunk with a dead lion."

So in February 1873, Comstock asked Jesup to send him to Washington to plead for a more stringent federal postal law. Jesup bought him a ticket and Comstock boarded the train with an assortment of offensive items from his trove. Congress was in turmoil. Republican president and Civil War hero Ulysses S. Grant had recently won a second term by a wide margin, trouncing his Democratic opponent, newspaper publisher Horace Greeley. But Democrats were attacking members of Grant's administration, including Schuyler Colfax, his vice president, for accepting bribes from a bank underwriting the construction of the Union Pacific Railroad.

Despite the scandal, or perhaps because of it, Republican leaders gave Comstock an enthusiastic welcome. Colfax allowed Comstock to set up an exhibit of his unspeakable wares in his Senate office. Comstock pleaded with members of the House and Senate to pass a stronger antiobscenity law that banned offensive newspapers, along with mention therein of contraception and abortion, from the mail. "All were very much excited and declared themselves ready to give me any law I might ask for, if only it was within the bounds of the Constitution," Comstock wrote in his diary.

William Strong, a U.S. Supreme Court justice, who had tried without success to insert the word "God" into the Constitution, helped Comstock craft a proper bill. Colfax promised that it would be passed before the end of the legislative session; Comstock stuck around Washington to make sure it did. He attended a reception at the White House where he shook President Grant's hand and gazed disapprovingly at the female guests. "They were brazen— dressed extremely silly—enameled faces and powdered hair—low dresses—hair most ridiculous and altogether most extremely disgusting to every lover of pure, noble, modest woman," Comstock scoffed. "How can we respect them? They disgrace our land and yet consider themselves ladies."

Comstock's bill cleared both the Senate and the House post office committees, but newspaper publishers complained that it threatened the freedom of the press and it was sent back to committee for amendments. Comstock worried that it might die there. House Speaker James Blaine told him not to worry; he would get it through before the end of the lame-duck session. Comstock stayed in the House past midnight on the final night. He waited as Blaine called for votes on hundreds of bills, but the speaker made no mention of his.

It was now early Sunday morning. Comstock felt compelled to abide by his mother's wish that he keep the Sabbath holy and he departed for his hotel, walking through chilly darkness full of rage. How could God have so forsaken him? Lying in bed, Comstock began to doubt his faith and could feel Satan in his hotel room, tempting him to abandon it. "The Devil seemed determined to claim me as his servant." he wrote in his diary. "He tempted me and made my heart rebellious. Yet a stronger hand was over me. I felt oh so crushed, so broken down, so tempted to sin against God. . . . O I felt almost like distrusting God, doubting and rebellious and then I went to bed, to pass the night beset by the Devil."

Comstock awoke exhausted and, assuming that he had lost his congressional battle, attended church. He didn't learn until early afternoon that the House had passed the antiobscenity bill at 2 AM. The Senate blessed it, and on March 3, 1873, President Grant signed what would become known as the Comstock law. There was more good news for Comstock. His admirers in Washington had persuaded John Creswell, Grant's postmaster general, to appoint him as a special agent in charge of enforcing the antiobscenity act. Comstock readily accepted the position, but he refused a government salary, saying the YMCA would take care of him financially. "I do not want any fat office created, whereby the Government is taxed or for some politician to have in a year or two," he wrote. "Give me the authority that such an office confers and thus enable me to more effectually do this work and the salary and honors may go to the winds."

Three days after the passage of the Comstock law, its namesake placed his hand on the Bible and swore to uphold his country's postal laws. He received an inspector's badge and a train pass entitling him to travel anywhere in the nation by rail, free, in pursuit of those who besmirched the mails. The Post Office now employed 63 special agents, but Comstock enjoyed an exclusive status. He didn't have to audit post offices; he was free to focus all his considerable energies on exciting investigative work. He targeted people who used the mail to peddle fake medicines and fraudulent financial schemes. Comstock is credited with shutting down the many so-called state lotteries that used the postal system to sell tickets, most notably the popular Louisiana lottery, whose leaders attempted to bribe Comstock with a generous donation to his society if he left them alone. Comstock politely declined the offer.

But Comstock was best known for his antiobscenity cases. Within a year of the Comstock law's enactment, he made 55 arrests under the new law, and he had a scar on his face from an encounter with a knife-wielding pornographer in Newark, New Jersey, whom he still managed to subdue, showing that he wasn't someone to trifle with. "The mail of the United States is the great thoroughfare of communication leading up into all our homes, schools and colleges," Comstock wrote. "It is the most powerful agent to assist this nefarious business, because it goes everywhere and is secret. It surely needs no argument here to convince the most exacting of all decent men, that no department of Government should be prostituted to serve this infamous traffic, nor become party to it, by continuing to serve these loathsome creatures after the character of their hellish business . . . is known."

No matter what Comstock did, the newspapers knew about it and generally lavished him with praise, though not everybody approved of his grandstanding. The YMCA thought the special agent attracted too much attention to the vice trade and severed its ties with his society. Comstock was happy to be free of the Y; he suspected that its leaders were jealous of him. He reconstituted his organization as the independent New York Society for the Suppression of Vice. Jesup remained on the board along with J. Pierpont Morgan, the powerful financier, and toothpaste magnate Samuel Colgate. Comstock encouraged the founding of satellite societies around the country. R. W. McAfee, another special postal agent, presided over the Western Society for the Suppression of Vice, with branches in Cincinnati, Chicago, and St. Louis. Thanks to the efforts of Comstock and his followers, states around the country enacted their own versions of the Comstock law.

By 1877, Comstock had largely shut down the obscenity trade. That year, the New York Society for the Suppression of Vice lamented in its annual report that there would be fewer front-page seizures of pornographic goods. The vice business had fallen on hard times. But Comstock still needed to make arrests so that his financial backers would continue to underwrite the society's annual $10,000 budget.

He went hunting for new forms of obscenity, harassing the publishers of medical volumes with anatomical studies of the human body and importers of European art books with nude portraits. Comstock also became the scourge of freethinkers who championed sexual liberation in Victorian America.

Ezra Heywood was a radical contrarian. A handsome, dark-haired graduate of Brown University, he was a staunch abolitionist, but refused to fight in the Civil War because of his strong pacifist beliefs. He insisted that marriage was unfair to women, calling it "legalized prostitution." Yet Heywood enjoyed a happy union to his wife Angela. Ezra and Angela, who lived in Princeton, Massachusetts, published the *Word*, a newspaper devoted to free love and labor reform. They were also among the founders of the New England Free Love League.

In 1876, Heywood published a turgidly written pamphlet entitled *Cupid's Yokes*, in which he assailed marriage and exalted sex in pseudoscientific terms. Heywood also lambasted Comstock, calling him "a religion-monomaniac" and advocating the repeal of the Comstock law, which he called "the National Gag-Law." *Cupid's Yokes* was no fun to read and probably would have been quickly forgotten if it hadn't attracted the interest of Comstock himself. Posing as "E. Edgewell of Squan Village, N.J.," Comstock ordered a copy of the pamphlet from Heywood through the mail along with Trall's *Sexual Physiology*, a book by a noted hydrotherapist. Once he received them, Comstock obtained a warrant for Heywood's arrest from a Boston magistrate. He didn't have to go to Princeton to serve it. Heywood was in Boston presiding over a meeting of the Free Love League.

Comstock gave a colorful account of what transpired in his book, *Traps for the Young*. When he arrived at the meeting, he found the Heywoods onstage in front of an audience of several hundred supporters. Angela Heywood delivered an impassioned speech in which she defended free love and assailed Comstock. Comstock left the building and stood outside on the sidewalk. "The fresh air was never more refreshing," Comstock wrote. "I resolved to stop that exhibition of nastiness, if possible. I looked for a policeman. As usual, none was to be found when wanted. Then I sought light and help from above. I prayed for strength to do my duty, and that I might have success. I knew God was able to help me. Every manly instinct cried out against my turning my back on this horde of lust. I determined to try. I resolved that one man in America at least should enter a protest."

Having fortified himself with such self-aggrandizing rhetoric, Comstock went back inside and endured more blasphemy. Just when he thought he could take no more, Ezra Heywood left the stage and wandered into the lobby. This was Comstock's chance. He followed Heywood and confronted him. "I have a warrant for your arrest for sending obscene matter through the mail," Comstock informed him. "You are my prisoner."

According to Comstock's account, Heywood made several attempts to escape. He told the special postal agent that he needed to inform the crowd that he was in police custody and would be departing sooner than scheduled, but Comstock would have none of that. Heywood next asked the vice suppressor if he would get his hat and coat. Comstock told a doorman to retrieve them. The doorman returned with Angela Heywood, who wanted to escort her husband to jail. Comstock had no interest in sharing a carriage with Mrs. Heywood. "I felt obliged out of respect to my wife, sister, and lady friends to decline the kind offer of her (select) company," he wrote. Heywood's supporters realized something was wrong and hurried to the lobby to see what it was. Comstock rushed his captive out of the building and shoved him into a carriage, ordering the driver to take them to the Charles Street jail. "Thus, reader," Comstock boasted, "the devil's trapper was trapped."

Heywood offered a terser version of his arrest. "In Boston," he wrote, "as I had momentarily left the chair in which I was presiding over a public convention to transact business in an anteroom, a stranger sprang upon me, and refusing to read a warrant, or even give his name, hurried me into a hack, drove swiftly through the streets, on a dark, rainy night, and lodged me in jail as a 'US prisoner.'" Heywood didn't discover until the next morning when his jailers finally showed him the warrant that it was Comstock himself who had arrested him. "Knowing the purity of my life and writings, the severely chaste objects and methods of my work, I scorn even to defend myself from 'obscenity' against the mercenary assassin of liberty!" Heywood raged.

United States District Court Judge Daniel Clark tried the case in 1878. Heywood's supporters filled the courtroom in Boston but Clark refused to let them testify about Heywood's character. He shut down the defense's efforts to call witnesses who would challenge the government's contention that *Cupid's Yokes* and *Sexual Physiology* were obscene. Clark wouldn't even permit the books to be read in the courtroom. He only gave the jurors copies with the objectionable parts underlined when they left the courtroom to deliberate. The jury didn't find *Sexual Physiology* indecent, but it accepted the government's contention that *Cupid's Yokes* was. Clark sentenced Heywood to two years of hard labor in Dedham jail in Massachusetts.

Comstock was elated. "Another class of publications issued by Freelovers and Freethinkers is in a fair way of being stamped out," he boasted in the Society's annual report. "The public generally can scarcely be aware of the extent that blasphemy and filth commingled have found vent through these varied channels. Under a plausible pretense, men who raise a howl about 'free press, free speech,' etc., ruthlessly trample under foot the most sacred things, breaking down the altars of religion, bursting asunder the ties of home, and seeking to overthrow every social restraint."

After the verdict, thousands of Heywood's supporters gathered for an "indignation meeting" at Boston's Faneuil Hall to condemn Comstock and the Post Office Department. Some contended that the special agent should confiscate the Bible, which overflowed with sex. Others insisted that Comstock was violating the sanctity of the mail by sending letters under false names to entrap people and opening packages that weren't addressed to him. "The two ways specially sanctioned by this learned judge are the post-office decoy system and the post-office espionage system," said Theodore Wakeman, a prominent Boston attorney. "Two plainer violations of the Bill of Rights—two meaner outrages upon liberty, decency, and morality—have never been perpetrated among our people! The learned judge did not invent them; they are old instruments of the Christian Inquisition. . . . Is this not a libel on our age and century, or have the Dark Ages returned?"

Heywood's admirers appealed to President Rutherford Hayes to pardon Heywood. Hayes didn't think it was a crime for a United States citizen to advocate the abolition of marriage. Nor did he find *Cupid's Yokes* to be "obscene, lascivious, lewd, or corrupting in the criminal sense." Comstock tried to change the president's mind, but it was no use. After six months in jail, Comstock's "devil trapper" walked out of Dedham jail a free man.

This seemed like an opportune time for freethinkers to lobby Congress to rescind the Comstock law. They collected more than 70,000 signatures and packed a hearing before the House of Representatives on the law. Comstock thought Satan's army had descended on the nation's capitol. "As I entered the committee room," he wrote. "I found it crowded with long-haired men and short-haired women, there to defend obscene publications, abortion implements, and other incentives to crime by repealing the laws. I heard their hiss and curse as I passed through them. I saw their sneers and their looks of derision and contempt." But neither the House nor the Senate wanted to overturn the antiobscenity law and face the wrath of Comstock and his followers around the country.

Comstock kept a watchful eye on Heywood, who had grown bolder since his presidential pardon. In the fall of 1882, Comstock pretended to be "J. A. Mattock of Nyack-on-the-Hudson, N.Y." and placed an order for *Cupid's Yokes*, an edition of the *Word* with Walt Whitman poems from *Leaves of Grass*, and another containing the offending advertisement for a birth control device mischievously called the Comstock Syringe. A grand jury indicted Heywood, claiming that *Cupid's Yokes* and the Whitman poems were "too grossly obscene and lewd to be placed on the records of the court." Even Whitman thought the publisher of the *Word* had gone too far. "Heywood is certainly a champion jackass," the poet wrote to a friend. "I am sorry for him, but his bed is his own making, and he should have known what Comstock would do to him. . . . I only hope we shall escape the consequences that follow."

This time, Heywood found himself in front of T. L. Nelson, a U.S. District Court judge less inclined to defer to Comstock. Nelson threw out the charge involving the Whitman poems, saying that neither was "grossly obscene and lewd." He ridiculed the charge related to *Cupid's Yokes*. "The court is robust enough to stand anything in that book," Nelson said. In the end, Heywood stood trial on a single count: advertising the Comstock Syringe. He took the witness stand and delivered a four-and-a-half-hour lecture, comparing himself to Jesus and John Brown and accusing Comstock of persecuting him because he advocated the repeal of the postal obscenity law.

The jury deliberated for two hours and found Heywood not guilty. The jurors said they would have acquitted him sooner, but they were entitled to one more free lunch courtesy of the federal justice system. When they heard the verdict, Heywood's friends in the courtroom cheered and embraced each other. Comstock sat among them, trying to contain his fury. "Upon the release of their Chief Free-lover, or more properly free-luster, what did the Liberals do?" he wrote. "How did they receive the man they helped release from the penalties of the law? THEY HAD A PARTY."

It was a rare defeat for Comstock, who continued for three more decades to arrest people for mailing literature that he found offensive. In 1892, a Post Office official acknowledged that the New York Society for the Suppression of Vice "has been so closely identified with the postal department that it is almost a part of it." But after the turn of the century, the public grew less prudish. Judges found Comstock's cases specious. Publishers and theatrical promoters welcomed his condemnations because they invariably translated into higher sales of tickets and books. The Irish playwright George Bernard Shaw coined the word "Comstockery" to describe the postal inspector's inability to distinguish between art and smut. "Europe likes to hear of such things," Shaw said. "It confirms the deep-seated conviction of the old world that America is a provincial place, a second-rate country town civilization after all."

Comstock responded with appropriate cluelessness. "George Bernard Shaw?" he told the *New York Times*. "Who is he? I have never heard of him in my life. Never saw one of his books so he can't be much."

The vice suppressor spent his final days pursuing Margaret Sanger, future founder of Planned Parenthood, who fled the country in 1914 after a federal grand jury indicted her for violating the Comstock law by mailing copies of the *Woman Rebel*, her monthly publication. Sanger argued that the founding fathers would have been aghast if they could have seen Comstock's abuses of the Post Office. "When the Constitution of the United States authorized Congress to establish post offices and post roads, it was not intended that the authority should go beyond this," she wrote. "It did not authorize it to censor the matter to be conveyed, nor to sit in judgment upon the moral, or intellectual qualities of the printed matter or parcel entrusted to it to deliver. The post office was, primarily, a mechanical institution, not an ethical one, whose business was efficiency, not religion or morality."

After he died the following year, Comstock became a laughingstock, ridiculed by F. Scott Fitzgerald and H. L. Mencken. But the Post Office would carry on his legacy for many more years.

Postal inspectors could still effectively censor books and magazines by banning them from the mail and showed the same inability to distinguish between literature and smut, between a D. H. Lawrence and a Larry Flynt. It would take a humiliating defeat in federal court to finally convince them to stop trying.

4

A Businessman
at the Post Office

After he won the presidential election of 1888, Benjamin Harrison scandalized the public with one of his cabinet appointments. In the past, presidents had awarded the job of postmaster general to men from the world of politics. While these men may not have known much about the mail, they knew who deserved a job in the department as a show of appreciation for their diligent campaign work. The public sometimes complained about the political nature of postal service hirings, but it generally accepted that this was the way the system worked.

Harrison took a decidedly different approach. He appointed John Wanamaker, a wealthy Philadelphia department store owner, to be his postmaster general. Wanamaker's sole qualification seemed to be that he had raised $200,000 for Harrison's triumphant campaign against Democratic incumbent Grover Cleveland. *Harper's Weekly* found the selection of Wanamaker puzzling. "Wanamaker is in no sense a leader of the party, and before the late election, he had been unknown in political life," it wrote.

The *Nation* was outraged by Wanamaker's appointment. "Would he ever have been thought of for a place in the Cabinet if he had not contributed or raised this money?" asked the liberal magazine. "Shall it be established for a precedent that a certain amount of cash entitles the giver or the financier to the position of Secretary of the Navy or Postmaster-General? If so, there will never be a campaign hereafter without a boodle candidate for a Cabinet position."

Cartoonists at satirical magazines such as *Puck* and *Judge* lampooned the new postmaster general, a bland-looking 51-year-old with a full nose, a slight chin, and thinning gray hair. Wanamaker was not only rich enough to fund a presidential election; he was deeply religious and went home to Philadelphia every weekend to teach at a Sunday school he had founded. The artists caricatured him as "Holy John," a hypocrite who preached the gospel from a Bible in one hand while using his other to spread corruption with his money, which was reportedly used to buy votes for Harrison (Wanamaker professed ignorance).

The skeptics mocked Wanamaker still further when he vowed to bring a more businesslike approach to the Post Office Department, which they assumed meant he planned to dispense contracts and jobs to Harrison's supporters. If that was Wanamaker's scheme, he was in the perfect place. In the private sector, he had been master of an operation with more than 4,000 employees and millions of dollars in sales. But now he presided over what he described as "the largest business concern in the world," with 150,000 employees and nearly 60,000 retail outlets. The year before Wanamaker's appointment, the Post Office delivered 3.8 billion pieces of mail and had sales of $53 million, or $1.4 billion in today's dollars.

Unlike Wanamaker's department store, the Post Office lost several million dollars a year. He said he could make the deficits disappear, but not right away. Instead, he made a series of proposals that shocked Harrison and the rest of his cabinet. Years later, Wanamaker gave an interview to journalist Samuel S. McClure, founder of the influential *McClure's* magazine. They sat in the former postmaster general's parlor, where a portrait of Harrison hung on the wall. "Harrison still speaks to me," Wanamaker said. "Now look at him. You remember him so well with that cold judicial appearance and his rather white skin. What do you suppose he is saying? 'Wanamaker, are you sure of your ground?' He says that to me every day."

Even after John Wanamaker was wealthy enough to afford a town house on Walnut Street in Philadelphia; a suburban estate in Cheltenham with stables, a bowling alley, and a 100-foot swimming pool; and a three-story oceanfront vacation home in Cape May, New Jersey, he referred to himself as a "country boy." It may have seemed strange but Wanamaker took pride in his humble beginnings.

John Wanamaker was born in 1838 in a farming community on the outskirts of Philadelphia called Gray's Ferry. The son of a perennially struggling bricklayer, he went to school for only two years and didn't get much of an education. "I never learned any more than simple arithmetic, for the teacher himself did not know any more," Wanamaker lamented. At age 14, he went to work full-time as a messenger at a bookstore near the city's waterfront to help pay his family's rent. He made $1.25 a week. The other messengers made fun of his rural ways, but Wanamaker was no hayseed. After several months, he got a job that paid nearly twice as much at a men's clothing store on the same block.

The new store's predatory environment fascinated Wanamaker. There were no fixed prices for clothes. Salesmen gave inflated quotes, and their customers refused to pay for anything without extended haggling. When a customer finally did purchase a shirt or a pair of pants, he couldn't return it. All sales were final in Philadelphia. Wanamaker wasn't sure this was admirable, but he become so adept at these methods that he impressed Colonel Joseph Bennett, owner of Tower Hall, the city's largest men's store, who hired him away.

Bennett paid Wanamaker six dollars a week and treated him like a son, buying him meals and listening to his plans. "John was certainly the most ambitious boy I ever saw," Bennett would later say. "He would tell me how he was going to be a great merchant."

Wanamaker was eager to make good on his promise. After three years, he quit when Bennett refused his demand for an ownership stake in Tower Hall. Wanamaker stormed out of the establishment, vowing to start one of his own and bury his former mentor.

Before Wanamaker could exact his vengeance, he became terribly ill. From the time of his boyhood, he had suffered from a respiratory ailment. Now Wanamaker could barely breathe. His doctor told him to flee the city and travel to a place with pristine air. A forgiving Bennett offered to pay his way, but Wanamaker refused and used his own savings to pay for a trip to Minnesota, where he regained his health.

Wanamaker returned to Philadelphia at the end of 1857 in a different frame of mind. Rather than open his own men's store as he had planned, he took a job as secretary for the newly constituted YMCA of Philadelphia. A devout Presbyterian, Wanamaker proved to be as good at attracting converts as he was at selling neckties. Within a year, the YMCA's membership had grown from 57 to 2,000 men. Wanamaker founded a Sunday school and considered a career as a clergyman, but he ultimately decided to return to the business world. "The idea clung to my mind that I could accomplish more in the same domain if I became a merchant and acquired means and influence with fellow merchants," Wanamaker said.

In 1861, Wanamaker opened Oak Hall, his own store on Market Street, with his brother-in-law, Nathan Brown. Their timing seemed inauspicious. The Civil War had begun, and young men were getting measured for military uniforms rather than sharply tailored suits. Wanamaker himself would have joined the Union Army, but his weak lungs made it impossible. "You are making a mistake in starting a business at such a time as this," George Stuart, president of the local YMCA, warned him. "The country is entering a great war, and there will be no business. Before long, grass will be growing in the streets of Philadelphia."

Oak Hall didn't attract many customers early on, at least not the purchasing kind. Wanamaker needed to lure more people into his store and get them to spend money, so he abandoned the sales methods he had learned at his previous jobs. He offered clothing at a fixed price. This wasn't entirely new. A. T. Stewart, a shrewd Irish immigrant, was already doing it at his New York department store. But Wanamaker added his own twist: a money-back guarantee. "Any article that does not fit well, is not the proper color or quality, does not please the folks at home, or for any reason is not perfectly satisfactory, should be brought back at once, and if it is returned as purchased within ten days, we will refund the money," Wanamaker promised. His competitors thought he had lost his mind.

Wanamaker also spent heavily on advertising at a time when other merchants felt it was a tawdry practice. He hired men to walk around with sandwich boards and ride around in coaches with bugle blowers promoting Oak Hall. One day, a representative of the Philadelphia City Directory visited Wanamaker and asked if he would buy an advertisement at the bottom of the page with the listing for Oak Hall.

"How about the top of the page?" Wanamaker responded.

The sales representative was taken aback. "We have never done that, sir," he said.

"Well, what if I took the top of every page in the book?" Wanamaker continued.

Wanamaker brusquely commanded the speechless salesman to get him a price. "If I put in an order like this," he added, "I shall expect also to have the cover page of the directory for a picture of our building."

In 1868, Nathan Brown died, and Wanamaker bought his share of the business. The following year he opened a fancier store called John Wanamaker & Company on Chestnut Street. The Civil War was over, the economy was booming, and once again people were spending freely. Wanamaker installed a skylight, laid plush carpets on the floors, and decorated the walls of the new store with paintings and mirrors, attracting fashionable Philadelphians who would have otherwise shopped in New York. Three years later, Wanamaker did $2 million worth of annual business at his two establishments.

Naturally, Wanamaker dreamed of doing something bigger. He visited Paris and toured its sprawling department stores like Le Bon Marché. He thought he could construct something commensurately grand in Philadelphia. In 1875, he purchased an entire city block from the Pennsylvania Railroad at Thirteenth and Market streets. Wanamaker tore down the old train shed on the site and built an enormous hall that had pagoda-like towers. He named it the Grand Depot and opened the doors in the summer of 1876 when visitors surged into Philadelphia for the country's centennial celebration.

In the beginning, the Grand Depot was a cavernous men's store. Wanamaker added women's clothing, linens, furniture, books, refrigerators, and washing machines. He promoted his money-back guarantee in full-page newspaper advertisements, but he understood that shoppers hungered for something more. They wanted an experience when they entered his door. So he gave them one after another. With the help of Thomas Edison, he illuminated the Grand Depot with electric lights, another Wanamaker first that dazzled customers. He installed the first in-store air-conditioning system, pumping a million cubic feet of cool air into his store during Philadelphia's humid summers.

The Sunday-school-teaching retailer wanted to enlighten his customers too. So he opened an in-store art galley with paintings from his personal collection and treated shoppers to free orchestral concerts. These innovations become part of his establishment's allure. Along with Chicago's Marshall Field, Wanamaker was part of a vanguard of retailers who ushered in a new era of American consumer culture that melded shopping with show business.

It was inevitable that Wanamaker, a loyal Republican and an admirer of Lincoln, would be drawn into politics. In 1884, Grover Cleveland was the first Democratic president to be elected in 24 years. Republican Party leaders wanted the White House back. Four years later, Matthew Quay, the powerful U.S. senator and Republican Party chairman, telephoned Wanamaker and asked him to help raise money for the Harrison campaign. Wanamaker threw himself into fund-raising with the same competitiveness that he showed in business. "We raised so much money the Democrats never knew anything about it," he boasted. "They had their spies out, supposing that they were going to do something. But before they knew what was what, they were beaten, not in November, not in October, but long before." The voters favored Cleveland by a slim margin, but Harrison trounced him in the electoral college with 233 votes to Cleveland's 168.

After the election, Quay let it be known that Wanamaker deserved to be rewarded for his hard work. In January 1889, the department store owner received a letter from Harrison. "My Dear Sir, we did not have the pleasure of meeting during the campaign, and I have had it in contemplation for some time to ask you to visit me," Harrison wrote. "Will it not be convenient for you to come at some early day? You are at liberty to name any time that is most convenient to you, as I shall always be at home. Very sincerely, Benj. Harrison." The president-elect misspelled his financial benefactor's name, which might otherwise have offended the detail-obsessed storeowner. Even so, Wanamaker made the journey to Harrison's home in Indianapolis, Indiana. "General Harrison sent for me . . . and offered me a position in his cabinet—one of the 'easiest' secretaryships," Wanamaker remembered. "But I said, 'I can't do it. I don't want a lazy place; if I take anything I will take the hardest place you have got,' and he put me in the Post Office Department."

Wanamaker took over at a time when the public's fascination with the Post Office had never been higher. In cities like Philadelphia and Baltimore, letter carriers made as many as seven deliveries a day, which meant they were a constant presence in the lives of urban Americans. Along with books, letters, and newspapers, carriers brought millions of greeting cards to their doors each year. Louis Prang, the lithographer credited with making the first commercially produced American Christmas cards in 1874, was printing five million a year by the 1880s. The Post Office made $1 million a year selling prestamped penny postcards, which had been introduced around the same time. These cards didn't have pictures on them—the department wouldn't formally admit that kind for another two decades. But the public embraced the penny postcards because they were a cheap and easy way to send a quick message.

More than 4,000 railway mail clerks sorted mail on trains, and they had a mascot now, a shaggy dog named Owney who had wandered into the post office in Albany, New York. Owney started riding on rails with the clerks and ended up traveling around the entire country with tags on his collar showing the many mail routes he had taken. The public became so enamored with Owney that Wanamaker arranged for him to get a small jacket on which his badges could be displayed more stylishly. When Owney died—he was either put to sleep after biting a clerk or mistakenly shot by a Toledo postmaster—the railway mail clerks had him stuffed and sent him to the department's headquarters, where he was proudly displayed; he can now be seen at the Smithsonian National Postal Museum.

Tourists flocked to the department's Dead Letter Office Museum in Washington, D.C., where the Post Office displayed the strangest of the seven million undeliverable items it received every year. Marshall Cushing, Wanamaker's secretary, described some of the things that the dead-letter clerks found: "The whole range of domestic life finds a full expression here: tiny little socks, delicately colored and ornamented; the juvenile necktie and the message-bearing valentine; the jewel box with its engagement ring; wedding cake in fancy boxes; infant's apparel again; soothing syrup; cholera mixture; little shrouds; coffin plates inscribed 'at rest'; flowers from a grave, —all come here when misdirected, unclaimed, with postage unpaid, without address, or not prepared for mailing in accordance with the regulations." Cushing also mentioned live toads, snakes, beetles, and tarantulas.

People who couldn't visit the museum could read magazine articles about Patti Lyle Collins, a widow from Mississippi who worked in the Dead Letter Office and became famous for being able to decode unreadable addresses. "One of the most valuable of the acquirements which are Mrs. Collins' possession is the knowledge of the city locality of almost every street in this and most other countries," the *Ladies' Home Journal* wrote. "One has but to mention a street to her, with the exception, of course, of those named Broad, High and Market, to have her, in ninety-nine cases out of a hundred, tell at once the city in which it is."

An address had to be almost impossibly difficult to read for the department to send it to Collins. Around this time, Mark Twain needed to send an early version of one of his stories, "Diaries of Adam and Eve," to a friend, but couldn't recall his address. So Twain wrote on the envelope, "For Mr. C. M. Underhill, who is in the coal business in one of those streets there, and is very respectably connected, both by marriage & general descent, and is a tall man & old but without any gray hair & used to be handsome. Buffalo N.Y. From Mark Twain. P.S. A little bald on the top of his head." That was more than enough for the post office to locate Underhill and give him Twain's manuscript.

Wanamaker still thought there was much that could be improved at the department. He embarked on a European tour to study the postal services of countries like England, France, and Germany. He was thrilled by what he discovered. The European posts carried mail to everybody in their nations, whether they lived in cities or in rural areas. They brought them packages along with letters and newspapers, unlike the U.S. Post Office Department, which wouldn't carry anything that weighed more than four pounds. England, France, Belgium, Russia, the Netherlands, and Sweden had savings banks in the post offices in which customers could deposit their money, knowing it would be safeguarded by the government. The foreign posts had also moved beyond paper-based communications, operating their nations' telegraph and telephone systems.

In his first annual report to Congress in 1889, Wanamaker argued that the Post Office Department should do all of these things. He asked Congress for funding to test rural free delivery, or RFD, as he called it. He wanted to put savings banks in 10,000 post offices in small communities where people typically hid their money under their mattresses because there were no financial institutions nearby. He wanted the Post Office Department to begin carrying parcels.

Wanamaker stopped short of proposing a government takeover of his country's telegraph and telephone systems, but he wanted to put telephones in post offices so people could make cheap calls. He also wanted the Post Office Department to speed delivery of mail by telegraphing letters between post offices. He hoped this would break the virtual monopoly of Western Union, which, he argued, overcharged for its services, denying ordinary people the opportunity to send fast messages. "We feel rather proud if we quicken a mail between New York and Chicago by three hours," Wanamaker wrote. "We smile with satisfaction if we induce a railroad company to put on a new mail train, which puts the businessmen of New Orleans, say, four hours nearer to the businessmen of Chicago. Here in the postal telegraph plan is a proposition that saves days and nights."

Before he took over the Post Office Department, Wanamaker could do whatever he pleased as long as he didn't bankrupt himself. If he wanted to make the Grand Depot sparkle with electric lights, he did so. If he wanted to station buyers in Paris, Berlin, and later Tokyo to keep track of the newest fashion trends, he did that too. But as postmaster general, Wanamaker didn't have the same unbridled freedom. Private bankers mobilized against his postal savings bank plan, saying it would undermine their industry. That was enough to kill the proposal.

Private express companies like Wells Fargo, American Express, Adams Express, and the United States Express Company mounted a similar campaign against Wanamaker's parcel post proposal, arguing that he was promoting it because it would help his department store's mail-order business. They had powerful congressional allies. In the U.S. Senate, Thomas Platt of New York looked out for the interests of these companies. His motives were hardly charitable. He was also president of the United States Express Company and didn't want the postal service encroaching on its business. In the U.S. House of Representatives, Speaker Joseph Cannon, an assiduous guardian of special interests, made sure that Wanamaker's parcel post plan quietly died in committee.

Wanamaker also incurred the wrath of Jay Gould, the Gilded Age financier who controlled Western Union. Gould went directly to President Harrison and told him to reign in his brash postmaster general. Gould had contributed as much as $100,000 to the Harrison campaign and warned in no uncertain terms that if he didn't get his way, he would not be so generous when the president ran for reelection. The *New York Times* reported that Harrison scolded Wanamaker for upsetting such a powerful ally. "I made no recommendation in my message warranting you to proceed as you have," Harrison reportedly said. "The effect of your work is to deprive my administration of valuable friends—friends who deserve better treatment and are not to be slighted. The friends you have slapped in the face were most valuable to us in 1888. And we need them in 1892. To attack them is political insanity. There is no need for it. This postal telegraph scheme might just as well be dropped; it never should have been begun." The *Times* attributed this information to unnamed Wall Street sources, which suggests that Gould and his allies wanted to publicly humiliate Wanamaker.

Wanamaker was known for his vigor and his optimism, but now he was becoming angry and frustrated. The Democratic press depicted him as a sleazy spoilsman. Wanamaker didn't help himself by firing 30,000 Democratic postmasters and replacing them with members of his own party, angering a rising Republican Party star named Theodore Roosevelt, who was Harrison's civil service commissioner and an opponent of the patronage system. Wanamaker subjected himself to further ridicule by declaring Tolstoy's *Kreutzer Sonata*, a novella about adultery, too obscene to be mailed. He realized his error and reversed himself, but the damage was done.

Like many postmaster generals before him, Wanamaker did nothing to stop Anthony Comstock from harassing freethinking Americans like Ezra Heywood. In 1890, the *Boston Daily Globe* wrote approvingly that "Anthony Comstock has renewed his fight against Cupid's Yoke and other radical social literature published by Ezra H. Heywood. He failed in the courts but now though Brother John Wanamaker, he is wielding the post office department against the wicked Mr. Heywood." Ten days later, Heywood was arrested by a Boston postal inspector for mailing him an issue of *The Word* with a mother's account of how she had explained sex to her daughter. Even Heywood's lawyer had warned him not to print this one.

In the ensuing trial, U.S. District Court Judge George Carpenter all but declared Heywood to be guilty. "It is right for us to hold that no person should think that purity, manliness and virtue could be promoted by sending through the mail a lewd, lascivious and obscene paper," Carpenter said in his instructions to the jury. "We have before us an example of a person who apparently, with the education of a respectable man, yet believes it." Heywood was found guilty of violating the Comstock law and was sentenced to two years of hard labor at Charleston State Prison on July 24, 1890. The verdict gave Wanamaker's critics more evidence that he was a hypocritical moralizer like Comstock himself.

Perhaps Wanamaker was on Comstock's side when it came to sexual matters, but he had a larger plan for the postal service that he wanted pursue if only Congress would let him. Three months later, Wanamaker won a victory, albeit a small one, when Congress gave him permission to conduct a one-year test of the "practicability" of home delivery in rural areas. He was authorized to spend only $10,000, but at least it was something.

City dwellers enjoyed all the benefits of modern life, such as paved streets, electricity, and frequent home visits by their letter carrier. Congress had lowered the price of sending a half-ounce letter to two cents in 1881. For 10 cents more, the sender could have the letter rushed to its destination by special delivery messengers. Yet for most Americans, this level of service was only a dream. Nearly two-thirds of the country's citizens lived in rural areas. These people still had to go to the post office to get their mail, and that often meant a long, bumpy trip over dirt roads, which they could make once a week at most. Most of them were farmers struggling to make a living. Without the regular delivery of a newspaper, they had no idea if it would rain the next day, so they didn't know when to plant their crops in the spring or harvest them in the fall. Without the newspaper, they didn't know what the market was paying for livestock or crops, meaning that buyers could easily get the better of them when they loaded their wagons and journeyed into town to sell to them.

This discrepancy in mail delivery contributed to the feeling among farmers that they were second-class citizens in the United States. Radical orators like Mary Elizabeth Lease stoked their resentment by telling them to "raise less corn and more hell." They threw their support behind the Populist Party, which championed postal reforms strikingly similar to Wanamaker's. The party's platform called for postal banks to protect the savings of small-town residents, a parcel post service to bring them goods at a reasonable price from the stores where city folk shopped, and government ownership of the telegraph and telephone systems. Wanamaker's opponents and even some of his friends in Washington may have called him a socialist for pushing such ideas, but the wealthy department-store owner found common cause with the people who tilled the American soil. They fondly referred to him as "Brother Wanamaker."

In 1891, Wanamaker tested rural free delivery in 46 small towns across the country from Dexter, Maine; to Roseville, California. RFD proved to be so popular in these villages that locals worried what would happen when the experiment ended and their customers had to return to their old ways. "The free delivery is a success in the broadest sense of the word," wrote the postmaster of Emporium, Pennsylvania. "We could not do without it, as the signature of every citizen here would attest if required." Wanamaker boasted that the Post Office Department made a profit of $4,000 on the trial because it inspired citizens to send more letters. "It is evident, then—indeed, we have proved it—that you can spend money for free delivery in these small communities and get it back and more too," he crowed.

Local chapters of the National Grange of the Order of Patrons and Husbandry, the influential farmers' advocacy group, sent petitions by the thousands to Congress clamoring for Brother Wanamaker's experiment to be extended. Small-town residents like J. B. Brown of Vernon Center, Connecticut, sent letters to the editor calling for RFD in their communities. "Bring the post office to the farmers' doors and you will take more hayseed out of their hair, put more comfort in their homes and money in their pockets than any one thing purchased at the same expense," Brown wrote. In Salisbury, Massachusetts, P. A. True sent a similar letter to his newspaper. "The United States mail is a great civilizer," True wrote, "and I do not know why the farmers of the rural town can not have it [delivered] free as well as the city mechanic." Naturally, newspaper publishers in rural areas called for RFD too, knowing it would increase their subscribers.

Once again, special interests rallied against Wanamaker. Merchants in small towns opposed rural free delivery, saying customers wouldn't come into town to shop as much. Saloon keepers argued that farmers would have less excuse to stop in for a drink after visiting the post office and the country store. The private expresses insisted that rural free delivery was just the first step in Wanamaker's scheme to destroy rural businesses. After all, they warned, once farmers got mail delivered to their homes, they would insist on ordering everything from Montgomery Ward and Sears, Roebuck & Company.

Some people said there should be no further RFD testing because letter carriers wouldn't be able to ride their bicycles on bumpy dirt roads. "I am glad to know this," Wanamaker responded indignantly. "R.F.D., like bicycling, will make for better roads, and that is the crying need. A nation's strength and progress are bound up with the improvements of communications, and it is the duty of the whole community, for social and patriotic reasons, to work hard on the roads. . . . If there are millions, as you say, to whom it will be difficult for rural carriers to get mail, how do the children of those towns get to school?"

In January 1892, James O'Donnell, a congressman from Michigan, introduced a bill to appropriate $6 million for broader testing. But the House of Representatives refused to approve the funds, and even killed an amendment that would have appropriated $100,000 for more limited tests. Once again, Wanamaker, who had become a millionaire by creating one of the world's greatest department stores, had been thwarted by politics. Rural free delivery was dead, and its chief evangelist couldn't have been more disappointed.

This is not to say that Wanamaker didn't have some more modest successes during his four years as postmaster general. He placed clerks on streetcars and ocean liners, turning them into traveling post offices as the department had done with trains. He introduced home mailboxes in cities. This meant a letter carrier no longer had to hang around outside people's houses waiting for them to return so he could give them their mail without fear of its being lost or stolen. Wanamaker introduced the postal service's first pneumatic tube system, sending a Bible wrapped in an American flag underground from one Philadelphia post office to another. Within a few years, the department had similar networks humming beneath the streets of New York, Boston, St. Louis, and Chicago. Wanamaker introduced the first commemorative stamps. And he created the country's first national postal museum in Washington with artifacts from mail systems around the world. "The footprint of the mail carrier is the signpost of civilization," Wanamaker declared at the opening ceremony.

Still, Wanamaker sounded melancholy in his final annual report to Congress in December 1892. He had failed to get funds that year for any new projects. "There was nothing to be done this past year except to trudge along the old roads, for Congress at its last session passed no bill affecting the postal service in any substantial way," he sighed.

Wanamaker scolded Congress for not supporting rural free delivery. "The old system is really colonial," Wanamaker said. "It takes pay for delivery of letters without delivering them. It obliges people to go or send for mail and that means in the winter or stormy seasons and for families of aged people, the deprivation of going without letters and periodicals (hardly less valuable) that lie in post offices for long periods not called for. We shall look back with astonishment before many years that the present system had to be suffered so long." Wanamaker called for the resurrection and adoption of his postal telegraph plan. "I am fully convinced that the Government will never properly do the postal work committed to it until it uses electricity in some form," he insisted.

Then it was time for Wanamaker to say good-bye. A month earlier, Grover Cleveland had run again and defeated Harrison in the 1892 presidential election. That meant Wanamaker and the other members of Harrison's cabinet would soon be out of work. For Wanamaker, it would be a relief to return to the private sector, where he no longer had to submit to the will of Congress. But he would miss the people at the Post Office Department, many of whom he had gotten to know and admired. Before he went home to Philadelphia,

Wanamaker personally signed more than 65,000 letters of appreciation to every postmaster in the country.

Wanamaker would construct a larger and even more iconic department store in Philadelphia and create another in New York. But he continued to pay attention to the Post Office Department, where something remarkable was happening. The second Cleveland administration opposed RFD, saying it would be too expensive. But farmers' organizations, small-town residents, and their allies continued to press for it, and in 1896, Congress approved $40,000 for a larger test. William Wilson, Cleveland's postmaster general, reluctantly created 44 RFD routes in 29 states.

Rural letter carriers delivered mail in the backwoods of Maine, the sugar belt of Louisiana, the fruit-growing districts of Arizona, the ranch lands of Colorado, the farms of upstate New York, and an island in Lake Champlain in Vermont. They made their rounds on bicycles, horses, buckboards, buggies, and two-wheeled carts, crossing over farms and fields to make their deliveries. People never complained when they saw a letter carrier traversing their property. Rural residents were delighted to get their mail at home.

Farmers fashioned makeshift mailboxes out of stovepipes, tomato cans, and feed boxes and hung them outside their gates. "One man has a lard pail hung out on a fence post; three or four have nailed up empty coal oil cans, and a few have utilized syrup cans," the Post Office reported. "These make very secure receptacles when placed on the side with the upper half of one end cut out."

Now that farmers received a daily newspaper in their mailboxes, they knew the weather forecast. "That saves us time and anxiety," wrote O. N. Caldwell, a farmer in Carpinteria, California. "The weather report is dropped in our box, and that is the first thing I look at, to see what it says about the weather tomorrow." They could keep track of the price of crop futures and get better prices for their livestock and vegetables. "I saw a big jump in the potato market," wrote J. S. Hollingsworth, a farmer in Snacks, Indiana. "Next day I left a postal card in a United States box at the crossroads for a farmer three miles distant to 'hold your big potato crop; a jump is on the market; don't sell too soon.' In two weeks from that date he sold 1,000 bushels at 20 cents above the October market." Rural free delivery raised property values too. "It's already had an influence on the price of land, which has increased $5 an acre," wrote S. C. McDowell of Fox Lake, Michigan.

RFD also made farmers feel more like full-fledged citizens. In Tempe, Arizona, one grateful farmer wrote: "I live three and a half miles from the Tempe post office, and have been sick for a week past, yet my mail is brought to my door every morning, except Sunday. I hope the Government is satisfied that the experiment is a grand success; for I assure you that we 'hayseeds' (as we are sometimes dubbed) are more than pleased with the system. It looks as if 'Uncle Sam' had at last turned his eye in our direction, and had determined to help the farmer." RFD was hardly profitable, as Wanamaker had promised that it would be. In sparsely populated areas, rural carriers traveled for miles to deliver a handful of letters, which meant that the postal service spent as much as six cents to deliver some two-cent messages. The cost was surely higher in Alaska, where the post office delivered mail by dogsled and operated what was described as the world's only reindeer route. "Here on a sledge made of whalebone, drawn by a team of domesticated reindeer, Uncle Sam's postman hurried over the trackless snow covered tundras—freezing and starving at times, and at other times forced to kill and eat his 'horse,' bent upon the same mission as the R.F.D. carrier in the happy, populated U.S.A.," wrote the *Chicago Tribune*. But regardless of the cost, the time had come for rural free delivery.

The political climate in the United States was changing. The efforts of farmers to turn the Populist Party into a viable third party had failed, but many of its ideas were picked up and improved upon by progressives like Republican president Theodore Roosevelt, Wanamaker's old adversary, who had become his ideological kinsman on postal matters. In 1902, Roosevelt made RFD a permanent service. "It brings the men who live on the soil into close relations with the active business world," Roosevelt said in annual report to Congress that year. "It keeps the farmer in daily touch with the markets; it is a potential educational force; it enhances the value of farm property, makes farm life far pleasanter and less isolated, and will do much to check the undesirable current from country to city." The cries of protest against free rural delivery now came from small-town postmasters who realized what RFD meant for them. Now that the Post Office Department had carriers going door-to-door everywhere, it didn't need as many outposts. In the first decade of the twentieth century, it closed 17,108 post offices, reducing the total number from 76,688 to 59,580. It was a sharp reduction and one that would never be duplicated at the U.S. Post Office in such a short span of time.

Wanamaker was elated by his vindication, and a few years later, he savored another. In 1910, Roosevelt's successor, William Howard Taft, defied the banking industry and signed a postal savings bill allowing Americans to deposit up to $500 at their local post office. As Wanamaker had predicted, people were eager to entrust their money to the federal government for safekeeping. Half a century later, the Post Office Department would become America's largest bank, with four million customers and $3.4 billion in deposits.

Shortly after that victory, Wanamaker celebrated another belated triumph. His foes in the private express industry had been prescient: now that rural people had free letter delivery, they wanted parcels bought to their homes too. Wells Fargo, American Express, and the United States Express Company wouldn't do that; it wasn't profitable enough. The best they could offer was to drop off packages at the nearest train station, which might be miles away from a farmer's home. That wasn't good enough in the era of RFD. A new breed of muckraking journalists discovered that the private expresses were connected to the big railroads through a web of joint stock ownership. The railroads charged the Post Office Department four cents a pound to carry the mail. However, the expresses paid less than one cent per pound to carry their parcels on trains. Both the railroads and their private express partners made vast sums of money from this arrangement. Rather than conducting themselves like paragons of private enterprise as they claimed to be, the railroads and private carriers were operating a cartel.

Two decades earlier, GOP bosses like Thomas Platt and Joseph Cannon stood in the way of Wanamaker's parcel post plan. But Republicans were swept out of office in the 1910 midterm election, when voters replaced them with progressive Democrats who had no love for the private express companies. The new Congress held hearings on the creation of a parcel post service, frequently lauding Wanamaker, who was now hailed as a hero rather than scorned.

In 1912, Taft signed the Parcel Post Act, and his administration asked Wanamaker to be one of the first to send a package when the new service began on January 1, 1913. On New Year's Eve, the 74-year-old former postmaster general arrived at the Philadelphia General Post Office in a dark, three-piece suit and a bow tie, looking rounder than when he had presided over the mail system. "I have been on the Parcel Post turnpike since 1889, when I made an earnest and urgent argument for it and other postal service in my first annual report to President Harrison," Wanamaker reminded everyone. "The cost of living and the prices of many things would not have been as high the last twenty years if Parcel Post, postal savings and cheapened telegraph service had been granted to the people when other nations had proved them and were successfully operating them." He had a gift for President Taft, a set of gold-plated spoons. At midnight, Thomas Smith, the postmaster of Philadelphia, handed Wanamaker's package to a mustached postman who rushed it to the Pennsylvania Railroad's West Philadelphia Station so it could be delivered to the White House.

Later that morning, people around the country lined up at post offices that had opened for the historic occasion and sent three million packages. In Gary, Indiana, a brick dealer named William Parry arrived at the post office with a thousand of his products, individually wrapped to get around the 11-pound limit. It was the kind of self-promotional stunt that Wanamaker might have attempted in his early days, before he had achieved respectability.

The parcel post was a boon to mail-order companies like Sears, Roebuck and Montgomery Ward. Previously, they had relied on the private expresses to transport their orders. But now they had an army of federal letter carriers who could transport their goods to every doorstep in the country, including those in rural areas where people were starved for the items in their catalogs. Thanks to parcel post, the mail-order industry's profits climbed from $40 million in 1908 to $250 million in 1920. Wanamaker contributed to this by shipping parcels at no extra charge for customers who spent more than one dollar at his stores. He called it "Wanamaker Free Delivery."

Postal customers sent all sorts of oddities through the parcel post just to see if they could get away with it. They mailed pitchforks, brooms, and bees. They mailed eggs, some of which arrived intact. In February 1914, the Pierstorffs of Grangeville, Idaho, sent their five-year-old daughter to visit her grandmother 75 miles away in Lewiston via parcel post, because it was cheaper than buying her a train ticket. Little May Pierstorff weighed 48 pounds, which meant that she was just under the Post Office Department's 50-pound limit for parcels. The Grangeville postmaster charged her parents 53 cents, attaching the appropriate stamps to the front of her coat. May traveled all the way to Lewiston in a railway baggage car under the watchful eye of a railway mail clerk. When she arrived, a mail clerk on duty drove her to her grandmother's house rather than leaving her at the post office for morning delivery. Soon there were more incidents of "child mailing," and finally the Post Office Department outlawed the practice.

It's unclear what John Wanamaker made of that, but he was fascinated by the department's next innovation. He wished that the technology had arrived sooner so he could have been the postmaster general who could have taken credit for it. "Why weren't the Wrights a little earlier with their flying machine?" Wanamaker wrote. "Then I would have had the credit for this innovation, provided always that Congress would have listened to me. It generally didn't."

5

Into the Sky

Otto Praeger waited anxiously on a polo field beside the Potomac River in Washington, D.C., clutching a cigar in his right hand. Short and balding, the 47-year-old Praeger had a pale, doughy face. He wore a hat and a three-piece suit that needed pressing. He looked as though he hadn't slept, and he had every reason to be nervous. Praeger was the second assistant postmaster general in charge of transportation, and his biggest project was the U.S. Post Office's new Air Mail Service, which was about to make its first official rounds on the balmy, cloudless morning of May 15, 1918.

The new service would make its debut before nearly 5,000 people who crowded onto the polo field. Schoolchildren had been given the day off so they could see the flying mailmen. Praeger circulated among 500 dignitaries in a roped-off area. They included Alexander Graham Bell, inventor of the telephone and an aviation enthusiast himself; artic explorer Robert Peary; Japanese postmaster M. K. Kambara; a young Franklin D. Roosevelt, who was then assistant U.S. Navy secretary; and Postmaster General Albert Burleson, a dour 54-year-old Texan referred to by his fellow cabinet members as "the cardinal," because even on days like this, he dressed in a dark suit and a round hat and carried a black umbrella to hide his gout-infected foot.

The U.S. Air Mail Service would be a joint undertaking of the Post Office and the U.S. Army. The Army would supply the pilots, mechanics, and planes. The Post Office would do the rest—mapping out routes, securing airfields, building hangars, and hiring an administrative staff. The public would receive speedier mail delivery, and military pilots would learn to fly long distances before journeying to France to battle German airmen in World War I, which the United States had entered little more than a year before. At least, that was the idea.

The Wright brothers had flown the first airplane only 15 years before, and while aviation had advanced considerably since then, it was still primitive by today's standards. Airmail pilots would be transporting letters in the Curtiss JN-4H, better known as the Jenny, a single-engine biplane with an open cockpit. Jennies cruised at a maximum speed of about 65 miles an hour, barely enough to earn a speeding ticket on modern highways. Their gas tanks held a mere 21 gallons, meaning a pilot could fly only 175 miles before having to land and refuel. That wasn't enough for Army pilots to make the 215- mile journey nonstop from Washington to New York. So Praeger had designed a relay system: a pilot would take off shortly from the nation's capital with 6,000 letters and carry them to Philadelphia, where he would hand his mailbags to another airman bound for Belmont Park in Hempstead, New York. At the same time, a pair of Army pilots would travel the route in reverse, carrying letters from New York to Washington.

There was a roar of applause as President Woodrow Wilson arrived in a car with his wife, Edith. Dressed in a finely tailored four-button suit, Wilson produced a letter addressed to New York City postmaster Thomas Patten, who would receive it later that day by plane. Wilson ceremonially deposited his letter in one of the four sacks that would be carried by Lieutenant George Boyle, an Army pilot. Wilson and Boyle posed for a picture.

Then it was time for Boyle to be on his way. He climbed into the plane. The maintenance crew turned the propeller. The engine sputtered, but it didn't start. They tried again with the same disappointing result. Wilson became impatient. "We're losing a lot of valuable time here," he muttered to his wife.

Praeger was mortified. He hurried over to the maintenance crew. "What's the matter?" he asked. He discovered that the mechanics had forgotten to refuel Boyle's plane when it arrived that morning. The crew swiftly siphoned gas from other planes and filled the aircraft's tank. They spun the propeller again; this time, the engine clattered noisily to life. Praeger would later tell people that he heard Wilson sigh with relief at the sound. Boyle wheeled his Jenny around and took off. He circled the field above the cheering crowd, and off he went.

An hour later, Boyle was lost. He had tried to follow the railroad tracks north to Philadelphia, but he got confused and ended up heading south. His journey ended in Waldorf, Maryland, 44 miles southeast of Washington, where he spotted a field and tried to land. When he touched down, he flipped his plane and snapped the propeller. Boyle was unscathed, but he would go down in history ignominiously as "Wrong Way Boyle." His shipment of mail had to be transported to New York by train, infuriating Otto Praeger.

It was an inauspicious start for the U.S. Air Mail Service. Yet within two years, the Post Office would show that it was possible to fly coast-to-coast in little more than a day, demonstrating the feasibility of commercial aviation at a time when the private sector was too fearful to take the risk. The man behind it all was Otto Praeger. He wasn't a pilot—he took his first plane ride several months after the service started—but he is considered the father of the U.S. airmail. "Praeger was twenty years ahead of his time," aviation historian Henry Ladd Smith wrote in *Airways: The History of Commercial Aviation in the United States.* "In a day of open-cockpit planes, he dreamed of transoceanic airways and multi-engine ships." Praeger didn't let anything get in his way, either. Congressmen wanted to shut down his operation, saying it was a waste of taxpayers' money. The Army tried to snatch it from the Post Office. Praeger was also frequently at odds with his pilots, who accused him of callously risking their lives.

The accusation was not without justification. The men who transported mail in the sky were truly brave and not a little reckless. They flew planes without two-way radios, which pilots would later use to remain on course in bad weather. When they lost their way, they landed and asked locals for directions. If the engines caught fire, they were probably doomed. Pilots didn't carry parachutes back then. Small wonder the U.S. Air Mail Service would become known among pilots as the "Suicide Club."

Fittingly, Benjamin Franklin makes a brief appearance in the earliest days of airmail delivery. In 1785, French inventor Jean-Pierre François Blanchard and Dr. John Jeffries, Franklin's friend from Boston, made the first voyage by balloon over the English Channel. They carried letters, including one to the father of the American postal service. When Blanchard and Jeffries arrived in Calais, they made sure he got it, making Franklin, some would say, the first American to receive an airmail message, another of Franklin's many firsts.

But aviation historians generally say the first instance of airmail sanctioned by the U.S. Post Office took place much later, on August 17, 1859, when Professor John Wise, a professional balloonist, attempted to carry mail in his balloon *Jupiter* from Lafayette, Indiana, to New York. We know the Post Office cooperated because Wise said so beforehand in an advertisement: "All persons who wish to send their letters to their friends in the East by balloon today must deliver them at the post office previous to 12 PM, as the Jupiter's mail closes at that hour. The letters must be addressed 'via *Balloon Jupiter*' added to the ordinary directions and prepaid. This mail will be conveyed by Mr. Wise to the place of landing with the balloon, when it will be placed in the nearly post office for distribution."

A crowd of 20,000 spectators applauded as Wise rose over Lafayette in his balloon. But Wise couldn't find any wind, even when he rose 14,000 feet. After five hours, he gave up and landed thirty miles away in Crawfordsville. "Knowing that if there were no currents below I could land safely and easily in the town, and in order to make the arrival more interesting I concluded to send my letter mail ahead," Wise later wrote in his memoir *Through the Air: A Narrative of Forty Years' Experience as an Aeronaut.* "Having with me a muslin sheet nine feet square, I attached to each of its corners strings of about five yards in length. These were tied together at their lower extremities, and to this knot was attached the mailbag, and then I dropped it overboard. It made an admirable parachute. A few minutes travel informed me that it would drift a considerable distance to the south of Crawfordsville, as there was a slight breeze below drifting it in that direction. I pulled the valve of *Jupiter,* and followed, and soon overtook the mail. We kept near together all the way down, as I could regulate the descent of the parachute, and both aerial machines landed within fifty feet of each other on the public road."

A postal agent picked up Wise's mail and put it on a New York–bound train. For more than a century, there was a debate about the significance of Wise's flight. It wasn't just that he didn't get very far; nobody could find any letters from his so-called "trans-county-nental journey" that had been postmarked, which would have proved that the Post Office blessed his effort. In 1957, however, one of them turned up and two years later, on the one-hundredth anniversary of Wise's flight, the Post Office issued an airmail stamp in his honor.

At the time, the Post Office didn't seem impressed. It wasn't until the advent of airplanes that the Post Office got serious about starting an airmail service. Frank Hitchcock, Taft's postmaster general, tried to get it going when he swore in pilot Earle Ovington as a letter carrier. Ovington carried the mail in the sky from Mineola, New York, to Garden City, a distance of 6 miles, for about a week in 1911. It was more of a publicity stunt than anything else, but he couldn't get funding for anything more. "The Post Office Department has been up in the air long enough, and now let us get down to terra firma for once," a skeptical congressman said in 1912.

Where Hitchcock failed, his successor Albert Burleson would succeed. Burleson cultivated an image as a simple rustic, but he was a masterful politician. He belonged to the group of southern Democrats in Congress who supported Wilson, the Democratic governor from New Jersey, when he ran for president that year. When Wilson defeated Republican Taft and Theodore Roosevelt, who was running as the Bull Moose Party candidate, he showed his gratitude to Burleson in 1913 by appointing him postmaster general and his liaison to Congress, a familiar role for the nation's mail chief. The tall, severe-looking Texan could often be seen in the House and Senate chambers, trading patronage jobs for votes. He once gave four postmaster positions to a Kansas senator to secure his support for Wilson's proposed tariff reform. "I had the bait gourd," Burleson said. "They had to come to me."

In the year Burleson took over the Post Office, it delivered 18 billion pieces of mail, including 300 million parcels in the first six months of the year. In cities like Atlanta and New York, postmasters were beginning to use trucks to carry parcels to people. The number of post offices had declined to 58,020 as the rural delivery routes multiplied; Burleson noted in his first annual report that 40 million rural residents were enjoying daily visits from their letter carriers. But even as the department closed rural post offices, it was constructing grand monumental buildings in cities, like the Washington City Post Office, which was completed in 1914 and now stands beside Union Station; and New York City's General Post Office, which is now known as the James A. Farley Post Office, designed by the architects McKim, Mead & White. The typeface for the famous quotation from Herodotus above the entryway is now believed to have been chosen by Ira Schnapp, a young designer from Austria who would later create the Superman logo for Action Comics.

Burleson held his position during Wilson's two terms in the White House, making him one of America's longest-serving postmaster general, and he was one of the most polarizing. The son of a Confederate officer, he was a segregationist who transferred black clerks in Washington to the Dead Letter Office, where they would have no interaction with the public. Burleson was no defender of free speech either. Anthony Comstock died in 1915, but his legacy lived on at the Post Office thanks to Burleson. Four years later, the Post Office seized editions of the *Little Review*, a literary magazine that contained excerpts from James Joyce's *Ulysses*, which was considered risqué in certain quarters and would be banned from the mail for another decade by the department. During World War I, Burleson withdrew second-class mail privileges for socialist publications like the *Masses* because of the party's anti-interventionist stand; this was tantamount to censorship because without the discount, most small publications couldn't afford to widely circulate copies.

Yet in other ways, Burleson was a firm progressive. He believed that the Post Office should own and operate the nation's telegraph and telephone systems for the benefit of the public rather than shareholders. (During the war, Burleson did take them over with disastrous results. Rates increased and service declined because of a telephone workers' strike; the public demanded their return to private hands as soon as the war ended.) Burleson was a champion of the parcel post, lowering rates and causing the department's yearly volume to skyrocket to one billion packages. He enthusiastically promoted a short-lived, but farsighted farm-to-table service, which enabled farmers to ship butter, eggs, and honey through the parcel post to people in cities. He also believed that the department could carry mail in the sky and he knew just the person to get a permanent airline service up and running: Otto Praeger.

The son of a hardware store owner who had emigrated from Germany, Praeger was born in 1871 and grew up in San Antonio, Texas, which was still a town out of the Wild West with gambling halls that never closed and saloons where patrons frequently got into shoot-outs. Buffalo Bill Cody came through town with his traveling Wild West show, telling tales of the Pony Express. It was a lively place and young Otto did his part to contribute to its live-liness. At San Pedro High School, he created his own newspaper, which made him the object of his fellow students' fear and envy. "Pupils talked about him in whispers," recalled his schoolmate, Moses Koenigsberg, the future head of the Hearst Corporation's King Features Syndicate.

Praeger dropped out of high school in 1888 to take a job as a cub reporter at the *San Antonio Express*, which was full of hard-drinking nomads who wandered from one newsroom to the next. Praeger enjoyed their company, but he had grander ambitions. In 1892, he persuaded the *Express* to let him travel through Mexico on a bicycle and sent accounts of his adventures back through the mail. He spent three months pedaling through the Sierra Madre and the Sierra Mojada desert. He made his way to Mexico City, where Mexican president Porfirio Diaz received him. When Prae-ger returned, the *New York Times* gave him a hero's welcome. "He has suffered starvation, and has been well nigh crazed with thirst," the paper wrote. "Praeger was compelled for days to plod his way with a bicycle strapped to his side over paths that even the Mexican muleteers will not attempt, and has come through it all improved mentally and physically."

Praeger was promoted to city editor and then news editor of the *Express*. He wanted to be editor in chief, but the paper's owner held the title and wouldn't relinquish it. So Praeger quit in 1904 to become the Washington correspondent for the *Dallas Morning News*, the largest paper in Texas. He enjoyed the bustle of the nation's capital, but found most members of Congress to be colorless and mediocre, except for Albert Burleson, a Democrat from San Marcos, Texas. The two men went on hunting and fishing trips, talking politics and becoming close friends.

After he became postmaster general, Burleson appointed Prae-ger postmaster of Washington, D.C. Why Praeger? Burleson wanted to prevent Secretary of State William Jennings Bryan from steering the job to one of *his* chums. However unmerited his appointment may have seemed, Praeger quickly distinguished himself. The department had tried to hire private trucking firms to replace the horse-drawn wagons used to transport mail in the Washington area, but the haulers wanted too much money. Burleson had a better idea; he wanted the Post Office to buy its own trucks, and it would be up to Praeger to test the feasibility of his plan. Praeger introduced the trucks in Washington and got the new system running so smoothly that Burleson named him assistant postmaster general in charge of postal transportation for the entire country.

Praeger spent much of his time on the road, introducing postal trucks in Detroit, St. Louis, and Philadelphia, carrying a toothbrush and little else. When his shirts became too soiled to wear, he purchased new ones and sent the dirty shirts home through the mail to be cleaned. In Chicago, a Republican congressman insisted that horse-drawn wagons were swifter than the shiny new postal vehicles in traffic, and didn't want the department to cancel a contract with a local hauling firm that used horses. Praeger settled the matter with a race between his drivers and the private carriers in Chicago's downtown loop. The trucks beat the horse-powered carts, and soon there were hundreds of gas-powered vehicles transporting packages and letters in the Chicago area.

On an overcast wintry morning in 1917, Burleson summoned Praeger to his office. They stood at the window, looking out over the slush-filled streets and the Capitol building, which could barely be seen through the clouds. "Do you think that airplanes could operate in this kind of weather?" Burleson asked. "You know, we have a lot of it in the winter months." Praeger didn't think so. He had seen only one airplane: it had been piloted by Orville Wright himself at a demonstration in 1909. Wright's plane hadn't been capable of flying very high, let alone navigating in this kind of weather.

"Shucks," Burleson replied. "We have come a long way since those flights. You make a study of this thing. I tell you what: if I am convinced that the airplane can operate dependably in any kind of weather—of course, no worse than this—I will put the air mail in the postal service. Don't you see how that would speed up the mails?"

The first days of the Air Mail Service were chaotic. Wrong Way Boyle got another chance to deliver mail, but ran out of gas and crashed while attempting to land on a golf course in Philadelphia, ending his time as an airmail pilot. Another pilot got lost in fog on the way from New York to Philadelphia and landed in a field of horses in New Jersey, swerving to avoid one and smashing into a fence. Such incidents only increased the public's fascination with the Air Mail Service. In Philadelphia, the Post Office had to hire security guards to handle the hundreds of people who regularly showed up to watch its planes take off and land.

However, there were some encouraging moments in the first two weeks of the Air Mail Service. Traveling from Philadelphia to Washington one afternoon in 1918, Lieutenant James Edgerton encountered a thunderstorm over northern Maryland; determined to be on time, he headed into it. Almost immediately Edgerton lost control of his plane. "One instant, the plane became a tremendous elevator, leaping skyward hundreds of feet. Promptly, the bottom seemed to drop out, the dizzy fall to cover hundreds of feet," he wrote rather poetically. "Attacked by solid waves of air, the plane reared, slithered and bucked."

Edgerton relaxed his grip on the controls, hoping the storm would guide him. To his wonder, it did. "I gave in somewhat to my enemy, and in turn, he gave in somewhat to me," Edgerton recalled. Remarkably, he was still on course when he emerged from the maelstrom, even though his plane was a wreck. A large piece of the propeller flew by his ear as he glided down to the airfield in Washington. Edgerton had done what had previously been thought impossible; he had flown through a severe storm and survived.

In July 1918, Praeger extended the air service to Boston and insisted that pilots fly in all kinds of weather. Only then, he argued, would the Post Office be able to provide reliable, uninterrupted service. Reluctant to risk the lives of its pilots before sending them to France to fight, the Army refused. Sometimes it grounded pilots on foggy days, but not always. Praeger was enraged one Saturday when he learned the Army had halted the airmail because of inclement weather, but permitted a pilot to fly from New York to Washington the same day for a personal matter.

Captain A. C. Weidenbach, who oversaw the Air Mail Service for the Army, received a furious letter from Praeger, sent by special messenger. "I am afraid that the officers who are flying these routes are laboring under the attitude of mind that this aerial mail service is merely for the purpose of carrying a handful of mail," Praeger scolded him. "The purpose of the trips as the Post Office Department sees them is to establish a daily aerial movement in the face of weather obstacles, feeling confident that the necessities and exigencies of the situation will speedily devise means to overcome present obstacles." Weidenbach wouldn't bend. Only three months after the service was launched, the Army pulled out of it. The Post Office would have to go it alone.

Happy to be in complete control, Praeger advertised for civilian pilots willing to brave any kind of weather and quickly hired four applicants. The first was Max Miller, a sandy-haired former Army flight instructor born in Norway. "I've covered as much as 300 to 400 miles a day, only stopping for gasoline and oil or necessary repairs," Miller wrote to the Post Office Department. "I have carefully considered the risk involved caused by bad weather conditions, and I would be willing to do my best under those circumstance and would be ready to go out at any time required." Miller got the job.

So did Eddie Gardner, a former race car driver from Plainfield, Illinois. Gardner was a show-off who entertained audiences with impromptu aviation stunts. His colleagues nicknamed him

"Turkey Bird" because his takeoffs tended to be wobbly. Gardner preferred the more manly "Turk Bird." Gardner wasn't particularly handsome, with his thinning hair, homely smile, and hooked nose, but he had no trouble getting dates. There was something irrefutably glamorous about the Air Mail Service pilots. When he suited up in his leather flying gear, even the Turkey Bird looked like a Hollywood hero.

Praeger and his pilots traveled to the headquarters of the Standard Aero Company in Elizabeth, New Jersey, where they tested new planes with bigger gas tanks and more powerful engines. Gardner thrilled the crowd with figure eights. Praeger scolded him when he landed, and Gardner promised never to do it again. The second assistant postmaster general told a group of reporters at the factory that the new planes would enable the Post Office to extend airmail across the country. "There is no guess work about it," he said. "It is just as feasible to operate a mail line from the Atlantic coast to the Pacific coast in relays of 200 to 250 miles as it is to operate a single line of 250 miles with the certainty with which the aerial mail has been operated between New York and Washington."

The first step was to carry mail from New York to Chicago. Praeger and Burleson believed their pilots would be able to make the trip between the two cities in nine hours, easily beating the fastest trains, which took 21 hours. In 1915, a pilot named Victor Carlstrom made the trip in a total of 8½ hours, but it took him two days. He got as far as Hammondsport, New York, before he was grounded for the night. Then he flew the rest of the way in the morning. Carlstrom never had the chance to try again. He died in a crash two years later while giving a flying lesson to a student in Newport News, Virginia.

Praeger wanted his men to make the nearly 800-mile journey between New York, and Chicago on a daily basis. Nothing like this had ever been attempted before. The Air Mail Service pilots would have to cross a section of the Allegheny Mountains in Pennsylvania that they called Hell's Stretch. Fog often shrouded the Allegheny peaks, and there was virtually no place to land safely if aviators had engine trouble. Still, Praeger pressed on with what he referred to as "Project Pathfinder," mapping out a route from Belmont Field in New York to Chicago's Grant Park, with refueling stops along the way in Lock Haven, Pennsylvania, and the cities of Cleveland and Bryan in Ohio.

Before the first flight, Benjamin Lipsner, the Post Office's recently hired superintendent of airmail, decided to turn Project Pathfinder into a contest between pilots Miller and Gardner. He invited them to lunch and told them of the plan. As Lipsner explained it, Miller would leave first and Gardner would follow. That didn't sit well with Gardner. "What do you mean follow?" he asked.

"Wait a minute," Lipsner said. "Don't get so excited about it, Eddie. It doesn't make the slightest difference to me who leads. You can lead the way and Max can follow."

"Oh Max can, can he?" said Miller sarcastically. "Why I couldn't follow him for a mile without running him down."

Lipsner flipped a coin. Miller called heads and won. Gardner was still miffed, but there was nothing he could do.

"Good luck, Max," Gardner said. "You deserve it."

Miller looked embarrassed. "I ought to be ashamed of what I said."

"Aw shut up," Gardner told him.

The sky was cloudy on September 5, 1918, when Gardner and Miller departed from Belmont Field. Gardner couldn't resist teasing Miller before he took off first at 6 AM. "Look me up when you get to Chicago, Max," Gardner said. "I hope I don't get sleepy waiting for you."

As soon as Miller departed, it began to rain. "Just our luck," said Eddie Radel, a mechanic who would make the trip with Gardner. "I'll bet Miller missed it."

"Forget it," Garner assured him. "A bad beginning is a good ending."

It quickly got worse. Gardner and Radel climbed into their plane only to discover that it had a bad engine. Gardner commandeered another aircraft over the objections of the maintenance crew. "But Eddie, that plane has never been tested," a crew member warned.

"I don't give a hang," Gardner said. "Is she full of gas?

"Yes."

"Then it's going to Chicago right now, tested or not."

Gardner turned to Radel. "Are you game?"

"You know me, Turk," Radel said. "Just say the word and I'm with you."

Gardner and Radel took off at 8:50 AM. As they crossed the Hudson River, Radel discovered that he had forgotten a fire extinguisher and the lunches he had prepared for the two of them. Praeger was furious about the troubles afflicting Project Pathfinder, and there were more to come. Miller made it safely to Lock Haven, but then his radiator started to leak, forcing him down in a field. A suspicious farmer with a shotgun confronted him. "You just get off my place or I'll blow you to pieces," he said. The next place Miller touched down, the locals were more hospitable. Nevertheless, he lost his way and didn't make it to Cleveland until sunset. He was infuriated when his superiors ordered him to spend the night in the city. Miller felt better when he learned that Gardner was stuck behind in Lock Haven for the evening because of his own engine trouble.

Miller awoke the next morning and waited for the mechanics to fix his radiator. He finally departed at 1:35 PM and arrived at 6:55 PM in Chicago, where a huge crowd awaited him. Miller posed for pictures, savoring his victory. Naturally, he was eager for Gardner to arrive so he could gloat, but Gardner's plane didn't appear in the sky. Then night fell, and Miller began to worry about his friend. Finally, Gardner telephoned to say he was turning in for the night in Westville, Indiana, because it was too dark to fly farther. "Hey, Turk. I thought you were going to look me up when you got to Chicago," Miller joked, before Gardner slammed the phone down on the receiver.

Once Gardner reached Chicago the following day, the two pilots forgot about the competition and enjoyed themselves. Politicians and business leaders invited them to lunches and dinners, raising champagne glasses in their honor. But in truth, the pilots hadn't accomplished much. Miller's trip had taken 37 hours; Gardner's journey had lasted 48 hours. They would have to do better to persuade Congress to permanently fund the new airmail route. Fortunately, Project Pathfinder wasn't over yet. The two pilots had to fly back to New York.

The weather was beautiful on the morning of September 10. Having already won the coin toss, Miller got to lead the way again. "So long, Eddie," he told Gardner. "I'll think of you when I'm walking down Broadway tonight." He left at 6:30 AM and got as far as Cleveland before his radiator started leaking again. Miller landed in Cleveland for several hours of repairs, and he didn't arrive in Lock Haven until 7 PM. Miller wanted to go on, but it was getting dark.

He called Lipsner. "Say, chief," he said. "I'm in Lock Haven, and everything's all right now. My radiator had only a small leak, but I think it'll hold all right until I reach New York."

"What?" Lipsner replied.

"I'm going to New York. I'll call you from Belmont Park before you go to bed."

"You'll do nothing of the kind."

"You wanted me to make it in a day, didn't you?"

"You'll stay right where you are," Lipsner commanded. "It's too much of a risk to finish the trip tonight."

Miller wanted permission to take off, but it was futile. "You're flying the mail for Uncle Sam and you'd better obey orders," Lipsner told him. "Do you think I want you flying over those mountains and New York skyscrapers at this time of the night? Besides, that radiator is very unreliable." Miller reluctantly gave in.

Gardner had better luck. He and Radel made it as far as Jersey City by nightfall. Rather than consult Lipsner, they crossed the

Hudson River and flew over Manhattan, dazzled by the illuminated city. "The metropolis was wonderful—lights twinkling everywhere," Gardner recalled. "Manhattan, the Bronx, Brooklyn—lights, lights, lights, and more lights." The lights, however, became a problem when Gardner tried to locate Belmont Field. "Desperately, I tried to find the landing flares at Belmont Park," he said. "It was like trying to pick a couple of stars out of the Milky Way. I was baffled by the lights. They all looked alike."

His plane nearly out of gas, Gardner searched for an open field and crash-landed in Hicksville, New York, 10 miles from his destination. When he came to, he pulled Radel out of the wreckage. Radel looked at Gardner strangely. "Gee, Eddie, you're all cut up," he told him. The local police arrived and summoned an ambulance to take the two men to the hospital, but not before Gardner was sure that his mail would be taken into New York on the next train. Praeger was elated. His pilot had flown from Chicago to New York in nine hours and eighteen minutes. Granted, Gardner hadn't made it all the way to Belmont Field, but he had gotten close enough. Praeger sent Gardner a telegram: "You made a great flight. Hope you and Radel will have a speedy recovery from your injuries."

The warm feelings didn't last long. Within a few weeks of his epochal flight, Gardner refused to make his appointed rounds on a foggy November day. Praeger sent an angry telegram: "START THE MAIL SHIP WITHOUT A MINUTE'S DELAY." When Gardner remained on the ground, Praeger fired him. The next day, Gardner traveled to Washington to plead for his job, but his boss was unmoved. Miller resigned in protest. Lipsner quit too, complaining to reporters about the imperious second assistant postmaster general. Newspapers lambasted Praeger for mistreating the heroic airmail pilots, but Burleson stood behind him and the controversy blew over.

Praeger soon regretted the departure of his star pilots. He tried to start regular service between New York and Chicago in December, but it was clear from the first day that he should have waited. His newer pilots weren't prepared for long flights over unfamiliar terrain. They got lost. They crashed. The newspapers declared the new route a lost cause. "All that remains of New York to Chicago air mail service, which began life fresh and full of vigor yesterday morning, is a trail of broken or lost airplanes," the *New York Tribune* lamented. After four days, Praeger canceled the new service altogether.

Politics intruded on Praeger's plans too. World War I had officially ended on November 11, 1918. The Army wanted to get back into airmail delivery so its pilots would have something to do in peacetime. It had powerful allies on Capitol Hill. The same month, Republicans gained control of Congress. Republican congressman and future New York mayor Fiorello La Guardia led a campaign to defund the U.S. Air Mail Service and turn its operations over to the military. La Guardia had been an Army pilot during the war on the Austro-Italian front and fancied himself an aviation expert. "The Areo mail of this country is doomed to failure," he warned. In the end, the Post Office retained control of the service and got more funding for it, but only because Praeger and Burleson spent a good deal of time on Capitol Hill, fending off the military's takeover attempt.

Remarkably, none of this discouraged Praeger. He resumed service between New York and Chicago on May 15, 1919, the first anniversary of the Air Mail Service. Now that the war was over, there were plenty of experienced pilots available. Much to his relief, Miller and Gardner returned to the service, although they didn't last long with the Post Office. Shortly after his return, Miller was flying over Morristown, New Jersey, when his plane's engine caught fire. The plane crashed, and Miller was burned beyond recognition when the gas tank exploded. "Max Miller was the best pilot who ever sat in a plane," a devastated Praeger said. Gardner left soon after and died two years later while barnstorming in Nebraska.

Republicans kept agitating for the cancellation of airmail, but Praeger ignored them. He was consumed with its potential to hasten the mail. He monitored the service obsessively, learning the names of every pilot, mechanic, and night watchman and keeping track of every plane's whereabouts. On Sundays, Praeger met with his administrative staff at the Washington office, where they sat around his enormous desk with their jackets off and ties loosened, debating possible improvements. The second assistant postmaster general always had the final word. "When he said, 'By Golly, that's what we'll do,' there was no appeal," recalled Leon Lent, Praeger's chief aviation adviser.

On May 15, 1920, the second anniversary of the Air Mail Service, Praeger boasted that his pilots had flown into New York in storms so fierce that ships couldn't enter the city's harbor, and they had delivered mail to Chicago when trains were snowbound. Now it was time to carry mail to San Francisco. "Commercial aviation has arrived, and it cannot be stopped," Praeger insisted.

Early airmail pilots had been frightened by the Allegheny Mountains in Pennsylvania, but those peaks were less than 2,000 feet above sea level. To reach San Francisco, they would have to soar 9,000 feet above sea level to cross the Continental Divide. Then on the border of Utah and Idaho they would encounter the Wasatch Range, which an aviation writer described as "a maze of canyons, deep narrow [gorges], and sharp crest ridges that offered little hope of a survivable forced landing." They could expect more unforgiving terrain beyond the Rocky Mountains. After pausing in Reno, Nevada, pilots would have to ascend 10,000 feet above sea level to get over the Sierra Nevada, which the department described as "a genuine no man's land of mountain cliffs, canyons, small lakes, creeks, and trees and generally rotten flying territory." The airmail pilots would also encounter frequent snowstorms, gale force winds, and subzero temperatures in this part of the country.

Praeger was convinced his men could overcome these obstacles. The Air Mail Service began coast-to-coast service in September 1920, transferring mail to trains at night when it was dangerous to fly and sending it back into the air at daybreak. The courageousness of the pilots who flew the transcontinental route cannot be overstated. In *Aerial Pioneers: The U.S. Air Mail Service, 1918–1927*, William Leary describes how pilot James Murray crashed in a snowstorm on the way from Salt Lake City to Cheyenne: "The aircraft was a complete write-off, but Murray crawled out of the wreckage with only minor cuts and bruises. The accident took place at 4:45 p.m. Murray decided he would have to walk to safety. With the aircraft's compass smashed, he used the setting sun as a reference and trudged eastward for an hour through two feet of snow until he reached a frozen lake. With snow still coming down and darkness approaching, Murray took refuge under a cedar tree for the night. The next morning he found an abandoned cabin but no food. Walking into the rising sun, he came across a road with a signpost pointing to Arlington [Wyoming], fourteen miles distant. . . . Eating occasional handfuls of snow, he continued on his way. The tired and hungry pilot reached Arlington at 2:45 p.m., having walked eight hours to cover the fourteen miles." Needless to say, other pilots who crashed under such conditions didn't survive.

Burleson and Praeger were running out of time. Tired of Wilson's progressive tendencies, Americans voted overwhelmingly in November 1920 for Republican presidential candidate Warren Harding, who promised a "return to normalcy" and vowed to veto any more airmail funding bills. Burleson and Praeger knew they would lose their jobs as soon as Harding took office, but first they wanted to demonstrate that their pilots could make the entire 3,000-mile transcontinental journey in the air, which would require night flying, of course. They drew up a plan for two teams of aviators to simultaneously take off from New York and California. Ideally, the pilots would make the trip in 36 hours, four times faster than the transcontinental railroad.

The weather on the East Coast was terrible on the morning of February 22, 1921, when pilots Elmer Leonhardt and Ernest Allison left New York and headed west. Leonhardt was forced down in Pennsylvania because of icy conditions. Allison made it to Cleveland and handed his mailbags to Walter Smith. Smith reached Chicago, but his superiors grounded him because they felt it was too dangerous to fly in the mix of snow, rain, and fog.

On the West Coast, the airmail pilots fared even worse. Farr Nutter and Raymond Little took off in separate planes from San Francisco just before 5 AM. They flew in the dark to Reno, where they passed their mail to Samuel Eaton and William Lewis. Eaton and Lewis took it to Elko, Nevada, and they changed planes. When they tried to leave, Lewis crashed and died during takeoff. Eaton gathered up his colleague's mail and flew to Salt Lake City, where he gave the sacks to James Murray. In Cheyenne, Murray met up with Frank Yager who took them to North Platte, Nebraska. The pilot waiting for him was Jack Knight, whose name would shortly become known to every American.

A former World War I flight instructor who grew up in Buchanan, Michigan, Knight looked a bit like Fred Astaire, with the same elegant, thin face, high cheekbones, and receding hairline. He had already set speed records carrying the mail, and he was dutiful. A few months earlier, Knight had crashed on the way from Chicago to Cleveland. Once he came to his senses, he persuaded someone to watch his plane and got his eight bags of mail onto a train. Then he hopped onto a trolley into Cleveland, and the next day he flew the mail to Chicago as if nothing had happened.

Now it was up to Knight to get the mail to Omaha, and he would have to do it in the dark. The Post Office had asked residents of towns along the way to light bonfires. Knight followed the blazing path. "I felt as if I had a thousand friends on the ground—Lexington, Grand Island, Columbus, Fremont slipped by, warm glows of well-wishers beneath the plane's wings," he recalled later. "Then I saw the lights of Omaha."

Thousands greeted Knight when he touched down at 1:10 AM. He was spent, but the pilot who knew the route from Omaha to Chicago hadn't shown up, so Knight volunteered to take the mail to Chicago. "We can't let it bust up here," he said. "I'm going to take it through, so get out the maps and I'll be on my way after that coffee and two cigarettes." He studied the maps for a few minutes and took off at 1:50 AM.

Knight's account of his journey to Chicago is haunting. "By this time I was flying over territory that was absolutely strange," he said. "I knew nothing of the land markings, even if they had been visible. I had to fly by compass and by feel. The throbbing rhythm of the motor didn't help matters. It was almost a lullaby. I gripped the control stick with my knees and began slapping my face to keep awake. I stuck my face over the side of the cowl and let the rushing zero wind bite my cheeks almost raw. . . . I got pretty lonesome. At times, the moon was totally obscured by a layer of clouds. It looked as if the whole blooming world was sleeping hard. There's a sense of isolation that's hard to describe. But my faithful old Liberty [engine] roared out, fighting the wind and dragging my ship along at about a hundred miles an hour."

He found Iowa City deserted except for the night watchmen. Everybody else had gone home, thinking the Post Office had canceled the remaining flights. Knight ate a ham sandwich and smoked a few more cigarettes before departing for Chicago. "I didn't dare eat any more for fear it would put me to sleep," he recalled. "It was 6:30 a.m., Wednesday. The rest of the way I flew by instinct. I just pointed the plane's nose for Chicago and kept going. Snow whirled around the ship for a while and the wind blew stiff from the east. It was hellishly cold. But as the day grew brighter, I saw the gray smoke of Chicago, mixing with the clouds, and it was the finest sight I have ever beheld."

NEITHER SNOW NOR RAIN

Knight arrived in Chicago in exuberant spirits. "I feel fine," he told a reporter. "I just need some eats and some sleep." He gave his mail to pilot John Webster, who flew it to Cleveland. Ernest Allison transported it the rest of the way, arriving in New York at 4:50 PM. Previously, it had taken the Post Office nearly four days to transport mail across the country on a special train. But now the *New York Times* proclaimed on its front page, "Continent Spanned by Airplane Mail in 33 hours." Praeger sent Knight a grateful telegram: "Accept my hearty congratulations for your splendid performance last night under most difficult weather conditions."

The Republican majority in Congress had slashed the Air Mail Service's proposed $1.25 million budget for 1921 and planned to eliminate the service entirely under Harding, but now they hurriedly reinstated the funds. Days later, Praeger left the Post Office. He worked for a while as a consultant to mail-order companies that wanted to better understand the mysteries of the Post Office. Eventually, the king of Siam recruited Praeger to set up an airmail service in his country. So Praeger boarded a steamship and set off for the Far East.

The 1920s were another transformative time for mail. Americans sent hundreds of thousands of picture postcards every year. J. C. and Rollie Hall, two brothers from Nebraska, started producing Hallmark greeting cards, which would become America's biggest-selling brand of cards for Christmas, Valentine's Day, Mother's Day, and birthdays, too. Pitney Bowes unveiled its postage meter, soon to be ubiquitous in company mailrooms, freeing their employees from the burden of visiting the post office to purchase stamps. Eventually, sales of Pitney Bowes labels would surpass those of traditional stamps, though the labels would never replace stamps as some feared.

It was also a busy time for the postal inspection service. In 1920, inspectors put an end to Charles Ponzi, architect of the modern day pyramid scheme, when they arrested him for using the mail to bilk his victims. Mail train robberies became so common that the Post Office issued surplus military weapons to railway mail clerks, but that didn't frighten off the De Autremont brothers, who boarded a San Francisco–bound train in Oregon's Siskiyou Mountains in 1923 with sawed-off shotguns, thinking that it was carrying $500,000 in gold. A railway post office clerk locked himself in the mail car, but the De Autremonts had come prepared with dynamite and they used it to blow open the door. As it turned out, there was no gold on the train. After killing the clerk and three others, the brothers escaped with only $1,000. Postal inspectors pursued them for three and a half years, looking for clues in Alaska, Mexico, and South America. After the De Autremonts were apprehended, they confessed and were sentenced to life in prison.

The decade was also the golden age of airmail. In 1923, the Post Office created the world's first night airway between Cheyenne and Chicago, placing flashing gas beacons every 300 miles and installing powerful searchlights atop 50-foot towers at airports to guide pilots. In 1923, it started night flight training in North Platte, Nebraska. Air Mail Service pilot Dean Smith recalled those days with wonder. "I wish everyone could have the pleasure and excitement of those first hesitant probes across the dark plains," Smith wrote. "We were like children venturing from home, each time daring a bit farther, then running back filled with awe at what we had done. It felt empty and lonesome out there, even with the beacons flashing, four or five visible ahead; we felt the fear of the unknown, the excitement of pioneering, and the satisfaction of accomplishment."

Regular transcontinental service began in July 1924, and a month later, the Air Mail Service broke its own record, transporting the mail from New York to San Francisco in 24 hours. "The U.S. Post Office runs what is far and away the most efficiently organized and efficiently managed Civil Aviation undertaking in the world," wrote C. G. Grey, editor of *Jane's All the World's Aircraft*. "That 3,000 mile trip, with its 1,400 miles in the dark, day in and out all the year around, is a wonderful affair."

National Geographic praised the Post Office Department more effusively. "There is a revolutionary fact abroad in the land: aircraft have gone to work," the magazine wrote. "And the nation is waking to find itself fast wedded to a new handmaid of progress—the United States Transcontinental Airmail. The story of this great overhead skyline trail linking East and West, along which, through storm or calm, in darkness or in light, a score of winged couriers relay the public mails across three thousand miles of continent in less than a day and a half, is a modern romance of transportation as fascinating as any that comes to us out of the colorful past." The *New York Times* was no less impressed. "One of the most wonderful things in the world is the United States Air Mail Service," it observed. "It has its equal nowhere for the distance flown and service rendered."

But the end of the U.S. Air Mail Service was rapidly approaching. In 1925, Republican president Calvin Coolidge signed a law permitting the Post Office to award airmail contracts to private airlines with the hope of spurring the passenger transportation business. The Post Office was inundated with bids from companies newly formed specifically to win such contracts, and began parceling out routes to the low bidders. On August 30, 1927, Post Office pilot Stephen Kaufman made the U.S. Air Mail Service's final flight, carrying a shipment of mail from New York to Cleveland. His arrival in Cleveland must have been a surreal experience for him. When Kaufman landed at 12:58 AM, ten thousand people were waiting, including a former Miss America with a champagne bottle in her hand. But they weren't there to greet Kaufman; they had come out on this summer night to cheer for National Air Transport, a private airline that had won the contract for the route and would take Kaufman's sacks the rest of the way to Chicago.

Once Kaufman had handed off his mail, the U.S. Mail officials disbanded. The Post Office Department gave its lighted airways to the Department of Commerce, which regulated the aviation industry. It donated its airports to the cities and towns in which they were located. It sold its planes to the new airlines that had contracts to carry mail. These same companies hired many of the post office's longtime pilots.

In 1927, Charles Lindbergh, himself a former airmail pilot who worked for a private contractor, made his famous flight from New York to Paris, inspiring an aviation craze. Thousands of young men took flying lessons in the hope of emulating Lindbergh, cities that didn't already have airports built them now, and the public sent airmail letters as it never had before. Parker Brothers even created a board game called "Aviation: The Air Mail Game" to take advantage of the fad. Many private airlines chose this moment to issue stock, which speculators devoured, causing it to soar to unsustainable levels.

When the stock market crashed in October 1929, airline shares plummeted, putting the nascent industry in jeopardy. Its unlikely savior turned out to be Walter Folger Brown, Herbert Hoover's postmaster general. A politically connected Republican attorney from Toledo, Ohio, Brown was an owlish-looking man who parted his dark hair in the middle and wore round glasses. He had helped elect Harding and Hoover and he wasn't about to let anybody push him around in Washington. As postmaster general, he ordered a high-ceilinged sedan that he could get into and out of without removing his stovepipe hat. His political foes started calling him "High Hat Brown," but he made no apology. Initially, Brown said, the Post Office had ordered him "a small Lincoln car," but it simply wouldn't do. "When I looked at the car," he said "I found that a man of my height, and I am below the average, could not wear a top hat and sit in this car," he said. "The occupant would have to keep his hat in his hand, because there was not clearance enough. We were greatly disturbed about that." So Brown sent the Lincoln back and ordered a more suitable vehicle.

Brown was just as unyielding when it came to awarding airmail contracts. At his urging, Congress passed the Air Mail Act of 1930, enabling the department to award contracts without competitive bidding. With his new powers, Brown set out to reorder the imperiled aviation sector, which still carried more mail than people. "Someone has got to try to solve this problem, or we are going to have a collapse of the passenger-carrying industry in this country," Brown insisted.

As far as Brown was concerned, the airline industry was too fragmented, and many companies formed to win airmail contracts were too weak to survive. In secret meetings at the department's headquarters that would later become know as "the spoils conference," Brown awarded contracts to the strongest airlines, forcing some of them to merge with a competitor, creating four large companies that would dominate the industry for decades to come: Transcontinental & Western Air (later known as TWA), American Airways, United Airlines, and Eastern Air Lines. Otto Praeger had proved the viability of commercial aviation; now Brown used airmail contracts to restructure the industry and ensure its survival in the Depression. But did Brown save the industry or did he abuse his power as postmaster general? Inevitably, there was a scandal, but it unfurled after the election of another president who doted on the Post Office unlike any other.

6

A Stamp Collector in
the White House

On March 4, 1933, President Franklin D. Roosevelt, his legs rendered useless by polio, made his way to the podium in Washington, D.C., on the arm of his son James to deliver his inaugural address with the now famous words, "Let me assert my firm belief that the only thing we have to fear is fear itself." The audience didn't applaud. The country was in the throes of the worst economic depression in its history. One out of every four Americans was unemployed. In the previous two months, 4,000 banks had collapsed, and depositors were hurrying to withdraw their money from the surviving ones, all but guaranteeing that more would fail. Crop prices had tumbled, and farmers were defaulting on their mortgages and losing their land. There were plenty of reasons for Americans to be frightened.

The following day was a Sunday, but Roosevelt sequestered himself in the White House working out a plan for a four-day bank holiday, which he hoped would calm bankers and their jittery depositors. A technical question arose: should Roosevelt declare the holiday with an executive order or by proclamation? Roosevelt summoned Wilbur Carr, a State Department official known for coming up with solutions in gnarly situations. Carr told Roosevelt that he favored a proclamation, which settled the matter. He got up to leave, but the president stopped him. "Don't go, Wilbur," he said. "Wait until the others have gone."

When the two men were alone, Roosevelt changed the subject. "Wilbur," he asked eagerly, "don't you get a good many interesting foreign stamps?"

"Yes, many," Carr replied.

"I would appreciate it greatly if you would sometimes bundle up a few and send them over to me," Roosevelt said.

This story has been recounted by at least one of Roosevelt's biographers as evidence of his ability to maintain his sense of humor in a crisis, a personality trait that helped him restore the confidence of the American people during the Depression and lead them to victory in World War II. But historians often gloss over his passion for stamps. Roosevelt was a devoted collector, and once he occupied the White House, he involved himself in the Post Office's stamp issuing process more than any other president before or after. Republicans accused Roosevelt of politicizing the process, and to some degree, they were right. But for stamp collectors, Roosevelt's election was a glorious moment. They were accustomed to being called nuts and maniacs. Finally, they had a president who shared their obsession.

In 1886, 24 men posed for a picture at the top of the stairway in an ornately decorated building in Manhattan. Many of them appeared to be in their twenties and looked rather boyish even with their facial hair. The badges pinned to the labels of their suit jackets indicated that they were members of the newly formed American Philatelic Society, which would become the country's largest stamp collectors' club. Their newly elected leader, John K. Tiffany, a handsome, mustached 44-year-old, sat in the front row. Born in Massachusetts and educated in France, Tiffany had amassed one of the world's best stamp collections and would shortly write the first book cataloging American stamps. But in St. Louis, where he spent his adult life, he was known for his legal practice. When the *St. Louis Times* mentioned Tiffany in an article about the growing popularity of stamp collecting and wrote of his collection of 13,000 stamps, it withheld his name as if trying to shield him from embarrassment.

The truth was that stamp collecting occupied a strange place in American culture. Within a decade after the Post Office issued its first stamps in 1847, people in the United States began hoarding them, and within two decades, more than sixty dealers advertised their services in publications like *Tiny Collector* and *Philatelic Squeal*. There were songs about the hobby, including "The American Stamp Polka," "The Philatelic Waltz," and "Stamp Galop," and even a romantic novel entitled *The Story of My Stamp Collection*. But in the mainstream press, stamp lovers were often described as a little crazy and perhaps not without reason.

The American stamps craved by the philatelists were dull by today's standards, featuring pictures of deceased presidents, vice presidents, senators, generals, admirals, and an occasional Indian or buffalo, and collectors were quick to assail the Post Office when it broke up the monotony. In 1869, the department issued more imaginative stamps that included a circular one bearing Franklin's image and others with pictures of a postal rider, a mail train, a steamship, and the signing of the Declaration of Independence. Rather than applauding, collectors scorned the new stamps, particularly a patriotic 30-cent one showing an eagle perched on a shield surrounded by American flags. The *American Journal of Philately* called it "the meanest looking stamp we have ever seen" and wrote that it "reminds us more of a bunch of rags hung out of a junk store than anything else."

The hobbyists responded with more vitriol when Postmaster General John Wanamaker introduced the first commemorative stamps in 1893 at the World's Columbian Exposition in Chicago, celebrating the four-hundredth anniversary of Columbus's voyage to America. Scrutinizing the stamps, collectors noticed that the explorer was clean-shaven when he sighted the New World from his vessel on the one-cent commemorative, but bearded on the two-cent stamp when he set foot onshore. Others accused the Post Office of trying to take advantage of them by charging $15 for the full set of 16 commemoratives. Collectors would come to revere the stamps, now referred to affectionately as "the Columbians," but it would take decades.

The collecting community also had a tense relationship with post office clerks. Collectors sought stamps in good condition, and it could take time to find the right ones. But clerks had long lines of customers and sometime became exasperated, like the postmaster of Newport, Rhode Island, who refused to fill a dealer's order for stamped envelopes. "If you want them for business purposes, I'll get them for you," the postmaster said. "But if it's for collectors, I can't bother with them."

By the 1920s, the number of collectors had swelled to 500,000 in the United States, and the Post Office realized it needed to treat them more deferentially. At the urging of Third Assistant Postmaster General Irving Glover, whose wife was a collector, the department created the Philatelic Agency in 1921, enabling collectors to order stamps through the mail in mint condition. It turned out to be a nice business for the Post Office. Collectors bought stamps and never used them, meaning the department kept nearly all the income from these purchases rather than incurring delivery costs. In its first year, the Philatelic Agency had sales of $20,906. Two years later, it made more than 10 times that amount as collectors overwhelmed its four clerks with orders. The Philatelic Agency was so successful that other countries emulated it, enabling collectors to fill their albums with stamps from around the world simply by sending a check and a stamped return envelope.

By the early 1930s, there were two million stamp collectors in the United States. Most major newspapers had stamp columnists. Gimbels opened stamp sales departments and started children's stamp clubs in 45 of its stores around the country. And in 1932, NBC began broadcasting *Ivory Stamp Club of the Air*, a children's radio show featuring "Captain Tim," former Australian Army captain

Tim Healy, whom it described as "the famous war veteran, soldier of fortune and stamp expert." Healy, who was in fact Australian but had recently worked as a street sweeper after losing his job at an oil company in the Depression, entertained his audience three evenings a week. "Do you know you can learn history and geography and the strange customs of strange places just by studying stamps?" he asked his listeners. Healy encouraged them to join his club by mailing in an Ivory soap wrapper for which they would receive a membership badge in return, along with an album and a package of stamps for starting their collections. Two and a half million children heeded his call. "Keep healthy and strong with Ivory Soap so you won't miss any of our programs," Healy urged them. "Whether I'm in America, Australia or the jungles of Africa, I take my daily bath with Ivory Soap."

It was great to have a champion like Captain Tim, but many Americans still thought of stamp collecting as an adolescent pastime. The most famous adult collectors seemed like cases of arrested development. Colonel Ned Green, a one-legged sybaritic millionaire, traveled to stamp dealers in a chauffeured limousine and stored his purchases in a New York apartment where they were guarded by his staff of nubile young women. Among Green's treasures were a number of coveted Inverted Jennies, stamps issued by the Post Office in 1918 on the day of the new service's debut. As it turned out, the famous biplane on the stamp was upside down on a number of sheets. Before the department discovered the error, a collector had bought a sheet of 100 at the Washington post office and sold it for $15,000 to a dealer who turned around and sold it to Green for $20,000. Green broke up the sheet and sold some of the stamps individually to his fellow collectors for tens of thousands of dollars. Some disappeared, despite the efforts of Green's alluring guards. There were rumors that he burned a few to show off for his friends. It has also been speculated that he lost 20 of the precious stamps when his yacht sank in Half Moon Bay. Either way, Green was no role model. American collectors longed for someone who would legitimize their hobby as King

George V, crowned in 1910, had done in England. They finally got their wish in 1932 when the Democratic Party nominated Franklin Roosevelt as its presidential candidate.

Born in 1882 in Hyde Park, New York, Roosevelt collected stuffed birds, model ships, and miniature books. He inherited his affection for stamps from his mother, Sara Delano, and it would outlast his other hobbies. He spent hours filling albums with stamps from faraway countries and making notes about their places of origin, which is how he gained his extensive knowledge of geography. He was especially intrigued with stamps from Hong Kong, where his aunt Dora resided. "Tell Uncle Will to save me foreign stamps as I have begun to make a collection," Franklin wrote to her.

His interest waned when he went off to Harvard College and later he married his fifth cousin once removed Eleanor Roosevelt. He entered politics in 1910, serving first as a New York state senator and later as assistant secretary of the Navy under Woodrow Wilson. He ran unsuccessfully for vice president in 1920 on a ticket led by Ohio governor James Cox. They were defeated by Republican Warren Harding and his running mate Calvin Coolidge, but Roosevelt was clearly a Democrat to watch, a charming young man with a radiant smile and a fine name even if some members of his party thought he lacked substance.

In 1921, Roosevelt was stricken with polio at his family's vacation home on Campobello Island, losing the use of both his legs. Stamps provided him with an escape as he spent weeks in bed coming to terms with his disability, and his attachment to them would never again weaken. Every night before he fell asleep, he spent half an hour organizing and annotating his stamps much as he had when he was a boy. When he seemed overwhelmed, his secretary Missy LeHand produced one of his albums and put him at ease.

When Roosevelt returned to politics, he made no secret of his passion. After he was elected governor of New York in 1928, he was photographed at his desk examining his collection, magnifying glass in hand. In 1931, he joined the American Philatelic Society, which was thrilled the following year when he entered the presidential race. "From the view point of the collector per se, the victory of Governor Roosevelt at the polls this November would be the most desirable ever in philatelic history," the *American Philatelist* wrote. "The resultant gain in prestige with the concomitant publicity that would necessarily follow would surely develop a world-wide boom in stamps. . . . The progress and spread of Philately in these United States would be of momentous proportions. And so, not as a Wet or Dry, not as a Democrat or a Republican, not as a liberal or a conservative, but simply as an enthusiast in Philately, we bespeak of favorable consideration by all the members of the A.P.S. of the candidacy of our fellow member, Franklin Delano Roosevelt, A.P.S. #11590 for the office of President of the United States!"

Roosevelt's opponent Herbert Hoover noticed the rapturous endorsement. Soon after, someone from the Hoover campaign wrote to the society to tell it that the incumbent had "a high opinion of philately" and that his sons were longtime collectors. This was news to the editors of the *American Philatelist*. They subsequently wrote that no matter who won the election, it was important for the society to sign up at least one of the Hoover boys. It was always good to have well-placed friends in Washington.

After winning the presidential race in November 1932, Roosevelt selected James Farley, his campaign manager, to be the nation's postmaster general—or, as the genial Farley liked to say, its chief "postage stamp salesman." Farley was six feet two inches tall, weighed 215 pounds, and was the picture of a machine politician with his double chin and bald head. The son of Irish immigrants, he was born in 1888 in the small town of Grassy Point, New York. As a teenager, he worked in his mother's tavern, tapping kegs, pouring drinks, and doing whatever he could to keep patrons happy. It was good training for his future career. Farley became known as a man who never forgot a face and had thousands of friends. "Some people have memories for figures, some for books," he said. "I happen to have a memory for people, not only their faces but their names. I have no doubt that this has helped me in making friends. People don't like to be forgotten. They want to be remembered."

Farley became a top salesman for the General Builders Supply Corporation, but he longed for influence more than commissions. In 1925, Governor Al Smith of New York appointed him to the New York State Athletics Commission, which regulated boxing. Farley knew little about pugilism, but he won many new friends by dispensing free tickets to prizefights. "Jim Farley passes fall like snowflakes on the deserving and the grateful," the *New Yorker* wrote in an early profile. Farley was also a prolific joiner, becoming a member of the Knights of Columbus, the Benevolent and Protective Order of Elks, the Improved Order of Red Men, and the Fraternal Order of Eagles.

The popular Farley held on to his athletic commission post and his club memberships when he managed Roosevelt's successful gubernatorial campaign in 1928. After the victory, Farley resuscitated the party in traditionally Republican upstate New York, writing letters to dozens of long-neglected Democrats in these areas and providing his assistance. Two years later, Roosevelt was reelected by a 750,000-vote margin and Farley floated his name as a presidential candidate. "I do not see how Mr. Roosevelt can escape becoming the next presidential nominee of his party even if no one should raise a finger to bring it about," Farley told the press.

Two years later, Farley masterminded Roosevelt's presidential campaign, traveling across the country to a national Elks convention in Seattle and stopping along the way to woo local Democratic leaders. On the night of his victory in 1932, Roosevelt celebrated with supporters including Farley and his wife, Elizabeth, at the Biltmore Hotel in New York. He whispered to Mrs. Farley: "Get ready to move to Washington." Elizabeth Farley said she didn't want to leave

New York. "Well, get ready anyway," Roosevelt replied. "Because Jim is coming down there after the Fourth of July." Roosevelt appointed Farley as both postmaster general and chairman of the Democratic National Committee, and the line between the two jobs tended to blur.

Democrats hadn't held the White House in 12 years, so party members descended on Washington seeking an audience with Farley. They took up residence in the waiting room at the Democratic National Committee's office, and they camped out on the green sofas in the reception area of the Post Office Department, where Farley had an office big enough to hold a basketball court, decorated with portraits of his mother and Benjamin Franklin. Job hunters stalked him in the hallways of the Mayflower Hotel, where he stayed in Washington. "I virtually had to slip back and forth to the office like a man dodging a sheriff's writ," Farley later wrote. There were requests from higher authorities too. Eleanor Roosevelt sent Farley a note on behalf of a relative: "Dear Jim, have we a Democratic postmaster appointed at Newberry, South Carolina? If not, I may have a candidate. A distant cousin has turned up. Very sincerely yours, ER." Farley told the first lady there would be no vacancy at the Newberry post office until the sitting postmaster's term expired in 1936.

Republicans condemned Farley as a political hack who filled the Post Office Department with more of the same, but he turned out to be an able administrator. The Depression had caused the Post Office's volume to fall between 1929 and 1933 from 27 billion to 19 billion items and its revenues to decline from $696 million to $588 million. The department lost $113 million in Farley's first year as postmaster general, but he trimmed the deficit by making his 242,971 employees take 11 payless furlough days. Department stores, utility companies, and some local governments started using private messengers to deliver bills and advertisements to people's mailboxes. Farley put a stop to this, persuading Congress to pass a law, still in effect, forbidding anyone but a government letter carrier to deposit anything in a home mailbox.

Farley was fascinated by the exploits of the post inspectors and how they caught members of the fearsome Touhy gang who were robbing mail trucks around the country. In 1933, four of its members—Basil "The Owl" Banghart, Ludwig "Dutch" Schmidt, Isaac "Ike" Costner, and Charles "Ice Wagon" Connors, all of whom wore handkerchiefs over their faces—stole more than $325,000 in cash and bonds from a truck parked by the loading dock of the main post office in Sacramento, California. With very little to go on, just the laundry mark on an abandoned glove, postal inspectors tracked the gang members down and recovered 85 percent of the stolen goods.

The following year, Farley was even more amazed when postal inspectors shepherded $2.3 billion worth of gold weighing more than 2,375 tons from the U.S. Mint in San Francisco to the Denver Mint on special trains that secretly moved across the country on different days. For Farley, it was "like a fantastic tale from the Arabian Nights or some other highly romantic piece of literature." He was less interested in censorship, abandoning the department's efforts to keep books like Joyce's *Ulysses* out of the mail.

While Farley acclimated himself at the Post Office, Roosevelt embarked on an unprecedented expansion of the federal government. He put unemployed people to work with jobs programs like the Works Progress Administration. He pushed through legislation to establish new regulatory agencies like the Federal Deposit Insurance Corporation, which protected people's savings; and the Securities and Exchange Commission, which policed Wall Street. Roosevelt also had to read a lot of mail. Hoover had need of only a single person on his staff to deal with his mail, but Roosevelt received more than 8,000 letters a day and needed a staff of 50 people to sift through it all.

Even with all that to keep him busy, Roosevelt wanted to see the designs for any new stamps that were being considered. So in

September 1933, Farley visited Roosevelt at the White House to discuss a new stamp honoring Rear Admiral Richard Byrd, the famous explorer who had led expeditions to Antarctica. Much to Farley's astonishment, Roosevelt spent an hour sketching a crude prototype with the routes that Byrd had taken to the south pole.

Farley couldn't help noticing how much Roosevelt relaxed as he worked on the drawing. Until then, Farley had assumed stamps were just a diversion for the president, but now he saw how they rejuvenated him. The president wanted stamps that might do the same for the Depression-weary public. He wanted to celebrate aspects of American culture that had rarely, if ever, been depicted on stamps. Working closely with Farley, Roosevelt helped design a series honoring America's national parks and another commemorating its poets, painters, composers, and inventors. When a women's group visited Farley and urged him to issue a stamp honoring suffragist leader Susan B. Anthony, Roosevelt told him to grant their wish. "By all means, authorize the stamp immediately before those ardent ladies reach the White House," Roosevelt joked. He was quick to pick up a pencil and sketch another prototype. Farley kept all the drawings, boasting that he had a complete collection of "original Roosevelts."

He may not have collected stamps himself, but Farley knew how to sell them, turning the appearance of each new stamp into a media event. He invited cameramen to the Bureau of Engraving and Printing to capture him tearing a proof sheet from the presses and autographing it for Roosevelt. "As you know, the president is an enthusiastic stamp collector," Farley told reporters early on. He also signed sheets for Roosevelt's chief of staff Louis Howe and Secretary of the Interior Harold Ickes, both ardent collectors like their boss, and set some aside for his own three children.

Inevitably, the flamboyant postmaster general became a political target. Airlines that had lost out on airmail contracts under the Hoover administration accused former postmaster general Walter Folger Brown of favoritism. In 1934, the Senate held hearings, excoriating Brown for approving the deals without competitive bids. The White House ordered Farley to cancel the contracts and arrange for the Army Air Corps to carry the mail, which he dutifully did.

It was an unmitigated disaster. Unlike those flying for private airlines, the Army pilots weren't prepared to fly in bad weather, and that's what they encountered as they took to the skies in February. There were blizzards in the West and gales in the central and eastern states. In the first week, five pilots died, three of them while still in training. The aviation industry seized the opportunity to assail the White House. The World War I ace Eddie Rickenbacker, now a vice president of Eastern Air Lines, called Farley's decision "legalized murder." Republicans joined the attack. "The summary, autocratic and dictatorial manner of canceling the air mail contracts without a hearing is worthy of fascism, Hitlerism or Sovietism at their best," said Hamilton Fish, a Republican congressman from New York. As the death count rose to 12, newspaper cartoonists depicted Farley leading a parade of dead pilots.

Meanwhile, former postmaster general Brown insisted on testifying before the committee and clearing his name. He explained what he had done to rescue the imperiled aviation industry and he said that even Farley had told him that he thought the hearings were bunk. (Farley denied this.) As public opinion turned against the White House, Roosevelt grounded the military airmail operation. "The continuation of deaths in the Army Air Corps must stop," he said.

The Post Office rebid the contracts and the same big airlines won them. Farley pointed out that the Post Office got a better deal; its yearly airmail costs fell from $20 million in 1933 to less than $13 million in 1934. The crisis focused attention on the need to overhaul the Army Air Corp in the years leading up to World War II. But Farley was privately furious with Roosevelt for not defending him against the attacks.

Farley also ran into trouble with the philatelic community over his stamp sheet giveaways. Prominent dealers complained that unlike ordinary stamps, the sheets lacked gum and perforations and were therefore quite rare. Indeed, no true maniac's collection would be complete without them. Columnists noted if the sheets ever turned up on the market, collectors would pay huge sums for them; therefore it wasn't fair for Farley to dole them out to White House insiders.

Farley insisted the collectors were fussing over nothing, but the complaints continued, and in January 1935, Roosevelt told Farley to stop giving the sheets away. "I do not think that this should be continued, even if such sheets are regarded merely as samples and not available for postage in the regular way," the president wrote to Farley in a memo. "Will you, therefore, be good enough to take steps to discontinue the issuance of any stamp or stamps except in the precise condition in which the issue is placed on sale at the Post Offices?"

Unfortunately, Farley had already given a sheet of Mother's Day stamps to William Wallace Atterbury, president of the Pennsylvania Railroad. Atterbury passed the sheet on to a relative in Norfolk, Virginia, who hung it in her living room where a dealer spied it and offered to buy it for $15,000. When she turned him down, he raised his offer to $20,000 and then $22,5000. The dealer got the stamps and took them to New York to turn a profit. The news spread quickly among collectors, and they condemned Farley for ignoring their warnings.

Farley didn't do himself any favors by dissembling. First he said he had no idea how the stamps had gotten into private hands. "When that Mother's Day stamp came out, I think Mrs. Roosevelt got one of the sheets and another got loose," he said. "That's probably the one that is down in Norfolk." Next, he insisted that the stamps were worthless "specimens" because the Post Office never sold them.

Republicans saw an opportunity to embarrass the man they called Roosevelt's "jobs-master." Charles Millard, a thick-necked, bespectacled Republican congressman from Westchester County, New York, called for Farley to appear before Congress to explain the stamp gifts. "The real question at issue is not whether certain philatelists or stamp dealers have been injured, but whether Mr. Farley or any official of the United States has used his official position to show favors and bestow valuable gifts upon a special group of people," Millard said on the House floor. Another Republican asked if the rugs were still on the floor in the postmaster general's office. The Democratic-controlled House overwhelmingly rejected Millard's request to interrogate the postmaster general and chairman of their party's national committee. "It was the biggest turnout since the opening day of Congress," the *Chicago Tribune* observed. But allegations of favoritism hung over the stamps that collectors now referred to as "Farley's Follies."

The politically shrewd Farley came up with a face-saving scheme. If collectors wanted proof sheets, he would furnish them. The Post Office announced that it would sell the same kind with neither gum nor holes to the public beginning on March 15, 1935. Thousands of happy collectors lined up at the Philatelic Agency's window and the Benjamin Franklin Post Office in Washington to purchase the stamps. One buyer hitchhiked all the way from Kansas the day before so he could sleep on the post office floor and be first in line for the sale. Postal workers told him he couldn't spend the night in the building, but he was outside when the sun came up, and he was soon at the front of a long line of men, women, children, and soldiers in uniform. The Post Office stationed inspectors to keep the peace, but the collectors didn't cause trouble; they just wanted their proof sheets. On the first day, the Post Office reaped $529,838. The *Washington Post* called it "the greatest stamp rush in history."

It was almost as if Farley had orchestrated the entire thing as a publicity stunt. Later that year the *American Philatelist* published a poem entitled "To Hon. James A. Farley, Master Salesman of the World."

A master salesman—Here's to Jim,
We never saw the likes o' him.
He doesn't need to advertise,
This politician, smooth and wise.
He changes the critic's stinging lash
To a half a million dollars—cash!
This Master Salesman shrewd and arch,
Who sold us stamps the ides of March.

Those sheets ungummed with center lines
And perforated gutter lines—
He gave us what we hollered for
And took our shekels by the score.
He saved the labor costs and gum—
So speed the presses, let 'em hum
A chance to sell—He would not muff it,
More than half a million profit.

The Devotees of Philatelum
Buy all the stamps that Jim will sell 'em.
(A half a million of the line
In half a day is doing fine.)
And Texas, Maine, and Delaware
And Foreign buyers, too, were there.
They had the cash—God bless their souls—
Jim sold 'em stamps—without the holes!

Farley also poked through departmental records and discovered that under Republican administrations, the Post Office had given entire albums of stamps to party leaders like President Theodore Roosevelt and bosses like House speaker Joseph Cannon and New York's U.S. senator Chauncey Depew. Farley found that Republican loyalist Anthony Comstock had also received free stamps from the department. "As long as the critics felt that I should be purer than the pure Anthony Comstock in regard to souvenir stamps, I had no wish to disappoint them," Farley would later write.

Throughout it all, Roosevelt remained in the good graces of collectors. In the summer of 1935, the American Philatelic Society held its fiftieth annual convention in Washington, D.C. Roosevelt allowed some of his stamps to be exhibited on the convention floor. The president invited Max Ohlman, his personal stamp dealer, to the White House for tea. The two men laughed at the news that Herbert Hoover had belatedly joined the society that day. Roosevelt promised to have his picture taken the next morning with conventioneers on the White House lawn. The following day, there was pandemonium outside the White House as hundreds of collectors tried to get past the guards to have their pictures taken with the president. The White House panicked and called it off. But the society's members forgave Roosevelt. Thanks to him, their hobby had never been more popular; Farley estimated that the number of American collectors was approaching 10 million. "The United States has become the stamp-collecting wonder of the world," wrote the *New York Times*.

Roosevelt's interest in the Post Office went beyond stamps. He wanted people to purchase them in nicer buildings. As part of his effort to create jobs and get the American economy moving, his administration built 1,731 new post offices, more than any previous administration. But Roosevelt wanted to do more than just put people to work. He wanted to create post offices that inspired stamp buyers and made them proud to be Americans. With his blessing, the Treasury Department funded and designed post offices that were more attractive than most of the ones built before. It constructed mission-style post offices in California, art deco ones in Florida, and colonial revival–style post offices in the older Northeast.

Many of these buildings are now historical landmarks and not just because of their lovely facades. Roosevelt wanted the lobbies of these buildings to be breathtaking too. So the Treasury Department created the Section of Painting and Sculpture (later called the Section of Fine Arts), which commissioned 1,200 murals and 300 sculptures for the new post offices by emerging American artists like Ben Shahn, Rockwell Kent, Philip Guston, and Milton Avery. Like the stamps of the Roosevelt era, these murals were meant to lift the spirits of Americans as they waited in line at the post office to buy stamps or mail a package.

Predictably, some of these murals were controversial. In 1937, Rockwell Kent completed a set of murals in the department's headquarters in Washington depicting an airmail pilot arriving in Puerto Rico with a letter from Alaska written in an Eskimo dialect. Kent tipped off a reporter that the letter in the pilot's hand contained a provocative message. The reporter had the letter translated and discovered it was a call for Puerto Ricans to rebel against their American rulers: "To the people of Puerto Rico, our friends! Go ahead. Let us change chiefs. That alone can make us equal and free."

Farley asked Kent to replace the message with something less controversial, preferably in English, and threatened to withhold the final $1,300 of the artist's payment. Kent refused and promised a suit of his own if Farley proceeded. The Treasury Department finally paid Kent in full because it said this would enable the federal government to take possession of the mural and sanitize it. The *Washington Post* warned the Roosevelt administration against this. "Hitler to the contrary notwithstanding, art can know no dictation—even when it impinges on propaganda," the *Post* wrote. "Mr. Kent's mural does just this, but a laughing and tolerant public will want it to stand. It happens to be good art, a verdict not always possible to hand down on most essays at mixing paint and politics." Though he was no art aficionado, Farley listened. The mural still hangs in the building, unaltered.

There were more disputes over murals. In Safford, Arizona, the chamber of commerce objected to artist Seymour Fogel's proposal to paint one showing Apache Indians performing a ceremonial dance. What was the problem? The chamber members said Geronimo had killed several of their Mormon parents. Puzzled Treasury Department officials explained that Geronimo was nowhere to be seen in the mural, which only upset local business owners more. Fogel ended up painting a mural showing the arrival of white settlers in Safford instead.

In Kennebunkport, Maine, locals protested Elizabeth Tracy's fine mural of bathers at nearby Old Orchard Beach, saying the women in the painting weren't sufficiently svelte. Senate Minority Leader Wallace White, a Republican from Maine, took up their cause. "The mural is a picture which, to speak frankly, depicts a group of fat women, scantily clad, disporting themselves on a beach," White said. He waved off the suggestion that his constituents were prudes. "Oh, I don't think those gentlemen of Kennebunkport have any objection to nudity," he said. "It was the bulges, fore and aft, they objected to." Sadly, Tracy's mural was painted over.

More often, postal customers welcomed the murals. In small towns, people who had never been to a museum lingered at the post office, watching as muralists brought scenes from their community to life on the wall. Parents asked where their children could get art lessons because the local schools didn't offer them. "The only trouble with the pictures is that they are so good they call for more of the same," lamented the *Pocahontas Times* in Marlinton, West Virginia. "It is pitiful to arouse taste and desire for the artistic and shut off the supply: in the nature of cruel and unusual punishment. Those stark cold walls were never forbidding until two corners of our post office lobby were warmed into life by the fine paintings."

An amateur architect, Roosevelt was deeply involved in the architectural design of post offices in six upstate New York towns including Hyde Park, where Springwood, his family's ancestral home, is located. Roosevelt wanted architects to replicate the region's vanishing Dutch Colonial buildings. "I never knew anyone to take as much interest in the public buildings of the neighborhood as my husband," Eleanor Roosevelt wrote in "My Day," her newspaper column. "He has watched every step of the Poughkeepsie Post Office building and now that they are starting a post office building in Rhinebeck, he is off this morning to discuss that."

Roosevelt got the same kind of pleasure from conceiving post offices as he did designing stamps. Roosevelt befriended the architect Rudolph Stanley-Brown, with whom he worked on four of the buildings. The president drove the architect and his wife out to visit a historic house in Rhinebeck with a distinctive curved roof that he had selected to serve as the model for the village's new post office. The Stanley-Browns rode in the back with two Secret Service agents. On the way, Stanley-Brown said he was sure the metal rods separating the panes of glass in the windows would be three-quarters of an inch wide. Roosevelt didn't think so. "I think you'll find, my boy, they are exactly one inch across," he replied. When they arrived, Stanley-Brown found that the president was right. "That's the kind of thing I remember," Roosevelt said. "Not particularly useful in politics, but absorbing to me."

Roosevelt dedicated the Rhinebeck post office on May 1, 1939. He stood on the front porch of the building on the cool, overcast day in his overcoat with Eleanor, Secretary of the Treasury Henry Morgenthau, Farley, and the crown prince and princess of Denmark, who were touring the United States. Roosevelt told the crowd that filled the streets that his great-great-grandfather had lived in Rhinebeck and served in the Revolutionary War militia. He also talked about how the Post Office exemplified his administration's ideals. "We are seeking to follow the type of architecture which is good in the sense that it does not of necessity follow the whims of the moment," Roosevelt said, "but seeks an artistry that ought to be good, as far as we can tell, for all time to come."

When Roosevelt was done, he handed a trowel to Crown Prince Frederik of Denmark so he could lay the cornerstone. Farley joked that the post office might not stand for long because the prince wasn't a member of the builders' union. Roosevelt was ready with a quip of his own. "I now announce this very historic cornerstone has been well and truly laid and also that His Royal Highness is an honorary member of the Union, in good standing," he said.

It's hard to imagine a contemporary president caring so much about a post office, but Roosevelt understood that a local post office was more than just a place where people bought stamps. Throughout the country, post offices anchored downtowns and instilled a sense of patriotism by flying the American flag. They were civic spaces where people of all races and income levels mingled and felt the touch of the federal government. The clerks at the counters could be doting or brusque, but everybody got the same treatment. What could be more democratic?

For 12 years, Roosevelt and Farley were a political team. They collaborated on so many new stamps that Republicans accused them of pandering to collectors to get votes. They strengthened the Democratic Party by dispensing postmaster positions and rural letter carrier jobs. But Farley wasn't a liberal ideologue like other members of Roosevelt's brain trust, including Secretary of Labor Frances Perkins and Harry Hopkins, director of the Works Progress Administration. He wanted to make friends, not enemies. He disagreed strongly with Roosevelt's divisive attempt to pack the Supreme Court with liberal judges who would support the New Deal and with his efforts to unseat Democratic senators who thwarted his legislative agenda. As the end of Roosevelt's second term approached, Farley thought he had the perfect candidate to run for president in 1940 and unite the party: himself. After all, he had so many potential supporters. "Someone once asked me if I thought I had 50,000 friends," Farley said. "Without wanting to brag, I think that 100,000 comes closer to the number. I can pick up this telephone on the desk and call up a friend in every city in the country from Maine to California and I know them all well enough to call them by their first names."

Farley wasn't taking any of them for granted either. On May 10, 1939, he departed to celebrate Postal Day at the San Francisco Fair. Along the way, he visited 13 states and delivered 20 speeches. Previously Farley had traveled the country as Roosevelt's advance man, but now he did so on his own behalf. "Jim Farley has done more favors and made more friends than any politician in American history, and his power is proportionately vast," *Life* magazine wrote. Farley refused to declare himself a candidate. The last thing he wanted was to be seen as disloyal to Roosevelt. But he encouraged speculation about his worthiness. "I've got as good a chance to be president as anybody in the world," he said privately. At the end of the year, Farley sent more than 200,000 Christmas cards, signing each one in his distinctive green ink. "This is going to be a huge job, but I feel sure it will be worth it," he wrote.

There was at least one obstacle to Farley's presidential candidacy. As the Democratic convention approached in July 1940, Roosevelt refused to say whether he might run again, putting Farley in a difficult position. He spent a sweltering afternoon at Hyde Park, pressing the president to reveal his plans, but Roosevelt would not be pinned down. "Jim, I don't want to run and I'm going to tell the convention so," Roosevelt said. Both men understood that this left open the possibility that the party might ignore his public demurrals and nominate him anyway, in which case the president might argue that he had no choice but to grant its wish.

That was obviously what Roosevelt hoped for. At the convention in Chicago, party leaders indulged him by choreographing what was supposed to look like a spontaneous outpouring of support for Roosevelt, complete with a 45-minute parade on the floor by his enraptured supporters. As a matter of pride, Farley submitted his name for the nomination. The delegates gave him a standing ovation, and the band played "When Irish Eyes Are Smiling," but it was no use. There was a roll call vote. Roosevelt received 946 votes compared with Farley's 72. Farley's friends, so many of whom were in the hall, had deserted him. He resigned from the Post Office Department and the Democratic National Committee and took a job as the head of the international division of Coca-Cola. He became one of Roosevelt's harshest public critics, calling him a despot and an untrustworthy friend, the worst kind in Farley's book.

Farley would never be president, but he would be the most famous postmaster general after Benjamin Franklin. In his farewell address, he told his employees not to be strangers and invited them to visit when he had settled in at Cola-Cola. "I should like to see any of you any time," Farley said. "Only don't crowd in at the same time."

Roosevelt replaced Farley at the Post Office with Frank Walker, another Irish Catholic. Walker had grown up in a mining camp in Montana and became a wealthy movie theater owner and one of Roosevelt's chief fund-raisers. Unlike Farley, Walker didn't court the press, which explains why he remained a stranger to many of his new employees "Let's get this straight," Walker said in a speech to several hundred of them in New York after several years on the job. "I am the postmaster general, despite the fact that a lot of people think Jim Farley still has the job." Walker later complained that Roosevelt had forced him into taking the job by publicly announcing his appointment at a campaign rally without giving him a chance to say no.

Like Farley, Walker soon found himself working with Roosevelt on stamp designs. After the Japanese attacked Pearl Harbor on December 7, 1941, Walker was inundated with requests for jingoistic stamps celebrating America's military might. A group of artists led by Paul Beranger, creative director of J. Walter Thompson, the New York advertising agency, drew up designs for stamps with tanks, bombers, and aircraft carriers and sent them to the White House for consideration. But Roosevelt didn't like them. "They're mighty fine designs," he told Ernest A. Kehr, the *New York Herald Tribune*'s stamp columnist. "But would such pictures reflect what we're trying to do? Wouldn't they convey to the minds of the people for whom we're fighting this war . . . that we are a militaristic and imperialistic nation?"

Instead, Roosevelt wanted individual stamps that celebrated America's freedoms and China's resistance to the Japanese. He called for a series of stamps with the flags of nations conquered by the Axis powers, including France, Poland, and Korea, and the image of a phoenix, the mythical bird that was reborn after its death. "It might tell those suffering victims in Europe that we are struggling for their own regeneration," Roosevelt said. The president purchased the first sheets of these stamps at the White House with the ambassadors of the occupied countries at his side. Walker was there beside him smiling awkwardly, unlike Farley who was a natural showman.

Walker also oversaw a campaign to airlift hundreds of millions of letters to American troops fighting overseas in World War II. Collaborating with the Army and Navy, the Post Office created V-Mail, a process enabling people to write short letters, which were converted to microfilm, flown overseas, and finally transferred back onto paper and delivered to soldiers. "An air-mail sack weighs about 70 pounds," Walker said. "By the use of V-Mail forms . . . the same 70 pounds can be reduced to two pounds." Within a year, the Army Post Office alone had delivered 25 million V-Mail messages.

The Post Office encouraged people to send V-Mail to boost the morale of American fighting men, but some correspondents answered the call with too much enthusiasm as far as the department was concerned. Shortly after the service started, the Post Office told women to refrain from kissing V-mail letters, saying their lipstick might cover the addresses. Some newspaper columnists saw Walker's influence in this edict. He was turning out to be quite a prude.

American soldiers loved *Esquire* magazine and hung its busty pinups in their barracks. In December 1943, however, Walker revoked the magazine's second-class periodical discount because he found the alluring images obscene. Fearing that its mailing costs would become unaffordable, *Esquire* sued the Post Office. Its editor Arnold Gingrich testified that he had been making monthly trips to Washington to show the magazine to postal officials before it went to press, a process he found burdensome and unfair. "It seemed like it was the only way to stay out of trouble," he said. "I would make all the required revisions on the spot, and some of the things I had to 'tone down' seemed to me to be a case of bending over backward to avoid offending even the most sensitive of sensibilities to a degree that was nearly ludicrous."

The case was covered extensively by the country's newspapers, which generally found Walker's objections laughable. The Roosevelt administration's enemies tried to turn the conflict between the postmaster and the men's magazine into a presidential campaign issue. Congressman Ranulf Compton, a Republican from Connecticut, accused Walker of setting himself up as "sole dictator over the nation's reading matter. The postmaster general has indicated that he had taken this outrageous action in order to force Congress to clarify the law," Compton fulminated. "That is comparable to a bank robber committing a murder in order to force the courts to determine whether murder committed in the commission of a felony is first or second degree. If every crackpot appointed by the New Deal decided to issue arbitrary and ridiculous interpretations of precedent law in order to force the hand of Congress, the nation will be in a sorry stats." The case eventually went to the U.S. Supreme Court and the eight judges issued a unanimous ruling in *Esquire*'s favor.

Roosevelt wisely stayed out of this fight. He was overseeing the U.S. invasion of Europe and meeting with America's allies to discuss how the continent would be reconfigured after Hitler's defeat, but he was never too busy to think about stamps. He called Walker late one night and told him he wanted an unadorned five-cent stamp with the words "Toward United Nations" to honor the first meeting of the United Nations in San Francisco on April 25, 1945. "The design has to be as simple as possible," Roosevelt said.

Roosevelt planned to attend the historic gathering and buy one of the first sheets himself in the city's main post office, but his health was deteriorating. He spent much of that month at his home in Warm Springs, Georgia, where he was secretly joined by his former girlfriend, Lucy Mercer Rutherfurd, with whom he had had an affair in the early years of his marriage. Rutherfurd invited her friend, the artist Elizabeth Shoumatoff, so she could paint Roosevelt's portrait. On the morning of April 12, Shoumatoff had the president sit in the living room and wrapped a navy blue cape on his shoulders. She could see that Roosevelt wasn't feeling well and thought she knew something that might lift his spirits. She had recently seen a new three-cent Florida centennial stamp and asked Roosevelt if he had anything to do with it. "Yes," Roosevelt said, brightening. "I certainly did." After about an hour, he raised his hand to his temple and said, "I have a terrific headache." He suffered a cerebral hemorrhage, and he died several hours later. Three months later, the Post Office Department released a memorial stamp in his honor at the post office in Hyde Park that he had helped design.

The Post Office arguably reached its zenith around this time. In 1947, it delivered 36 billion items, including 713 million post-cards. The department's annual income had surpassed $1 billion and it employed more 300,000 workers. Postal savings bank deposits peaked at almost $3.4 billion. The department had never been bigger or more prominent.

The public's sentiment for the Post Office had never been stronger either. *Miracle on 34th Street*, one of the year's most popular movies, highlighted the Post Office's Letters to Santa program, which allows people to buy gifts for needy children who mail their Christmas wishes to Santa Claus at the North Pole. In the film, New York postal workers deliver 50,000 of the children's letters to the judge who is ruling on the sanity of Kris Kringle, a kindly old man who claims to be the real Santa Claus. Previously, the judge has been skeptical, but once the uniformed carriers dump bags of letters on his desk, he changes his mind. "Since the United States government declares this man to be Santa Claus, this court will not dispute it," the judge says. "Case dismissed!"

"Thank you so much, your honor," Kringle says, "and a very merry Christmas to you."

Yet as the Post Office's deficits swelled, Jesse Donaldson, Harry Truman's postmaster general, reduced the number of daily residential deliveries from two to one to save money, ending what now seems like a wondrous time in American history. Telephones were becoming ubiquitous. In 1950, AT&T handled 51 billion calls compared with the Post Office's delivery of 45 billion pieces of mail. People no longer needed to be able to send a letter in the morning and get a reply in the afternoon. They could just pick up the phone and instantly talk to their families and friends. A Gallup Poll showed that 47 percent of the public disapproved of Donaldson's service cut while 53 percent thought it was a good idea or just didn't care.

The spread of telephones, however, didn't do anything to diminish the amount of mail flowing into people's homes. Businesses still relied on the Post Office to deliver their bills. Magazine publishers needed it to carry their thick, glossy product, and mail-order companies needed it to transport their catalogs. In 1940, the average American received 211 pieces of mail a year; a decade later, that number rose to 292.

In 1953, President Dwight Eisenhower appointed Arthur Summerfield, a Flint, Michigan, car dealer who had been his campaign manager, to be postmaster general and deal with this flood. In some ways, Summerfield was a buffoonish character. He made headlines with his short-lived effort to send mail by guided missile. "Before man reaches the moon," Summerfield said, "mail will be delivered within hours from New York to California, to England, to India or to Australia by guided missile." In fact, the postal service did this only once, firing a missile with 300 letters from a naval submarine to an air station on the Florida coast.

Summerfield was also obsessed with pornography. He kept a collection of obscene magazines and films confiscated from the mail in a special room and showed it to visitors. Channeling the spirit of Anthony Comstock, Summerfield ruled in 1959 that D. H. Lawrence's 1928 novel *Lady Chatterley's Lover* was too offensive to be mailed and confiscated copies. "Any literary merit the book may have is far outweighed by the pornographic and smutty passages and words so that the book, taken as a whole, is an obscene and filthy work," Summerfield said.

Barney Rosset, the publisher of Grove Press, which had published the book in the United States, sued the Post Office in a federal court in New York. His attorney called upon famous literary critics like Malcolm Cowley and Alfred Kazin to testify about the importance of Lawrence's book. Federal District Court Judge Frederick van Pelt Bryan ruled against the Post Office. "The Postmaster General has no special competence or technical knowledge on this subject which qualifies him to render an informed judgment entitled to special weight in the courts," Bryan wrote. The *New York Times* would later say that this was the day that obscenity became art in the United States. The Post Office would try again in the coming years to ban other books from the mail, but after Bryan's ruling, this became a futile effort.

In other ways, however, Summerfield was prescient. He could see that the system was breaking down. The decline of the railroads was forcing the Post Office to abandon the Railway Mail Service, which meant that it had to fly the mail between cities and then move it in trucks in downtown post offices through crowded urban streets. The change inevitably slowed down delivery and led to widespread customer dissatisfaction. During the Depression, the Roosevelt administration had poured money into the Post Office's infrastructure, but there hadn't been much investment since then. Summerfield saw the effect as he traveled around the country. "Almost everywhere work was being done with shopworn equipment in run-down, overcrowded, poorly lighted postal buildings constructed years before," Summerfield wrote in his memoir *U.S. Mail*. "Most tasks were being done by hand, too slowly and too expensively, in the same way they had been done in the days of the first postmaster general—Benjamin Franklin." Summerfield pleaded with Congress to raise stamp prices so he could modernize the Post Office. In 1958, Congress raised the price of sending a one-ounce letter to four cents, its first increase since 1932. For Summerfield, it was too little and too late. He left the Post Office in 1961 much as he had found it.

7

Mount Semrow

In the summer of 1963, when people went to their local post office to purchase stamps, many encountered a wide-eyed, orange-faced figurine clad in a letter carrier's blue uniform. His name was Mr. Zip. When they pressed a button on his side, they heard the brassy-voiced Broadway star Ethel Merman deliver a special version of "Zip-A-Dee Doo Dah." "Welcome the Zip Code," Merman half sang and half shouted in her inimitable style. "Learn it today. Send your mail out the five-digit way!"

Mr. Zip symbolized the five-digit zip code, the most radical address change since a century before, when Abraham Lincoln's postmaster general Montgomery Blair required people to put street addresses on their envelopes. Not that a street address was always necessary. The acerbic Washington columnist Drew Pearson once received a letter addressed to "S.O.B., Washington" from a reader upset about his criticism of Harry Truman. But between 1940 and 1960, the amount of mail delivered by the Post Office more than doubled, from 28 billion to 64 billion pieces a year. Clerks could no longer sort it all fast enough under the old system.

The zip code was supposed to be the solution. The first number represented one of 10 delivery zones around the county, starting with zero in the Northeast and ending with the number nine on the West Coast. The second number often indicated a state, and the third usually represented a big-city post office where mail was sorted. The fourth and fifth typically indicated the closest post office to a letter recipient's home. In other words, a clerk could look at a zip code and pinpoint almost exactly where a given piece of mail was going without squinting to read a sender's scrawled handwriting.

The Post Office wanted Mr. Zip to become as familiar as Smokey the Bear. Small-town postmasters arranged for him to ride on floats in parades and appear at country fairs. The Post Office held beauty contests around the country, crowning the winners Miss Zip Code. Dick Tracy, the popular square-jawed comic strip detective, appeared in an advertisement telling postal customers, "Protect your mail. Use Zip Codes!" The Post Office also recruited Hugh O'Brian, star of ABC's *The Life and Legend of Wyatt Earp*, to promote the code. Mr. Zip also appeared in a board game ("Zip Code: The Last Word in Games!") and on lunch boxes, on coffee mugs, and as a bobble-head doll.

Hoping to take advantage of the folk music craze which had spawned the ABC show *Hootenanny*, the Post Office ran public-service ads featuring an ensemble called the Swinging Six whose members wore turtlenecks, strummed acoustic guitars, and urged the public to use the zip code or else. "There's been a mail explosion!" the Swinging Six sang. "They've got a terrible load! You've got to help them right away before the U.S. Post Office explodes!" But the Swinging Six had good news: the Post Office had developed a computerized machine that could instantaneously read and separate letters based on the five-number code. They called it "the fantastic zip code scanner!"

The zip code would eventually become a fixture in American life, something everybody used to send letters and packages. Initially, however, people thought the zip code seemed like another step toward an Orwellian future when the federal government and large corporations would reduce everything in people's lives to numbers. AT&T had recently angered the public by requiring people to use entirely numerical telephone numbers rather than the old ones with distinctive two-letter prefixes, like BUtterfield or MUrray Hill, that stood for their neighborhoods. With the zip code's introduction, people wondered if small towns like Truth or Consequences, New Mexico; Wounded Knee, South Dakota; and Boring, Oregon, would forfeit their quirky names and become 87901, 57794, and 97009.

Postal workers didn't care for the zip code at first either. Clerks who had previously had to memorize complicated numerical "schemes" representing towns, neighborhoods, and streets worried that the zip code would dumb down their profession. Letter carriers felt insulted by the cartoonish Mr. Zip. "I'm tired of the image of the American Letter Carrier being held up for public ridicule," complained a carrier from Fort Worth, Texas. "No Letter Carrier I have ever seen looks as absurd as Mr. Zip." Yet before the end of 1963, the *Washington Post* declared the Post Office's campaign to create public awareness of the zip code an overwhelming success. "Even if they're not using it," the *Post* wrote, "they're talking about it."

The Post Office really did have a fantastic zip code scanner. In the 1950s, the department's research division created a device called an optical character reader, which sorted mail using an electric eye that could separate 36,000 letters an hour by zip code. The machine couldn't decipher handwriting yet. But business mail now accounted for 80 percent of America's postal volume. Companies spewed it out using computerized address lists and mailing labels. And the scanner could read a computer-generated zip code.

The Post Office was counting on the optical character reader to help it cope with the surging volume of mail. It knew that half of this mail came from 25,000 companies. The department would give them a three-year deadline to adopt the zip code. If it could install optical character readers in 200 large post offices, which handled 60 percent of America's mail, the Post Office wouldn't be swamped with letters. There was one problem. The Post Office had only one optical character reader, and it was a prototype still being tested at the Detroit post office. At the rest of the department's 34,000 post offices, clerks still sorted mail by hand as they had done in Benjamin

Franklin's time. The Swinging Six weren't exaggerating. The Post Office really was about to explode.

Harry Semrow, the postmaster of Chicago, was known in the city as "the world's happiest postmaster." Some even called him "the swingingest postmaster we've ever had." A handsome, six-foot-four conservatory-trained pianist with a quick wit and a toothy grin, he could sing and play the accordion with almost professional ease. He was also a talented politician who had made himself indispensable to Mayor Richard Daley, Chicago's political boss. Thanks to Daley, the 48-year-old Semrow had already served five years as a state legislator. His current position at the Post Office was just another in a string of political jobs, which, coupled with his outside business interests, would make Semrow quite wealthy. Of course, he was happy.

On the evening of December 28, 1963, Semrow was onstage at the Chicago Stadium in front of an audience of 13,000 postal workers hosting their annual holiday party. It was a very special occasion. Semrow introduced the gospel singer Mahalia Jackson, one of the evening's featured performers. He clowned around with movie star Jimmy Durante and even sang a song himself about the perils of postal work, accompanied by a letter carrier in a dog costume. The Chicago post office marching band performed in new red-white-and-blue uniforms paid for out of something called the Chicago Post Office Welfare Fund, as did the Chicago post office chorus, whose 70 members wore shiny new robes. Before Semrow joined the stars to sing "Auld Lang Syne," he thanked his audience for another fine year. But perhaps he spoke prematurely.

Semrow's Chicago post office was the largest mail processing facility in the world. It was known as "the hub of the American postal universe." Most of the mail traveling across the country passed through the massive building that spanned two city blocks and contained three million square feet. Inside, 14,900 clerks sorted

21 million pieces of mail a day, but it was a constant struggle. The amount cascading through the Chicago post office was twice as much as the monumental building was designed to handle when it opened in 1934.

On the night of the holiday gala, the Chicago post office was bursting with Christmas packages. Trucks were backed up for blocks outside the building, unable to drop off their loads because there was a backlog of parcels inside that couldn't be sorted quickly enough. Employees called it "Mount Semrow." Tons of packages wouldn't arrive at people's homes until after Valentine's Day. "We were really in a bind," said Clairborne Bolton, Semrow's assistant director of operations. "We had nearly 100,000 sacks of Christmas packages unprocessed. Some of it was stored in a garage. We had mail piled up all over the place." Semrow joked that businessmen must have been mailing presents when they should have been attending their holiday office parties.

Semrow probably would have been fired if he had worked at a private company, but postmasters did more than just keep track of the mail. They got out the vote on Election Day for their political patrons, and in Semrow's case the patron would have been Mayor Richard Daley. Rank-and-file clerks and letter carriers were no longer patronage hires, but none of them got promoted without the blessing of their postmaster, who kept files on the political affiliations of his or her employees. As long as Semrow was taking care of that side of his job, he would weather a Christmas mail backup.

Not surprisingly, then, Semrow stayed on the job until 1966 when he left to run for a seat on the Cook County Board of Review, which handled property tax appeals. That year, President Lyndon Johnson appointed Chicago's first African American postmaster. His name was Henry McGee, and he was a broad-shouldered 56-year-old who may not have played the accordion like Semrow but knew a lot about mail delivery. He had started out in 1929 as a substitute carrier making 65 cents an hour and earned his bachelor's degree by going to college at night. He wrote a thesis entitled "The Negro in the Chicago Post Office," which condemned its discriminatory employment practices and called for replacing them with a merit system.

McGee had barely settled into his new position when there was another logjam at the Chicago post office, one that would make the previous breakdown look almost laughable. The Post Office Department had given most businesses until January 1, 1967, to begin mandatory zip code usage. After that, they would be required to presort their mail by zip code so the Post Office could move it faster. That wasn't a problem for magazine publishers and banks; they had computerized their mailing lists long ago. But it was arduous for junk mailers whose systems weren't as sophisticated. Hoping to beat the deadline, they flooded the system with uncoded advertisements and circulars. Much of this mail ended up at the Chicago post office. Inside the building, piles of mail rose as high as 40 feet, dwarfing Mount Semrow. At the pinnacle of the crisis, there were 10 million unsorted pieces of mail languishing in the building. "We had mail coming out of our ears," McGee lamented. Tractor-trailer trucks laden with mail were backed up for blocks outside the building. Trains full of it sat idle on the tracks beneath the post office. The magazine *Saturday Review* called it "the most incredible snarl in the mail movement since the inauguration of the U.S. postal system—and, in the view of some experts, a nightmarish preview of mail service horrors that lie ahead."

Finally, the department closed the Chicago post office for 10 days and sent in a team of troubleshooters to unclog the world's largest mail processing facility. They diverted mail to post offices in Nashville, Milwaukee, and Kansas City so it could be sorted there. They got the first-class mail out of the building before anything else. What about the heaps of unsorted junk mail? The Post Office telephoned mailers and asked if the department could burn it. Afraid of setting a precedent for incinerating their product, the junk mailers insisted that the Post Office deliver it anyway. So in the following weeks, letter carriers around the country dropped flyers into people's mailboxes for promotions and sales that had expired weeks before.

Reporters from national publications descended on Chicago to find out what had gone wrong. They found plenty to write about. On a typical day, 10 percent of the employees at the Chicago post office were out sick. Those who showed up disregarded the 10-minute coffee break limit, lingering in the cafeteria for half an hour. For years, a parcel clerk had run a loan-sharking operation during work hours under the noses of his supervisors. Postal inspectors finally arrested him after they noticed dozens of his fellow workers queuing up at his window on payday. The Chicago post office was also plagued by racial tension. White supervisors complained that their black employees, who made up 65 percent of the workforce, were ignorant and lazy. Black employees accused white managers of engineering the crisis to make the city's first black postmaster look bad. Some people blamed the crisis on female postal workers. "There's no doubt they slow things down," a union leader claimed. "A man can carry a heavy tray of mail from one place to another like nothing, but a woman has to make three trips."

Racial tension, chronic absenteeism, and criminal activity contributed to the crisis, of course, but Lawrence O'Brien, Lyndon Johnson's postmaster general, testified before Congress that the real reason for the breakdown in Chicago was more fundamental. "The conditions that produced chaos and the mail logjam are not confined to Chicago," O'Brien said. "We are trying to move our mail through facilities largely unchanged since the days of Jim Farley."

Like James Farley, O'Brien was the son of Irish immigrants and a man who was accustomed to getting things done. Born in Springfield, Massachusetts, in 1917, O'Brien grew up in a political household. His father was a Democratic Party organizer who frequently hosted household visitors like James Curley, Boston's legendary mayor and political boss. O'Brien himself became an able party operative, one who knew how to charm crusty, older, working-class

Democrats and their college-educated children. In 1952, Joseph Kennedy asked O'Brien to manage his son Jack's campaign for the U.S. Senate against Republican Henry Cabot Lodge Jr. "Larry, Jack is a man of destiny," Kennedy's father told O'Brien over lunch one day at the family's home in Hyannis Port, Massachusetts. "He is going to defeat Lodge and serve with distinction in the Senate, and eventually, he is going to be president of the United States." O'Brien was more bemused than impressed. He later wrote, "I thought to myself, 'Fine, but why am I knocking myself out helping to build a political operation for Kennedy if destiny is going to take care of everything?'"

O'Brien used what he referred to as "womanpower" to gather votes for Kennedy. He sent Jack Kennedy's mother Rose and his glamorous sisters Pat, Eunice, and Jean out to campaign for him. Kennedy's cousin Polly organized receptions around the state (the press called them "tea parties") where the handsome and still single candidate spoke to groups of adoring female voters. O'Brien also recruited female campaign workers, something that wasn't done much at the time. Mothers with young children might not be able to come in and work the phones at the Kennedy campaign office, but they had telephones at home. O'Brien had them call each person on a single page of the phone book, ask for their support, and promise to transport them to the voting booth on Election Day. Kennedy defeated Lodge. Six years later, O'Brien organized Kennedy's successful reelection campaign, in which he won by 874,608 votes, then a record in Massachusetts.

Naturally, Kennedy turned to O'Brien in 1960 when he ran against Richard Nixon for president. After Kennedy won by a slim margin, he asked O'Brien to become his liaison to Congress. O'Brien did well enough that *Time* magazine put him on the cover in September 1961, calling him "one of the most important of the New Frontiersmen" and celebrating him as a quintessential backroom operative who smoked three packs of Pall Malls a day and consumed "a Niagara of coffee" while prodding lawmakers to support Kennedy's agenda. O'Brien also served as a buffer between the president and the many supplicants who wanted things from him. When people on the Hill pressed Kennedy for favors, Kennedy responded, "Have you cleared this with Larry?"

O'Brien was in the motorcade in Dallas on November 22, 1963, when Kennedy was shot, and he was at first lady Jackie Kennedy's side at the hospital when Vice President Lyndon Johnson showed up. Johnson begged O'Brien to stay on and work for him. "I need you more than you need me—and more than Jack Kennedy needed you," Johnson told him. At first O'Brien wasn't sure. He was devastated by Kennedy's slaying and couldn't believe that Johnson was making his plea at a time like this. Like many members of the Kennedy administration, O'Brien also didn't especially care for Johnson, an old-school Texas politician. But O'Brien succumbed to the new president's persistent overtures and became his man on Capitol Hill and the manager of Johnson's landslide victory over Republican Barry Goldwater in 1964. When O'Brien tried to leave the White House the following summer, Johnson named him postmaster general, announcing it at a press conference at his Texas ranch before O'Brien could say no, just as Franklin Roosevelt had done with Frank Walker two decades earlier. When O'Brien telephoned his sister in Massachusetts to tell her the news, Johnson snatched the receiver from his hand. "Well, what do you think about this?" Johnson told her. "Your brother's got two jobs now."

Johnson wanted O'Brien to take the oath of office at an old-fashioned post office in Hye, Texas, where the president claimed to have sent his first letter. When they arrived, Johnson introduced O'Brien to Levi Deike, the long-serving local postmaster. "I want you to meet your new boss, the postmaster general," Johnson told him. "Tell him who appointed you as postmaster."

"Jim Farley," Deike told him.

That wasn't the answer Johnson was looking for. In 1934, he told O'Brien, *he* had arranged for Deike get the job. Apparently,

Deike had forgotten all about it. Johnson ended the conversation abruptly, and posed for a picture instead with O'Brien, who couldn't have been more entertained by the exchange.

O'Brien moved into Jim Farley's expansive former office in the Post Office headquarters on Pennsylvania Avenue in Washington. A portrait of Ben Franklin already hung over one of the two fireplaces. O'Brien hung a picture of Farley over the other. Even before the Chicago crisis, he could see that the mail system was breaking down. But after the logjam in America's second-largest city, there was no longer any question. The country's magazines, most of which were delivered by the Post Office, were full of stories about the deteriorating mail system. "Time is running out and trouble is spreading," *Fortune* wrote. A *Reader's Digest* article bore the headline "Crisis in the Post Office." *U.S. News and World Report* asked, "Can Anything Be Done About U.S. Mail Service?"

The Post Office needed more optical character readers. Detroit still had the only one. O'Brien asked Congress to fund a $100 million modernization plan to increase the number of these devices in large post offices in the next few years. But he didn't think it would be enough. Service was deteriorating around the country, and there was little O'Brien could do about it. He was running an organization with $4.8 billion in sales, more than any American companies except AT&T; Sears, Roebuck & Company; and A&P. But he couldn't appoint a postmaster in a large city without congressional approval. He couldn't raise stamp prices or give his employees a raise without a vote on Capitol Hill. O'Brien literally risked imprisonment if he spent a dime of stamp money without congressional permission.

So he asked four of his closest advisers what they would do if they could create the Post Office from scratch. He announced their conclusions in a speech before the Magazine Publishers Association and the American Society of Magazine Editors on April 3, 1967, at the Shoreham Hotel in Washington. The speech must have stunned his listeners, who were some of the country's biggest postal customers. O'Brien said the Post Office was being strangled to death by congressional micromanagement. "If we had run the telephone system in this way, the carrier pigeon business would still have a great future, and I would sell my shares in AT&T—if I had any," O'Brien said. "If we sought to build the atomic bomb in this way, we'd still be surveying sites in Tennessee, Washington, and New Mexico—or arguing whether we should survey the sites. Ladies and gentlemen, the Post Office Department, as presently constituted, reminds me of the classic definition of an elephant—a mouse built to government specifications."

O'Brien said the Post Office should be removed from the president's cabinet and transformed into a government corporation run by a chief executive selected by a board of directors appointed by the president of the United States. Rather than pleading with Congress for funding for new buildings and new equipment, O'Brien argued that the Post Office should be able to set its own prices and raise money by issuing bonds just as private companies did. He also said the new postal service's managers and employees should be paid salaries comparable to those enjoyed by their counterparts in private industry. And O'Brien didn't want anybody to think that he was making this proposal because he was looking for a raise. "In case there is any doubt, I want to state that while I am advocating the abolition of my job, I will not under any circumstances take an executive position in the government corporation I am proposing," O'Brien said.

Five days later, Johnson appointed a commission to study O'Brien's proposal, led by none other than Frederick Kappel, the recently retired chairman of AT&T. Who better to come up with a plan to fix the Post Office than the man who had run the world's largest telephone company? AT&T had taken over the role the Post Office had once played in America as the country's primary communications provider. In 1964, AT&T handled 251 million calls a day, more than twice as many as the pieces of mail the Post Office delivered. Unlike the Post Office, however, AT&T was considered a beacon of American innovation. In his final years at AT&T, Kappel had introduced the soon-to-be ubiquitous touch-tone phone. He also unveiled the picture phone, which would go down in history as one of the company's greatest failures. But AT&T could afford a few missteps. It made three times as much money as the Post Office and it generated nearly $2 billion in yearly profits, compared with the Post Office's annual deficit, which was approaching $1 billion. More people held shares in AT&T than in any other company in the world.

A native of Albert Lea, Minnesota, with a farmer's square jaw and reserved demeanor, Kappel strongly believed in the inherent virtuousness of the American corporation. His life story seemed to attest to this. He started at AT&T in 1924 as a pole digger earning $25 a week and rose through the corporation's ranks to become chief executive in 1954 and then chairman in 1961. Like many chief executives in that era, Kappel lived in less than grand style, in a four-bedroom house in Bronxville, New York, with six telephones. He listed his home number in the telephone directory, as did the 25 presidents of the 25 regional companies that made up AT&T's Bell Telephone system. Kappel worshipped at a local Dutch Reformed Church on Sunday and played bridge every week.

Otherwise, he devoted himself to his company. "A.T.&T. is a pure meritocracy, run by men who started at the bottom and worked up, step by step, winning the nod of many bosses along the way," *Time* magazine wrote in a 1964 cover story about Kappel and his corporation. "The executives at A.T.&T. combine in themselves dedication, sense of service, awareness of public responsibility, invocation of old-fashioned virtues, puritan earnestness, Rotary Club friendliness, and a touch of self-righteousness. They consider themselves a breed apart —and they are. They value continuity and gradualism in management more than most, and, though at ease in handling vast sums, run their company with a peasant's fear of debt and the thrifty conviction that every piece of installed equipment ought to be good for 40 years. Most of all, they view their job—helping the people to speak—as an almost priestly calling."

Most of the other 10 members of what became known as the Kappel Commission came from the same corporate world. They included a Harvard Business School dean; a vice president of the Ford Foundation; and the presidents of General Electric Company, Campbell Soup Company, Cummins Engine Company, and Bank of America. The only outlier was George Meany, the cigar-smoking president of the AFL-CIO, who rarely attended meetings and was the only commission member who didn't endorse its eventual findings.

Even Meany, however, agreed that the Post Office was a mess. Customers were unhappy. Rates didn't make sense. (The commission found that while first-class mail and airmail paid their own way, junk mail covered only 76 percent of its costs and magazines and newspapers paid for a mere 26 percent.) The department's buildings were crumbling. Employees were frustrated. Worst of all, the men (and they were almost all men) who were supposed to be running the Post Office were powerless to prevent any of this. As a postmaster in a large midwestern city told the commission, "How do I manage this operation? My friend, I don't manage it, I administer it."

For Kappel, the solution was to empower the postal service's managers to make decisions as their counterparts did at AT&T or Campbell's Soup. The majority of the commissioners believed that the Post Office would have functioned best as a private company with few governmental restraints. But Kappel lamented that this wasn't possible. Who would buy a deficit-ridden government agency that needed an estimated $5 billion to modernize itself? America was still two decades away from the privatization wave that would be cheered on by President Ronald Reagan. Moreover, as the commission delicately put it, there was still a widespread assumption that mail delivery should be the government's business just as it had been for nearly two centuries. "If I could, I'd make it a private enterprise and I would create a private corporation to run the postal service and the country would be better off financially," Kappel later said. "I can't get from here to there."

But the committee said there was another option. The federal government had set up so-called authorities or government corporations providing services that generated income and therefore could be self-supporting. Some of the biggest and most successful were created by Franklin Roosevelt, like the Federal Deposit Insurance Corporation, which collected fees from banks and used the money to protect their customers' savings if the institutions failed; and the Tennessee Valley Authority, which generated electricity for people in rural Tennessee, Alabama, Georgia, Kentucky, Mississippi, North Carolina, and Virginia. The presidentially appointed directors of these agencies had more budgetary and managerial freedom than the heads of federal departments. The Kappel Commission believed the Post Office would flourish if it were restructured along these lines. In fact, these corporate savants predicted that such a reconfigured Post Office would be profitable within a few years.

So in June 1968, Kappel stood at a press conference in a dark suit with a pointer in his hand gesturing at a flip chart showing how the reconstituted Post Office would work. Newspapers around the country praised the commission's work, but Lyndon Johnson was reluctant to bless the plan. Johnson had recently announced that he would not run for reelection that year. Democrats disapproved of his handling of the Vietnam War and civil rights issues, dooming his chances of winning his party's presidential primary. After Johnson announced his decision not to run for reelection, O'Brien left the administration to run Robert Kennedy's presidential campaign. Marvin Watson, the new postmaster general, told people that the Kappel Commission's plan was "going nowhere."

Republican presidential hopeful Richard Nixon disagreed. He praised the commission's findings on the campaign trail, and after he was elected in 1968, Nixon appointed Winton Blount to be his postmaster general and act on them. A wealthy contractor from

Montgomery, Alabama, Blount was a lanky 47-year-old with big ears and no lack of self-esteem. His friends called him "Red." Unlike Frederick Kappel, Red Blount flaunted his wealth. He and his wife Mary lived in a Georgian-style mansion on 60 acres of land outside the city and owned a second home on nearby Lake Martin where they entertained guests on a real Chinese junk. Red drove a Jaguar. Mary preferred a Lincoln Continental.

Like most postmaster generals, Blount hadn't given the Post Office much thought until Nixon tracked him down at a University of Alabama football game and offered him the job over the phone. But Blount was intrigued. He had dreams of running for office himself and would undoubtedly enhance his chances as a Republican candidate if he shook up the Post Office Department, long described by his party as a sclerotic, patronage-ridden mess. Blount studied up by reading the Kappel Commission report. At his first meeting in the White House with Nixon to discuss his appointment, Blount gave the president an ultimatum. "Mr. President," Blount said, "if you want to reform the Post Office, I'd be delighted to do it. If you want a postmaster general like the rest of them, I'm not interested." That was fine with Nixon. "Who's going to make the appointments in the Post Office?" Blount challenged him. Nixon pointed his finger at Blount. "You are," he said.

Nixon had more pressing things to worry about than the Post Office. The Vietnam War was escalating. The U.S. economy was weakening. He had to desegregate southern schools without alienating his supporters in the region. Nixon also didn't think Blount would get the votes for postal reform as long as Democrats controlled both houses of Congress. He underestimated Blount's determination. Blount moved into Jim Farley's cavernous office, bringing along his African American chef Jesse Butcher to cook grits, quail, and other southern specialties for him.

It wasn't long before Blount upset people on Capitol Hill. With Nixon standing beside him, Blount announced at a press conference that all Post Office hiring would be merit-based from now on. House Republican leader Gerald Ford endorsed the proposal, but individual party members were furious about it. They had just regained the White House after eight years, and they were eager to reward their campaign workers with jobs. "That son of a bitch takes away all the job opportunities Republicans have been crying for a generation," said H. R. Gross, a Republican congressman from Iowa. Bryce Harlow, Nixon's congressional liaison, told Nixon that he would be "committing hari-kari" if he supported Blount's misguided scheme.

Nixon didn't waver, and neither did Blount. Blount asked Ford to let him address the Republican caucus in a closed session. For two and a half hours, members of Blount's own party berated him for taking away their patronage appointments. "We called together all of the Republicans in a private off-the-cuff discussion," says Paul Carlin, Blount's legislative aide. "They all gathered in one room, and Red spoke to them for two hours. There was no one in there except the congressmen, Red, and me. They were so vividly angry. I mean, they shouted and jumped up and down."

At the end of the meeting, the Republican lawmakers weren't satisfied. So 10 days later, Blount returned for another gripe session. This one lasted an hour and a half, but when it was over, Blount's fellow Republicans understood something about the new postmaster general: they could yell all they wanted to, but it didn't mean a thing to Red Blount.

Congressional foes of postal reform soon discovered that Blount was determined to go over their heads to the public. He formed the bipartisan Citizens Committee for Postal Reform to spread pro-reform messages in their districts. The commission was chaired by former Kentucky senator and Republican Party chairman Thruston Morton and Larry O'Brien. O'Brien detested Nixon, but he couldn't let Republicans run away with postal reform. So he swallowed his pride and attended a press conference in support of Blount's initiative at Nixon's home in San Clemente, California. "Larry, why don't you stand here to my right?" Nixon said.

O'Brien replied, "Just as long as it's not too far to your right."

The committee took out newspaper advertisements promising that corporatization would speed delivery and improve working conditions for postal employees. Blount also enlisted a public relations team to spread negative press about the agency. One of the results was "The U.S. Mail Mess," a 1969 *Life* magazine cover story that explained how the modern Post Office delivered letters more slowly than the Pony Express. "No one really runs the Post Office," Blount told the magazine.

Like O'Brien and Kappel before him, Blount warned of a catastrophe if Congress didn't restructure the Post Office soon. "The volume of mail continues to increase," Blount told a Senate committee. "At some point in time, we are going to reach the point where this system cannot continue to operate as it is presently constituted. It will break down of its own weight. That kind of breakdown could happen, not only in Chicago, but in many of the urban areas of this country; it could happen all at once, and we would have economic chaos." If senators and representatives didn't get the message, Blount tried to deliver it to them personally. Nixon kept a yacht called the *Sequoia* on the Potomac. Blount used it to entertain lawmakers. He invited them in groups of five or six to breakfasts in his office, where Butcher served them his delectable grits and quail. "If we don't pass postal reform and get Blount out of town, he's going to kill us with those grits," complained one of Blount's guests.

Blount's doggedness impressed a lot of people, but it wasn't enough. Frederick Kappel thought Blount was alienating Congress with his aggressiveness. "He wouldn't budge on anything," Kappel later said. "He was too rigid." Blount was up against a group of foes who were equally unyielding: the leaders of seven postal worker unions. The presidents of these unions had become some of the most active lobbyists and biggest contributors on Capitol Hill. They didn't think their members were getting paid enough, but they preferred to deal with Congress rather than take their chances with a postal corporation. The union presidents didn't always get along with each other, but they were united in their opposition to Blount's plan.

The only union leader the White House thought it might be able to convert was James Rademacher, the tall, charismatic leader of the National Association of Letter Carriers (NALC). Unlike his counterparts, Rademacher had endorsed Nixon in the 1968 race, but Rademacher and Blount had a toxic relationship. They weren't just diametrically opposed when it came to postal reform; furthermore, they hated each other. Rademacher had attacked Blount's public relations campaign, calling it "one of the smoothest and most massive attempts at public brainwashing since the German glory days of Joseph Paul Goebbels."

Blount accused Rademacher of willfully distorting his reform plan and refused to meet with him. "From time to time we have been asked why the postal unions are opposed to the Postal Service Act," Blount said. "Mr. Rademacher's reckless misrepresentation suggests a possible answer." As long as Blount and Rademacher were in a stand-off, the future of the Post Office was in jeopardy. Ultimately, they ended up working together and bringing about the most sweeping organizational change in the department's history, but first there was a postal crisis that dwarfed the one in Chicago.

8

The Day the Mail Stopped

In 1941, James Rademacher, a recently married 19-year-old with a pregnant wife, sat in the Redford, Michigan, post office just outside Detroit, waiting for work. There was no guarantee when he arrived each morning that he would get any. He was a temporary substitute, which meant he filled in for the permanent letter carriers when they were sick or took a holiday. Rademacher begged the other employees to take pity on him. "We're expecting our first child," he told them. "Could you possibly take a day or two off so I could get some money?"

One day, the carrier who delivered mail in the Dime Bank building in Detroit answered his plea and took a day off. Rademacher got his route. When he arrived at the building, he was astonished to find a pile of mail two feet taller than he was. He was so nervous that he ducked into a stairwell and threw up. When Rademacher emerged, the supervisor had given the route to another substitute.

Five months later, Rademacher became a full-time substitute, which meant he had steady hours. He was drafted in 1944 and served for two years in the U.S. Navy in World War II. When he was discharged, he became a regular carrier just like his father. The pay still wasn't much, but Rademacher and his fellow carriers took pride in their work. They wore ties and jaunty caps. This was a time when the Post Office delivered mail several times a day, and carriers were expected to get it there on time. There was a street mailbox on every block. Rademacher remembers emptying the mailboxes at 11 PM so that letters could be delivered the following day.

Back then, letter carriers had a close relationship with people on their routes. The community Rademacher served sent flowers to the hospital when he and his wife, Martha, had their two children. At Christmastime, they gave Rademacher presents to take home to his children. "That's how much they care about you if you treat them right," he says. "Not every carrier treats them right, of course, but the majority do."

But Rademacher didn't want to deliver mail the rest of his life. He tried to get a management job, but that didn't work out so he got involved in the union. When a representative from the Detroit branch of the NALC came around to collect dues, Rademacher pressed him about what he was getting for his money. The dues collector answered that if he was so curious, he should come to a meeting and find out. Rademacher showed up at the next one with 15 other young carriers from his post office. William Nonen, president of the Detroit branch, was so impressed that he made Rademacher the union representative at the Redford post office. Rademacher found that he enjoyed taking on the management. In one of his first cases, he defended a carrier who had been suspended for three weeks for putting a letter in the wrong mailbox. Rademacher said that the carrier had delivered mail for 25 years without a complaint. Wasn't the punishment too harsh? "We've got to have good service at this station," the supervisor told him.

"Is what he did any worse than when you ordered the mainte-nance man in this post office to go down in this cellar and burn all the A&P ads at Christmas?" Rademacher asked.

The supervisor thought it over. "I don't think that man deserves a suspension," he said.

In 1949, Rademacher ran for branch secretary and won. The next year, the Post Office fired Nonen for his alleged ties to the Com-munist Party, and the branch's 1,500 members chose Rademacher to replace him. Rademacher was 29 years old, which made him the youngest president in the history of the Detroit branch. He would go on to lead the NALC through a period of unprecedented turmoil and transformation. Years later, one of the union's press officers would describe Rademacher as "a modern-day Moses" who led postal workers out of an industrial dark age. This was certainly how Rademacher saw himself. But other letter carriers called him a sellout and burned him in effigy in Times Square.

Letter carriers think of themselves as a special breed. They are the organization's more visible employees, and they tend to be extroverted. They spend the day visiting people, and they always have something to give them. It might be a flyer from a local car dealer, and it might be the phone bill, but they also bring birthday cards, magazines, and packages. Is it any wonder that people are happy to see their letter carriers and sometimes even offer them a cool drink in the summertime or a warm beverage in the winter?

These outgoing postal workers have historically enjoyed each other's company too. As soon as Montgomery Blair, Lincoln's postmaster general, started hiring carriers to provide free city delivery in 1863, they formed benevolent societies and brass bands. Unlike clerks, who historically had a closer relationship with management because they worked in postal facilities and were more likely to be promoted to supervisors, letter carriers were free spirits who worked outdoors and were on their own most of the day. Their allegiance was to each other.

Early on, carriers were political appointees who could get fired anytime their party lost control of the White House. That changed after a frustrated federal job seeker shot and killed President James Garfield in 1881. Two years later, Congress passed the Pendleton Act creating civil service protection, which covered a growing number of federal workers, including letter carriers and postal clerks, so that these jobs would be awarded on the basis of merit rather than political affiliation. Even then, however, letter carriers had 12-hour days and no paid holidays or pensions. They all had to watch out for postal inspectors who followed them as they made their deliveries and sometimes had letter carriers fired.

Given their mutual regard, it's no surprise that letter carriers were the first group of postal employees to form a union. In 1889, in a meeting room above Schaefer's Saloon on Milwaukee's Water Street, sixty carriers from around the country formed the National Association of Letter Carriers and elected William Wood, a thin-faced Detroit mailman with dark eyes and a bushy white mustache, to be their first president. That is why the Detroit chapter became the NALC's Branch No. 1. Two years later, there were 231 branches around the nation, and the number rose to 333 the following year. The NALC now represented over 5,000 carriers, and it was a political force. President Grover Cleveland had signed a law mandating an eight-hour workday for full-time letter carriers, but the Post Office disregarded it so the NALC sued. In 1893, the U.S. Supreme Court ordered the department to pay $3.5 million in unpaid overtime to letter carriers. The NALC wasn't just bringing them together; it was delivering results.

Predictably, other kinds of postal workers formed their own unions, hoping to emulate the NALC's success. After President Theodore Roosevelt declared rural free delivery a permanent service in 1902, the men and women who delivered the mail to farmers formed their own lobbying organization, called the National Rural Letter Carriers' Association. "It has been suggested by the city carriers that we cast our lot with them," said one of their leaders. "The city boys are a splendid lot of fellows and have troubles of their own, but their troubles are as dissimilar as the work of the two branches and it has been the generally expressed judgment of our best men that each delivery will be better served by its own organization." Like their city counterparts, the rural carriers wanted higher wages, but they also wanted smoother roads and a stipend to cover the cost of their wagons and horse-drawn buggies, which they used to haul the mail.

Postal clerks tried to organize too, but they were a fractious bunch. In 1899, a group of clerks who called themselves the United National Association of Post Office Clerks (UNAPOC) met in New York and adopted a constitution. Seven years later, another faction convened in Chicago and created the competing National Federation of Post Office Clerks (NFPOC). The two organizations talked about merging but spent much of their time bickering instead. The New York–based clerks called the ones in Chicago radicals. The clerks headquartered in the Midwest dismissed their East Coast adversaries as management stooges. Meanwhile, railway mail clerks, who considered themselves a cut above the average post office clerk, formed their own association, but it was for whites only. So black workers had to start their own advocacy group, which was called the National Alliance of Postal Employees.

None of these organizations had much power at first. The Post Office wasn't legally required to discuss anything with them and generally ignored them altogether. Albert Burleson, Woodrow Wilson's postmaster general, fired union presidents for criticizing his policies. When 25 workers at the Fairmont, West Virginia, post office quit to protest the local postmaster's firing of an elderly carrier, Burleson accused them of conducting an unlawful strike and pressed charges against them. One alleged striker, a letter carrier named W. H. Fisher, was so traumatized that he hung himself in his jail cell on the eve of his trial.

Burleson roiled the Post Office further when he introduced industrial efficiency expert Frederick Winslow Taylor's system of scientific management. With stopwatches in their hands, managers observed postal workers as they went about their daily routines, calculated the average amount of time they took, and tried to hold everybody to the same standard. The clerks didn't seem to care, but letter carriers hated the system that became known pejoratively as

Taylorism. The NALC accused Burleson of trying to turn its members into robots and tried to have Taylorism banished from the Post Office, but Burleson was too powerful.

So the NALC focused instead on Congress, whose members tended to be more susceptible to pressure from postal employees, especially letter carriers who visited the homes of their constituents every day. To keep these gregarious postal workers happy, Congress periodically passed pay raise bills. But presidents often vetoed them, as Calvin Coolidge did in 1926. When President Franklin Roosevelt took office in 1933, he trimmed the salaries of federal workers by 15 percent and made postal workers take nine furlough days. As far as the NALC was concerned, FDR was no friend of the workingman. The union fared better in the postwar years. President Harry Truman dutifully signed a bill in 1945 increasing the top pay for letter carriers to $2,500—the equivalent of $33,047 today—and subsequently signed another bill raising it by an additional $400 ($5,288 today).

Newsweek took notice of the NALC's growing clout on Capitol Hill. "Congress suffers from a strange occupational ailment," the magazine wrote. "Postmanitis is marked by a high fever and a fluttery stomach; although not fatal, it nevertheless is terrifying. It recurs whenever the legislators start thinking about what might conceivably happen if they ever did anything to make the nation's mail carriers angry. The only cure for it, as far as Congress knows, is simply to vote for everything the postal employees' lobby wants."

In 1947, Truman appointed Jesse Donaldson, a former letter carrier from Shelbyville, Illinois, to be his postmaster general. It was the first time a president had promoted a career postal worker to be the country's top mailman, and the NALC celebrated the decision. But letter carriers came to despise Donaldson as much as they did Albert Burleson. When Congress shaved $24 billion from the Post Office's budget in April 1950, Donaldson responded by reducing home delivery to once a day. This was quite a change for densely populated places like New York where people were accustomed to getting mail four times a day at home. In the New York suburbs, the carriers visited three times a day.

Polls showed that most people didn't care about getting mail once a day but letter carriers were furious about it. Previously, they had delivered mail in the morning, returned to the post office for a leisurely lunch, and then departed for the afternoon tour. Now they spent most of their day on the street. NALC's president William Doherty, a white-haired former carrier from Cincinnati who weighed more than 300 pounds, called Donaldson's decision "the rape of the Post Office" and mounted a campaign to restore two deliveries a day. Some members of the U.S. Congress sympathized. "Fifty million tired taxpayers have been hit in the mailbox with this ruling," protested Senator Alexander Wiley, a Republican from Wisconsin. "I, for one, think it is disgusting because there is need for more mail service rather than less."

Much to the NALC's disappointment, Congress decided not to overturn Donaldson's decision. From then on, the union became more combative. "When we are angry (and we have had many occasions to be angry in recent years), we say so in no uncertain terms," Doherty wrote in his memoir *Mailman U.S.A.* "We do not pull punches." Not that it did much good. In the 1950s, President Dwight Eisenhower vetoed four pay raise bills. Toward the end of Eisenhower's second term, however, Doherty organized what he called the "Crusade for Economic Equality" and persuaded Congress to override the popular Republican president's last veto in 1960.

For all Doherty's tough talk, he was also conspicuously weak on race relations. In southern cities, the NALC typically had two branches, one for its white members and another for the black ones. Doherty wearily argued that the union needed to maintain a policy of segregation if it wanted to increase its membership and its lobbying strength. "I suppose [segregation] has been debated endlessly in all democratic forms of government since long before the War Between the States or the Civil War," he said. "*It is just one of those things.*"

* * *

In Detroit, James Rademacher became one of the young, rising stars of the new assertive, NALC. He enjoyed challenging the Post Office's management, and he did so often. Not long after he became president of Branch No. 1, he referred to a supervisor as a "sadist" in the local newspaper for refusing to let a carrier out of work to be with his hospitalized wife. The postmaster of Detroit saw the article and tried to have Rademacher fired for using such language. Rademacher didn't want to lose his job so he went to see the branch's attorney. While he was waiting in the lawyer's office, Rademacher spotted a dictionary on the shelf. He looked up the word "sadist" and saw that it meant "slave-driving boss." Rademacher wrote the postmaster a gleeful letter: "Dear Mr. Baker, this is where I got the information to call him a sadist. I quoted Funk & Wagnall's. Yours very truly." The postmaster backed off.

Soon, Rademacher found a larger stage to perform on. At the 1954 NALC convention, he and some of his Detroit men paraded down one of Cleveland's main streets with a coffin to protest Eisenhower's recent veto of a salary increase bill. Three years later, he became nationally known within the union for filing a federal lawsuit against the Post Office when the Eisenhower administration briefly halted Saturday mail delivery because of a budget shortfall. "They just hated me," Rademacher laughs.

The Post Office could have lived without Rademacher, but the NALC wanted more of him. In 1960, Rademacher was elected national assistant secretary-treasurer and moved to Washington. He got to know Democratic presidential candidate John F. Kennedy, who wanted to improve the federal government's labor-management relations. Two years later, President Kennedy signed an executive order requiring federal agencies to negotiate with officially recognized employee unions. But the NALC would never be on that list as long as it had dual chapters for blacks and whites. Rademacher was given the job of combining them.

Rademacher traveled to Atlanta first and was stunned when he got off the plane. Having grown up in Detroit, he had never seen separate water fountains and washrooms for blacks and whites. Carriers of both races toiled side by side in the southern city's post office, but they couldn't gather together after work. The only place Rademacher could meet safely with all of them was a federal courthouse. The whites took seats on the left side of the room and the black letter carriers clustered on the right. "Now close the doors, and keep them closed," Rademacher commanded. He motioned to some of the whites to move to the right and some of the blacks to take seats on the left. "That's it," he said. "You don't want a union? Go . . . now . . . get out! We fought hard to get this executive order. We don't want to lose it." The carriers started talking and, by midnight, they agreed to form a single unit.

In a Louisiana city that he refuses to name, Rademacher had a harrowing experience when he talked to black and white carriers in the basement of a local branch president's home. Someone interrupted and told him to look out the window. There was a flaming cross on the front lawn. The branch president told Rademacher he needed to leave right away and drove him to the airport, avoiding the main roads where he feared that the Ku Klux Klan might be waiting for them.

In the end, the NALC did away with the dual chapters and won recognition as an official bargaining unit along with six other unions representing clerks, rural letter carriers, mail handers, maintenance workers, truck drivers, and special delivery messengers. The clerks should have had the biggest union of them all. After all, clerks made up nearly half of the department's 716,000 employees in 1968. A decade earlier, the two main clerks' organizations had stopped fighting with each other and merged their two lobbying groups into the

National Federation of Postal Clerks. Yet the federation had only 143,000 members. (One of the reasons was an unrecognized organization known as the National Postal Union, which represented a large number of clerks in New York City.) Meanwhile, all but a handful of the Post Office's city carriers were dues-paying NALC members, making it the biggest postal workers' union. The same year, James Rademacher was elected national president of the NALC, which made him the most powerful of the seven union presidents.

All of them opposed the Nixon administration's effort to turn the Post Office into a corporation, but Rademacher was the most vehement critic, calling it "unnecessary and dangerous." He compared Winton Blount's public relations campaign to Joseph Goebbels's big lie. He claimed that AT&T was pushing the plan because it secretly wanted to destroy the Post Office and take it over: "Why then, there will be little old AT&T ready and willing, oh so willing, to pick up the pieces and inherit the entire communications complex of the United States of America."

If this wasn't provocative enough, Rademacher warned that there would be a letter carriers' strike if his members didn't get substantial raises soon. Postal service employees were legally forbidden to walk off the job, but Rademacher testified before the House post office committee in June 1969 that his restless members were likely to disregard the law and there was nothing he could do about it. "The time has come," Rademacher predicted, "when responsible union leaders can no longer control the troops."

For all of his calculated bombast, Rademacher was being truthful about the mood of his members. They were growing more militant, especially in New York, where the cost of living was higher than in the rest of the country. The starting salary of a letter carrier was $6,000—or the equivalent in today's dollars of $38,000 a year—compared with the $10,000 that a New York trash collector made. Why were the garbage men doing so well? The trash men had gone on strike in 1968. Postal workers in New York, many of whom worked two jobs, talked about striking too. Sure, it was against the law, but what did they have to lose? It was the sixties; everybody was protesting—blacks and Hispanics, students, women, gays and lesbians. It was time for postal workers to stand up for themselves too.

Rademacher was treading a fine line. He was indulging his members with his strike talk, but he didn't know what the Nixon administration would do if his people walked off the job. They might all end up in jail. So he sent carriers out after work in 400 cities to retrace their routes and deliver stamped postcards with the message: "SOS: Save our Service! Notify President Nixon right now to sign a pay bill." The White House received three million of these cards, a number the administration couldn't ignore.

Blount refused to have anything to do with Rademacher, but political operatives in the White House thought it was worth reaching out to him. The task was assigned to Nixon aide Charles Colson, who lived near Rademacher in a Maryland suburb and knew him causally. Colson telephoned Rademacher and invited him to the White House. "We got your message," Colson said. "We'd like to discuss this with you. When can you come over?" The two men met secretly over lunch at the White House on December 5, 1969, in the basement cafeteria beneath the Oval Office. At one point, Colson tried to impress his guest. "Do you hear those footsteps?" he asked. "That's the president of the United States." Rademacher informed Colson that he had been to the Oval Office for dinner the previous year with former President Johnson. "Okay, let's start fresh," Colson said.

The two went over Blount's proposal. "What's the problem with it?" Colson asked. Rademacher and Colson discovered they actually shared a lot of common ground. They agreed that the unions needed the right to collectively bargain with the Post Office rather than appealing to Congress for raises. Rademacher wanted to make sure his members kept their civil service status and the pensions they had built up over the years. "That's easy," Colson assured him.

Rademacher had also been keeping track of the votes for an administration-backed postal reform bill in the House post office committee. At first, it looked as if the bill didn't stand a chance because of union opposition, but the votes were getting closer and closer. Blount was doing more than feeding committee members grits: he was offering to build new post offices in their districts, as Jim Farley might have done to secure votes in the Roosevelt era. If Rademacher couldn't stop the bill, he wanted to shape its outcome. He figured that he could trade his endorsement for an immediate salary increase for his members.

So Rademacher broke with the other postal union leaders and blessed Blount's plan. On December 18, he returned to the White House and had his picture taken with Nixon in the Oval Office. Nixon was surprised to learn that Blount had been keeping Rademacher at arm's length. But once the union president was on his side, Blount invited Rademacher to one of his rich southern breakfasts. Blount's aides chuckled when the union president, an inveterate bargainer, demanded an extra biscuit, but they made sure he was satisfied. They needed his support if they wanted to get the reform bill passed.

Blount and Rademacher still didn't like each other but they lobbied Congress in tandem. On March 12, 1970, in a 17-6 vote they nudged through the House post office committee a reform bill with a 5.4 percent pay increase. Rademacher sent a telegram to his 600 branch leaders, "Cool it," he told them. "We're making progress." Rademacher was especially concerned about New York's Branch No. 36, the NALC's biggest branch, which represented 7,200 letter carriers in Manhattan and the Bronx.

Branch No. 36's president Gustave Johnson, an amateur painter who had recently grown an artist's mustache and goatee, told Rademacher not to worry; he had everything under control. But that night, when Johnson told his members about the proposed pay raise at a meeting, his agency members started chanting, "Not enough! Not enough!" and then "Strike when? Strike when?" One of the fed-up carriers made a motion for a strike vote, which passed. Johnson reluctantly scheduled the vote for March 17. He appeared on television to discourage letter carriers from voting for a walkout, warning them that an unlawful strike would be a catastrophe.

The vote was held on a Tuesday night at Manhattan Center, a former opera house that now served as a union meeting hall near the New York General Post Office. By 7 PM, the room was packed with 2,600 boisterous letter carriers. They booed Johnson when he arrived at 8:40 PM to get the voting started. Then he headed across the street to a bar called Farley's Gin Mill to confer with Moe Biller, president of the Manhattan-Bronx Postal Union, a renegade union without official recognition that represented 25,000 clerks and mail handlers.

An old-school labor agitator from the Lower East Side, the tall, balding Biller had been fired from the Post Office in the 1950s for his alleged Communist ties and later reinstated by the U.S. Supreme Court. They were joined by Jack Leventhal, president of the NALC's 6,000-member Branch No. 41 in Brooklyn. The three presidents needed to figure out what to do if Branch No. 36 called for a strike. Gus Johnson assured them that it wouldn't happen, but the other union heads weren't so sure. No matter what, the three men agreed not to make any decisions without conferring with each other.

Around 10 PM, they returned to Manhattan Center and took seats onstage. Johnson announced the outcome of the vote. It was 1,555 in favor of a strike and 1,055 opposed. "Well, we voted," he declared, banging his gavel. "That's it. This is a democratic union. There will be no mail delivery tomorrow in New York."

The same men and women who had booed Johnson less than two hours ago roared in approval. Jack Leventhal pledged the support of his members. "Your brothers and sisters across the river in Brooklyn are with you 100 percent," Leventhal said. "We're shoulder to shoulder."

Moe Biller was stunned. Johnson and Leventhal had promised not to do anything without talking to him, but they couldn't resist the chance to be heroes. When it was his turn to talk, Biller said he couldn't call a strike on his own and urged the letter carriers to wait until his union voted. The Branch No. 36 carriers hissed at Biller. "This is a letter carriers' strike," one yelled. "What I want to know is whether the clerks are going to cross our picket line."

"It's illegal for me to direct my members not to cross a picket line," Biller cannily answered. "But I'm sure as good union members, they will respect any picket line."

That mollified the letter carriers. After the meeting adjourned, some of them walked across Manhattan, grabbed some wooden barriers lying along the streets after the St. Patrick's Day parade, and set up a picket line outside the Grand Central post office. At midnight, hundreds of Biller's union members arrived for the late shift and refused to cross it. Johnson called Rademacher at home that night to give him the news.

"What am I going to do?" Johnson asked.

"Let it blow," Rademacher replied. The Great Postal Strike of 1970 had begun.

On Wednesday morning, letter carriers and clerks had set up picket lines outside nearly every New York post office. Winton Blount ordered the sealing of street mailboxes in New York and placed an embargo on all mail headed into and out of the city. He summoned Rademacher and the other six union leaders to his office for a 10 AM meeting and told them the department would seek a preliminary injunction in federal court declaring the strike illegal and enabling the Post Office to sue anybody participating in the walkout. "The Post Office will use every means in its command to punish, fine, and imprison leaders of the walkout," Blount warned.

Rademacher was in a bind. He sympathized with the strikers. After all, he had been complaining for months about their woes. But he feared that Blount might destroy his union. Congress was also on

A post office circa 1809, where all sorting was done by hand. (*Above*)

Benjamin Franklin, architect of the American colonial post, and first postmaster general. (*Above*)

In 1835, a mob in Charleston, South Carolina, broke into the post office and burned abolitionist newspapers. Postmaster General Amos Kendall condemned the American Anti-Slavery Society for mailing "exaggerated" accounts of slavery. (*Right*)

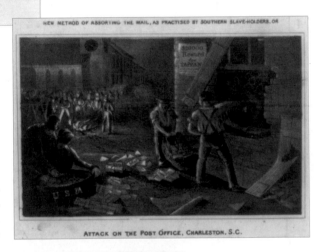

Before railroads, the Post Office sent mail to California via steamship. (*Left*)

Patrons in San Francisco crowded the post office. (*Above*)

The Pony Express, one of the most famous chapters in the history of the Post Office, was unprofitable and short-lived. (*Above*)

The Post Office faced competition from private carriers such as Adams Express, shown here in 1861 with packages for soldiers in the Civil War. (*Left*)

By 1867, postal routes stretched far across the country. (*Below*)

BEAUTIES OF THE FRANKING PRIVILEGE.

Member of Congress, *soliloquising*. "Seven cotton shirts, three flannel, six pairs of socks, one collar, five pocket-handkerchiefs, three pair of drawers, two linen coats—that's all, I guess; and the mail's just closing, that must do for to-day."
[Mails his clothes-bag under his frank, and has his linen cheaply washed at home in Wisconsin.]

The abuse of franking has a long history. (*Above*)

Railroads increasingly connected the country and sped the mail. (*Above*)

A city letter carrier in 1885. Free home delivery had begun in 1863. (*Left*)

In the early twentieth century, mail was regularly carried by dogsled in Alaska. The last scheduled run ended in 1963. (*Right*)

Wanamaker's "Cast Iron Palace" in New York, at 10th Street and Broadway. (*Below*)

Department store magnate John Wanamaker raised $200,000 for William Henry Harrison and was named postmaster general in 1889. (*Left*)

Mail was delivered to homes two times a day until 1950. This image from 1904 is captioned "a letter to Papa." (*Left*)

Rural free delivery, which Wanamaker advocated, was opposed by small-town merchants. It was finally made permanent in 1902 by Theodore Roosevelt. (*Right*)

Mail volume steadily increased, with sorting done as it was a century before: by hand. (*Left*)

AS TO THE PARCELS POST.

Wanamaker pushed for a parcel post, but the Post Office was kept out of the business until 1912, a situation lamented in this cartoon that appeared in an issue of *Puck* in 1910. (*Left*)

The Post Office adopted new technology, like the automobile, but were still using horse carts in some cities in 1917. (*Right*)

The use of horses on rural routes lasted for decades after the Post Office's adoption of the automobile, like here in New Mexico in 1940. (*Left*)

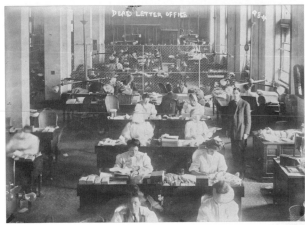

Benjamin Franklin created the Dead Letter Office, pictured here circa 1900. (*Left*)

After the creation of the parcel post, there were enough incidents of "child mailing" that the Post Office had to outlaw the practice. (*Right*)

Carriers laden with Christmas mail in 1910. (*Left*)

Interior of a Railway Mail Train.
Neg. # 29241.

The Post Office developed a system of sorting mail on trains in the nineteenth century. Special train cars were used, like this one in 1909. (*Above*)

Puck ridiculed Anthony Comstock, the crusading moralizer who used federal postal laws to stamp out "obscenity," as "St. Anthony Comstock, The Village Nuisance." (*Above*)

The postal savings bank, proposed by Wanamaker in 1889, was created by William Howard Taft in 1910. This photograph shows some of the first depositors. Half a century later it was the largest bank in America. (*Left*)

Pneumatic tube systems were introduced in the late nineteenth century in Philadelphia, Boston, Chicago, St. Louis, and New York, pictured here in 1914. (*Right*)

Mail being boxed by hand in New York in 1914. (*Left*)

Clerks in Washington, D.C. test the Gehring Mail Distributing Machine in 1923. With a keystroke, the clerks could sort letters into boxes for 120 cities or states, but the machine was never used and widespread mechanization wouldn't happen until the 1950s. (*Right*)

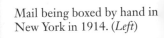

Downtown Manhattan

cago

Washington, D.C.

town Manhattan

Philadelphia

The late nineteenth and early twentieth centuries saw the building of lavish post offices.

Otto Praeger, father of the Air Mail. (*Above*)

Lt. George Boyle would go down in history as "Wrong Way Boyle," after piloting the first Air Mail flight south to Waldorf, Maryland, instead of north to New York. (*Above*)

The original Air Mail pilots were a glamorous, courageous bunch. (*Above*)

Postmaster General Albert Burleson and Woodrow Wilson
at the ceremonial inauguration of Air Mail Service in 1918. (*Above*)

Mail being loaded onto the plane for
the inauguration. (*Right*)

Early Air Mail
flights, like this
one from 1918 in
a Curtiss JN-4H
"Jenny," were
dangerous. (*Left*)

Franklin Delano Roosevelt was a devoted collector of stamps, and even designed new issues while president. (*Above*)

Roosevelt's campaign manager James Farley was named postmaster general in 1932. Farley was the consummate machine politician, but ran into trouble with the stamp-collecting community. (*Above*)

During the Roosevelt presidency, the Treasury Department's Section of Painting and Sculpture commissioned 1,200 murals in post offices, including these in the new U.S. post office building, which opened in Washington D.C. in 1934.

From top to bottom: "Country Post," (1938) by Doris Lee; "Mail Service in the Tropics," (1937) by Rockwell Kent; "Sorting the Mail," (1936) by Reginald Marsh.

A Works Products Administration poster. The Depression caused mail volume to drop. (*Above*)

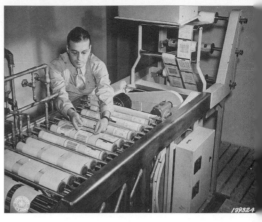

During WWII, V-Mail enabled more mail to be sent in less space. Letters were photographed and transferred to microfilm, then printed overseas. (*Above*)

The post office was the source of many jobs for minorities and women, here sorting mail in 1966. (*Above*)

From 1940 to 1960, mail volume doubled to 64 billion pieces a year. Zip codes were supposed to be the solution. (*Above*)

Mr. Zip helped sell zip codes to a reluctant public. (*Above*)

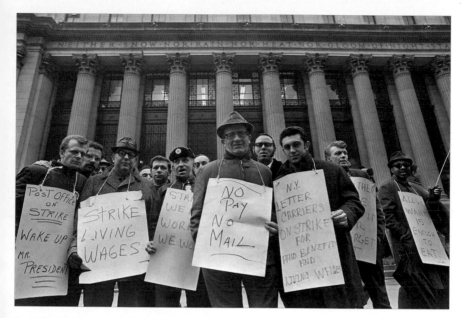

In 1970, the largest wildcat strike in American history crippled the post office and much of the country. (*Above*)

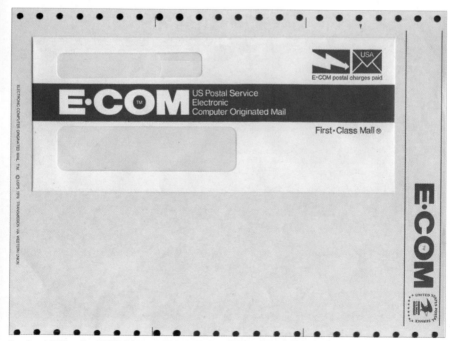

In the 1980s, the USPS knew the mail would be affected by computers. Electronic Computer Originated Mail, or E-COM for short, was intended as an answer, but it was hamstrung, and was cancelled in 1985. (*Above*)

After much delay, the USPS developed sophisticated, technologically advanced systems for mail, only to see first class volume decline precipitously.

the verge of passing a postal reform bill that would take care of his members. The bill would do more than just give them an immediate raise; it would give them collective bargaining. Rademacher worried that it would all fall apart if the strike continued, so he sent a telegram to Johnson ordering Branch No. 36 to go back to work.

It didn't, and the strike spread over the next two days to Philadelphia, Boston, Cleveland, Detroit, and Milwaukee. In Chicago, 6,000 letter carriers gathered for a vote, waving their fists and chanting "Postal power—strike!" They overwhelmingly decided to strike. "Our members are so militant, so upset they will stay out 'til hell freezes over," said Henry S. Zych, president of the Chicago NALC branch. A doleful letter carrier marched through the snow in St. Paul, Minnesota, carrying a sign that said: "Money for the moon, but none for the mailman." A *Washington Post* columnist summed up the fundamental irony of the postal strike: "President Nixon comes face to face today with his most pressing domestic crisis in a showdown forced not by students, restless blacks, or the new left, but by the most solid and dependable corner of middle America— the mailman."

At 10:40 AM on Friday, Rademacher was putting on his coat and getting ready to leave his office when his secretary told him that Secretary of Labor George Shultz was on the line. "We'd like to meet with you as soon as possible to try to settle whatever the problem is," Shultz said. Rademacher told him he was headed to a meeting with 300 of his branch presidents and state leaders at the Continental Hotel to discuss the strike. "Well, can you let them know we're ready to sit down?" Shultz said.

Rademacher replied that he would and headed off to the Continental, where the branch leaders were waiting in a ballroom. The attendees gave Gus Johnson and Jack Leventhal sustained ovations and wanted to know if Rademacher was going to declare a national strike. Rademacher said he didn't know yet; he had to go to the White House first and talk to Shultz. And off he went.

At 2 PM, Rademacher returned to the ballroom to shouts of "No sellout!" and "Let's walk!" Rademacher's supporters yelled, "Let him speak!" and "Shut up and listen!" After quieting everybody down, Rademacher said the White House was ready to negotiate, but not until striking postal workers returned to their jobs. The branch chiefs reluctantly voted to give Rademacher five days to reach a deal with the administration. If he didn't get what they wanted, Rademacher promised to call a nationwide walkout.

Again, Gus Johnson conveyed the message to his members in New York, but Branch No. 36 was no longer listening. Some of its members waved signs that said, "Dump the Rat" and "Impeach Rat-emacher." Others held a rally in Times Square and burned the NALC president in effigy. Rademacher started receiving death threats. When his wife, Martha, heard about it, she suffered a nervous breakdown. Nixon sent his personal doctor to the hospital to see if he could help.

Frustrated, Rademacher held a press conference on Sunday and blamed the walkout in New York on infiltrators from Students for a Democratic Society (SDS), a radical left group. This only further alienated members of Branch No. 36. Many were middle-aged World War II veterans like Vincent Sombrotto. "That's the greatest compliment they ever paid me," Sombrotto later recalled. "I was 41 years old and they were calling me a student."

Postal inspectors investigated and found that nobody in the branch had ties to the SDS. When real student radicals showed up to lend their support outside the General Post Office in New York, the strikers couldn't have been less welcoming. "We're from the SDS," said an emissary for the group with long hair tied behind his head with a string of shells. "We've come to help you."

He was immediately surrounded by unfriendly postal workers. "You're not part of our cause, and you are just going to mess it up," one of them growled.

"I'm with you guys," another SDS member assured them. "You know, if we weren't spending all that money in Vietnam we could all get good salaries."

"I got a boy in Vietnam," a postal worker replied.

"Look, mister, butt out," another striker said. Police officers had to intervene and escort the radicals to safety.

At the Post Office's headquarters in Washington, Blount's aides kept track of the strike's progress on an electric map of the United States. Red lights glowed in cities where the strike had halted delivery. Yellow lights illuminated the ones where service had been slowed. Green lights sparkled in areas where delivery was still on schedule, and blue lights were supposed to flash in places where strikers had returned to work, but that was rare. At the strike's peak, 200,000 workers had deserted their jobs in the Northeast, the upper Midwest, and California, bringing the mail to a standstill in 10 of America's largest cities including New York, Philadelphia, Chicago, San Francisco, and Los Angeles.

If ever there was a moment when people were aware of the role that the Post Office played in their daily lives, it was now. On a typical afternoon before the strike, the loading docks of any big city post office bustled with activity. Banks dropped off mountains of mortgage statements and credit card bills. Utilities trucked in stacks of bills. Employees from department store mailrooms showed up with monthly statements for their charge account customers. Magazine companies handed off their glossy periodicals and bills for their subscribers. Mail handlers wheeled it all inside to be sorted by clerks on the evening shift and delivered the next morning by carriers.

But now the inexorable flow of paper stopped. Banks had to get by without interest payments. In New York, Consolidated Edison and New York Telephone and Telegraph lost millions of dollars a day. Department stores feared they wouldn't make their payrolls. Meanwhile, the IRS couldn't collect $1 billion a day in taxes. The stock market plunged, and there was talk of closing it down because it, too, depended on paper to function. Traders mailed each other paper stock certificates to consummate their transactions. Without the massive postal bureaucracy, Wall Street was imperiled. "A modern economy is sustained by an endless flow of carefully directed paper," *Newsweek* observed. "The U.S. postal system, for all its creaky inefficiencies, simply has no parallel in performing this vital function."

Then there was all the routine business correspondence that normally circulated through the postal network. With a strike crippling the Post Office in major cities, executives from IBM, Standard Oil, GM, and Ford could be seen in airports carrying mail pouches instead of their usual briefcases. Pressed into service as a temporary carrier, Thomas Purcell, a salesman for Shield & Company, a New York securities firm, took 30 pounds of paychecks, research reports, prospectuses, and other documents on a flight from New York to Buffalo, stopping in Albany on the way. "It was all I could lug," Purcell said. The Post Office told businessmen they could also entrust letters to the porters on Amtrak trains. "These people are remarkably honest," said a department official.

Western Union was overwhelmed with telegraph orders. "It's terrible," said a manager at the Times Square office. "We can't handle it." Hollywood wasn't immune from the strike's effects either. Gregory Peck, president of the Academy of Motion Picture Arts and Sciences, told his members in New York to deliver their ballots for the Academy Awards to the local office of Price Waterhouse. Otherwise, Peck warned, they might miss the deadline for choosing the year's best picture.

There were countless stories of ordinary post office users who were inconvenienced too. In New York, a woman getting married in Wisconsin feared that her wedding invitations wouldn't be delivered in time to out-of-town guests so she went to John F. Kennedy International Airport and pressed them on outbound travelers who promised to put them in the mailbox wherever they landed. In Whitefish Bay, Wisconsin, a man walked into the post office with several canisters of film that he needed to mail immediately to Madison. The clerk told him there was an embargo on Madison-bound mail because postal workers were on strike there. "You can't do that!" the man shouted. "This is the U.S. Post Office!" He tossed the metal containers onto the counter and stormed out of the building. A man with a dazed expression stood outside the Minneapolis downtown post office with a box in his hand. Someone told him the building was closed because of the strike. "Yes, but this is different," the man said. "These are cookies for my boy in Vietnam." A drunk stood in front of the post office in nearby St. Paul, hollering at the picketers. "Get back to work," he commanded. "You can't hold up my mail. It's illegal. How'm I gonna get my relief check?"

Polls showed that the public sympathized with the striking postal workers, a sign that Americans still had warm feelings for the men and women who brought them their letters and sold them stamps, but how long would this last? In one week, the government needed to send Social Security checks to 20 million retirees. Blount already had a court order declaring the strike illegal. Now he urged Nixon to send the National Guard into New York to break it. On Sunday, March 22, Nixon declared a state of national emergency and said he would send 27,000 soldiers into the country's largest city to restore order. "Essential services must be maintained," Nixon said in a televised address from the Oval Office. "As President, I shall meet my constitutional responsibility, to see that those services are maintained."

Rademacher pleaded with Nixon to change his mind, predicting violent clashes between the strikers and the guardsmen. But union leaders in New York told their members to stay calm and they waved on Tuesday when the National Guard arrived in the city in a convoy of trucks with orders to sort by zip code the 60 million pieces of mail that had piled up in New York's main post office, setting aside prescription drugs, welfare checks, and personal letters so they could be delivered quickly. Some of the troops had mixed feelings about their mission. "I'm a little embarrassed," admitted Arthur Solomon, a former New York postal clerk. "A lot of my friends are up here at the Post Office."

Major General Martin Foery, commander of the Forty-Second Infantry Division of the New York Army National Guard, didn't think there would be any trouble. "We know that people are hired temporarily at Christmas time to work in the post office and it works then," he said, gnawing on a cigar. "Besides, 50 percent of my men are college graduates." But when the troops took up their positions on the floors of the General Post Office in midtown Manhattan, the Church Street post office in the financial district, and the Brooklyn post office, they were overwhelmed by the magnitude of the job.

Usually, these cavernous rooms were filled with clerks who could throw as many as 60 letters a minute into their proper cubbyholes while conversing with each other about politics or sports or the shows they watched on television. "We would exchange verses from *Don Quixote* and *Rime of the Ancient Mariner* and other classics," says William Burrus, a former postal clerk in Cleveland who would later become the first African American president of the American Postal Workers Union (APWU). "On Tuesdays and Thursdays, we devoted all of our discussions to racial issues and some of the atrocities that had occurred in our country between the races."

But the troops didn't have any training or experience. David Andresen, a 21-year-old guardsman from Suffield, Connecticut, stood in front of hundreds of pigeonholes in the New York General Post Office trying to figure out where to put a letter. "I never expected to be doing this," he said. Kenneth Hancock, a 19-year-old from Roanoke, Virginia, sounded similarly mystified. "I just don't know where it goes," he sighed.

The National Guard didn't do home delivery, but it carried two million pieces of mail to businesses and nonprofit groups. The troops who made these rounds sometimes had trouble finding office buildings, even the very tall ones. Strike sympathizers called them "scabs" and "fascists pigs." But when the guardsmen showed up at the right addresses with the mail, they received a hero's welcome. Secretaries offered them coffee. Bosses dropped what they were doing and came out to shake hands.

The servicemen stayed in New York for two days, but by then Nixon had made his point. Around the country, strikers returned to their jobs and even the Branch No. 36 dissidents finally gave in. Some regretted it and wanted to walk out again, but Nixon kept 10,000 National Guard troops in New York to discourage any recidivists.

The same day the strike ended, the Nixon administration and the postal unions began their negotiations. The White House was willing to give the workers a salary increase in return for the unions' endorsement of postal reform. As far as Rademacher was concerned, it was largely a matter of what the number would be. But other postal labor leaders were still furious at him for breaking with them in December and joining forces with the White House. They wanted to discuss a raise first and postal reform later, and they chose the AFL-CIO's president George Meany, the grand old man of the labor movement, to negotiate for them. Rademacher didn't mind: the unions all belonged to the AFL-CIO. But he was soon at odds with Meany's people. James Gildea, Meany's executive assistant, told Rademacher not to appear on television while the two sides were talking. Rademacher refused. "This is a letter carriers' strike," he said. "I'm not getting off TV. I'm telling the public our story." And he did, too. The other union presidents tripped over the cables that television crews had unspooled on the floors of the AFL-CIO's headquarters so they could do live interviews with Rademacher during the breaks. "It's like a three-ring circus," one complained.

The two sides agreed to an immediate six percent raise. Then it was time to discuss what it might cost for the postal unions to support a reform bill. The White House offered an additional six percent raise, but Rademacher says he insisted on eight percent. "We got eight percent in addition to six percent, which is 14 percent," he says. On April 6, Meany and the postal union leaders sat at a large round table at the White House with Nixon and signed a memorandum of understanding finalizing the deal. Nixon said he would ask Congress to raise stamp prices from six cents to 10 cents to pay for the raises—the second of which would go into effect only after Congress passed the reform legislation.

Now that the strike was over, however, neither the House nor the Senate felt the need to move swiftly, and union militants started talking about another walkout. In a speech on April 27 at the National Press Club, Blount predicted there would be an even bigger strike if Congress didn't act. "We are going to have chaos and it's going to be widespread in the postal system if we don't change the system," he warned. "We are not going to be able to get through the next upheaval as quickly as we got through the last. There's nothing I can do. There's nothing the president can do, there's nothing anybody else can do more than we have—we can advise, suggest, recommend and we can please, and we've done all that but only Congress can decide."

Meanwhile, Rademacher tried to persuade his members to go along with the deal, telling them how much better everything would be under the new system. "One of the first things that this administration, that is only two years old, wants to do is get out of the stranglehold that Congress has on us," he said at an NALC banquet in Michigan. "We've got to get away from Congress and sit down at the bargaining table; not on a one, two, or three percent increase basis, but on meaningful increases. I favor reform because it takes us out of Congress and puts us at the bargaining table."

On August 12, 1970, Nixon signed the Postal Reorganization Act at the department's headquarters before an audience of 150 people, including six former postmaster generals, among them James Farley, who posed for a picture with the Republican president. Nixon reminded his listeners how skeptical he had been less than two years earlier when he first talked to Blount about reconfiguring the Post Office. Nixon said he knew of several of Blount's predecessors— among them Lincoln's Montgomery Blair—who had fought to stay in the president's cabinet. "I think what distinguishes the present Postmaster General is that he is probably the first who holds this office who instead of fighting to stay in the President's Cabinet has fought to get out," Nixon said.

Blount stood behind Nixon grinning as the president took out his pen and signed the bill. He would claim responsibility for ridding the Post Office of the patronage hiring that had plagued the department since Andrew Jackson's day. Blount was disappointed that Congress insisted on creating a Postal Rate Commission to approve stamp price increases, but he went along with it because he wanted to get the bill through.

Rademacher sat a few rows back in the audience. He had been politically damaged by the strike, but he had done more for his members than any of his predecessors. He had gotten them a 14 percent raise. They would be able to reach the top of their pay grade after eight years instead of waiting for 21 years. What's more, they would finally be able to directly negotiate with management, the holy grail of the labor movement. "We finally got collective bargaining instead of collective begging," Rademacher says.

Everybody at the event deserved to feel good about what they had done so far. As Nixon said, it was a day to celebrate bipartisanship and the ability of people with very different philosophies to work together. But there were flaws in the legislation that would soon become obvious. It was one thing to pass a bill depoliticizing the Post Office, but it was still a federal agency subject to the whims of Congress. The difficult work of transforming the agency was just beginning.

9

Interlopers II

In 1972, a curious article appeared in the *New York Times* under the headline "Carload of Mail, Lost in '70, Found." The story reported that a boxcar full of packages and junk mail bound for Birmingham, Alabama, on the Penn Central Railroad had gone missing somewhere between Philadelphia and Washington two years earlier. Postal inspectors had been searching for the boxcar since then and were mystified when they finally located it on a rarely used track in Perryville, Maryland. "Our inspectors made a two-year car by car search all over the Washington area," a USPS spokesman said.

However, the Penn Central Railroad said its employees, not the postal inspectors, had found the mysterious boxcar and that the agency had never notified it about the missing mail. Either way, this was a lot of late mail, and it seemed to indicate a larger problem at the newly reconfigured postal service.

As soon as the reorganization act passed in 1970, Winton Blount set out to transform the Post Office, which would be renamed the U.S. Postal Service. He recruited a board of governors from the private sector led by Frederick Kappel, the architect of the restructuring plan, and the heads of major corporations like Texas Instruments, Marine Midland Bank, and Humble Oil. Blount purged the upper ranks of the postal service of 2,000 long-serving bureaucrats, replacing them with bright young managers from the outside, some of whom he sent to Harvard Business School for training.

They would need it. The newly independent postal service faced a Herculean challenge. In 1971, its managers presided over an organization with 728,911 employees and a $9 billion annual budget. Even with a telephone in every household, the amount of mail was growing at a daunting pace. That year, the USPS delivered 87 billion pieces, 22 billion more than it had a decade earlier, but the system desperately needed to be modernized. So much was still broken from the previous decade.

More than anything else, the USPS needed to get first-class mail moving faster. In 1971 it delivered 50 billion letters, which accounted for 57 percent of its total volume. The agency continued to experiment with high-speed optical character readers, but these machines couldn't read handwritten addresses yet. So Blount accelerated the use of mechanical letter-sorting machines, which were operated by a dozen clerks who sat at their stations punching in the first three numbers of zip codes as letters zipped past them at the rate of one per second. These machines weren't as fast as the optical character readers, but they enabled a dozen clerks to process 36,000 letters in an hour, which was a big improvement over hand sorting.

The USPS also embarked on a $1 billion plan to construct 21 new bulk mail centers to sort packages and large qualities of magazines and junk mail. It was the biggest investment in the service's history, but Blount hoped new facilities equipped with conveyor belts and chutes would enable the postal service to win back business from United Parcel Service, a private company, which had been delivering packages for department stories like Macy's since the 1930s and was expanding around the country.

In October 1971, Blount resigned to run for the U.S. Senate in Alabama as the man who had fixed the Post Office, which had always seemed to be his plan. He lost. At least one southern editorial cartoonist suggested that Blount hadn't saved the postal service, but had left it a smoldering ruin. As the case of the missing boxcar showed, service hadn't improved. For decades, clerks had passed letters through the system with just a name and sometimes just a city. When people sent letters addressed to "John Wayne, Hollywood, California," clerks directed them to the right post office, where they were promptly delivered. The system may have been slow, but much of the time it worked.

Now clerks learning the mechanical letter-sorting machines keyed in numbers incorrectly, sending letters to the wrong cities. "These days, it seems, just about everybody has some personal horror story to tell about the U.S. Postal Service," *Fortune* wrote in 1973. "A check mailed by a woman in Charlestown, West Virginia, to Ravenswood, fifty-two miles away, took nine days to arrive—by which time she received a delinquent-payment notice. On Valentine's Day a resident of Elizabeth, New Jersey, received a Christmas card postmarked December 10. . . . On occasion, letters embark on extraordinary detours. A real-estate agent in Coral Gables, Florida, mailed a contract to a lawyer five blocks away. It arrived five days later, having made a round-trip journey to Los Angeles. More entertaining was the experience of an Atlanta businessman who last April was invited to a ceremony at the local post office. The invitation reached him ten days after the event."

The expensive bulk mail centers also turned out to be a disaster. Charles Wilson, a congressman from California, paid what he described as a "midnight visit" to the Detroit post office and found tens of thousands of mangled packages that had passed through the new system. In a hearing, Wilson complained that Americans were paying more money for lousier mail service, which was becoming a common lament. Other federal agencies like the Internal Revenue Service and the Government Printing Office started sending their fragile items through UPS rather than entrusting them to the USPS, further embarrassing the government mail service.

Then there was the spiraling cost of the USPS's employees. In 1971, the agency's managers negotiated its first contract with the seven unions. A year before, the postal service had given its workers a 14 percent raise, but now the union leaders demanded more money and members threatened to strike again, terrifying banks and magazine companies that depended on the mail to conduct business. These large customers pressured the USPS to keep the workers happy. Between 1971 and 1975, the postal service signed three collective bargaining agreements that raised an experienced postal worker's annual salary from $9,700 to $15,000 or $66,000 in today's dollars. Was the USPS giving away too much? After the signing of the third contract, the *Wall Street Journal* asked Francis Filbey, president of the American Postal Workers Union, which now represented 300,000 clerks, maintenance workers, special delivery messengers, and truck drivers. "I don't consider it generous," Filbey said. "It is the best the Postal Service could do under the present circumstance."

The public might have disagreed. In 1975, the USPS lost $1 billion, twice as much as the year before. Meanwhile, the price of a first-class stamp reached 13 cents more than double what it had been four years earlier. Nobody expected the USPS to become financially self-sufficient right away; Congress had given it until 1985 to erase its annual deficit. But now lawmakers began to worry that the USPS might never pay its own way.

Predictably, there was a backlash. Members of congress who had voted for postal reform regretted it. Some introduced bills that would restore the old system. "No one expected the transition of the Post Office Department to the U.S. Postal Service to be easy, but on the other hand, neither did anyone expect it to be catastrophic," said New York Democrat Thaddeus Dulski, chairman of the House Committee on Post Office and Civil Service. James Farley, the best-known postmaster general of the twentieth century and perennial defender of the patronage system, laid the blame for the agency's troubles on the restructuring. "I thought it was a mistake when they made the change and put it into a separate agency way out of the cabinet," Farley said. "I said so at the time and I think that's responsible in a large measure for what's happened to the department."

The *New York Times* offered its own gloomy prognosis in an April 1977 editorial entitled, "Delivering the Bad News." "It is clear now that turning the United States Post Office into an autonomous public corporation in 1971 has failed to realize the hopes of its proponents," the *Times* wrote. "Mail service has not improved; many believe it has actually deteriorated." The *Washington Post* was similarly skeptical: "Consider a corporation whose volume is stagnating; whose labor costs rose 63 per cent between 1971 and 1976, while productivity improved only 1.3 per cent; whose major new parcel post processing system may bring no return at all. . . . Any analyst would call that a corporation in big trouble."

Around the country, private mail companies with names like PF Brennan Mail Delivery, Marathon Postal Service, Post Haste Delivery, Independent Carriers of America, and Union Postal Systems of America materialized to take advantage of the public's discontent just as William Harnden had done more than a century earlier. The USPS shut down small private carriers, even going after Kenny Maguire, a 14-year-old boy in Charleston, South Carolina, for delivering letters in his neighborhood on his bicycle. It had a harder time with Larry Hillblom.

As a law student at the University of California at Berkeley in the mid-1960s, Larry Hillblom had long, curly brown hair and wore tight shirts and jeans, blending in with the radicals on the campus, but he wasn't one of them. Hillblom mocked their sit-ins, saying they would never achieve anything unless they adopted Mao Zedong's ruthless methods of consolidating power. It wasn't what the other students wanted to hear, but Hillblom didn't care.

Having grown up poor in Kingsburg, California, a small town near Fresno, Hillblom was more interested in money. He paid his own way through law school and in his second year at Berkeley, he found a job working as a messenger for a firm that transported documents for law firms and insurance companies between San Francisco and Los Angeles. Every evening after classes, Hillblom would take a full pouch on the last flight from Oakland to Los Angeles. The next morning, Hillblom would make the same trip in reverse and be back in time for classes at Berkeley. He looked as if he had slept at the airport, and he probably had. Hillblom often did his homework in flight.

Hillblom could see there was a bigger opportunity here. American companies were extending their reach around the world. They couldn't wait for the USPS to transport their contracts, blueprints, and legal documents to foreign countries. Hillblom could meet their needs by purchasing a plane ticket and hand-delivering their paperwork, bypassing both the postal service and foreign posts.

In 1969, he founded an overnight courier company called DHL with Adrian Dalsey and Robert Lynn. All they had between them was $500 in cash and a credit card. Lynn was a real estate investor who extricated himself from the fledgling company within a year because he didn't think it had a future, leaving Dalsey and Hillblom to run DHL. The two remaining partners squabbled constantly; Hillblom would eventually force Dalsey out of DHL, but for the time being they complemented each other. Hillblom was a strategist who preferred to work behind the scenes. Dalsey was a middle-aged salesman who knew how to get his foot in the door and see the right people at companies like Bank of America, IBM, and Standard Oil, and at the Federal Reserve, all of which became clients. In DHL's early years, the two founders and their friends and relatives often carried documents on planes, which made it a fun place to work. Soon, DHL had opened a headquarters in Honolulu and satellite offices in Guam,

Tokyo, Manila, Sydney, Hong Kong, Japan, and Singapore. By the mid-seventies Hillblom was a millionaire.

Then he ran into trouble in 1975, Hong Kong postal inspectors forced their way into DHL's office in the red-light district of that city, seizing its pouches and criminally indicting the company for violating its monopoly on letter delivery. So Hillblom flew to Hong Kong and hired Henry Litton, a prominent local attorney, to defend his company. Litton's case was simple: he argued in court that most of what DHL carried for its clients—blueprints, computer tapes, IBM punch cards, and checks—didn't fit the antiquated definition of a letter on which the colony's postal officials relied. A judge exonerated DHL, but it wasn't the end of the battle for DHL.

Hong Kong's post office immediately sought legislation to expand its legal authority. Hillblom hired a publicist who orchestrated a campaign to get the post office to reconsider. The press agent invited Hong Kong's postmaster to debate Henry Litton at a posh downtown hotel. When the postmaster declined the invitation, Litton debated an empty chair, much to the amusement of the executives from multinational corporations who used DHL and had come out to show their support. Up until now, the colonial legislature had backed the postmaster, but now the legislators decided not to intervene. It was safe once again for DHL to do business in Hong Kong.

The victory prepared Hillblom for a similar battle in the United States. Rather than raiding on DHL's offices, USPS inspectors visited the mailrooms of its customers, seeking back payment for items sent outside its network. Postal service salesmen usually showed up the next day, telling these companies they could avoid prosecution by using the USPS's Express Mail service. "They were thugs," says James Campbell, a former DHL attorney. "They were selling protection. They were basically intimidating people." Some DHL customers calculated how much it would cost to send a package through the U.S. mail system and put the appropriate number of stamps on their packages before sending them through DHL, much as Wells Fargo customers had done a century before in California.

Hillblom was determined to get the USPS to back off, just as he had done with Hong Kong's postal authorities, but it would be harder this time. The U.S. Postal Service had issued new regulations in 1974, defining a letter broadly as "a message directed to a specific person or address and recorded in or on a tangible object." The postal service exempted items like newspapers and telegrams, but the new rules applied to just about anything that DHL might carry.

After studying postal law further, Hillblom was convinced that the postal service was extending its power far beyond what the founding fathers had in mind when they created it. DHL couldn't afford to wage a legal battle against the USPS and its large staff of lawyers. But he felt certain that he could persuade Congress to intervene on his behalf. So Hillblom embarked on a lobbying campaign, recruiting other private carriers, most notably Federal Express's Frederick Smith.

Fred Smith's transformation of Federal Express into one of America's most admired companies is one of the great entrepreneurial success stories of the late 1970s. He was the son of a wealthy entrepreneur in Memphis who had started the Dixie Greyhound bus line and a chain of restaurants called the Toddle Houses. Smith's father suffered a heart attack in 1948, when Fred was four years old, leaving young Fred and his two half sisters a multimillion-dollar trust fund. As a boy, Smith suffered from Perthes' disease, a hip ailment that required him to use crutches until he was 10. But in high school, he played football and learned to fly.

In 1962 Smith went to Yale University, where he came up with an idea for an overnight delivery company. It's fleet of planes would pick up packages, fly them to a central hub where they would be sorted, and then transport them to their final destination by the next morning. Smith laid out the concept in a paper for his economics class. He got a C. "I remember reading it," Smith's roommate Dennis

Tippo said. "When he got it back, I think Fred joked about the grade. This idea always seemed to be in the back of his mind. In some of our bull sessions, all of us talking about life and things in general, several times he brought up the concept of Federal Express."

After Yale, Smith did two tours in Vietnam as a marine, fighting in some of the war's bloodiest battles and earning numerous medals. He would later say that he acquired his management skills in the military and certainly learned how to deal with pressure. "Some people do well under stressful conditions, dangerous conditions," one of his superiors, former lieutenant colonel Donald Rexroad, told Vance Trimble, author of *Overnight Success: Federal Express and Frederick Smith, Its Renegade Creator*. "He was one of that kind."

When Smith returned to the United States, he moved to Little Rock, Arkansas, and tried to put his college business plan to work. In 1970, he went to the Federal Reserve with a proposal to fly checks between its member banks so they would clear faster. While he awaited a decision, Smith borrowed $3.5 million, bought two twin-engine jets, and came up with a name for his company: Federal Express. But the Federal Reserve turned him down, leaving Smith with two idle planes and a significant amount of debt.

Rather than abandoning his idea, Smith went ahead and founded Federal Express. Dark-haired, handsome, and exuding self-confidence and southern charm, he persuaded older executives at established companies to quit their jobs and work for him, promising that they would get rich. He persuaded manufacturers to sell him more planes, even though they wondered sometimes if he would be able to close the deals. Smith also talked local bankers into lending him more money.

The planes had to be small. The Civil Aeronautics Board tightly regulated the aviation industry at the time and rarely approved the creation of new airlines. Smith ultimately got around that by purchasing small, French-built Falcons, which allowed Federal Express to operate as an air taxi service. Early on, the company made most of its money by flying mail for the U.S. Postal Service. "They needed service primarily in the northeast where they were having some problems getting mail moved rapidly on an overnight basis," says Roger Frock, a former Federal Express senior vice president. "We bid and we were awarded six routes."

In 1973 Smith moved Federal Express to Memphis, which had a larger airport, and established its headquarters there. The company threw together a makeshift hub in an old World War II–era hangar. It opened offices in seven cities, hired ground couriers, and found vans for them to drive. Smith's salespeople told him there would be plenty of orders in March when Federal Express started its overnight service. He was crushed when the planes arrived around midnight with only six items, including a birthday present Smith had purchased for an employee and a bag of dirty laundry.

Smith decided to ignore the failure and "officially" launch the service five weeks later. This time, the Federal Express fleet of 14 Falcons delivered 186 packages to 25 cities. The business grew steadily after that, but the company was constantly starved for cash. Every Monday, it had to pay its jet fuel suppliers $24,000; its pilots sometimes had to put it on their credit cards. One Friday night, Federal Express had only $5,000 in the bank. The following Monday, Roger Frock discovered that its balance had miraculously risen to $25,000. Smith confessed that he had flown to Las Vegas over the weekend and won $25,000 at the blackjack table.

"You mean you took our last $5,000?" Roger Frock said. "How could you do that?"

"What difference did it make?" Smith shrugged. "Without the funds for the fuel companies, we couldn't have flown anyway."

In late 1974, Smith raised $52 million in venture capital for Federal Express, a record for a start-up company at the time. But shortly after, he told his board that he was about to be indicted for allegedly forging his attorney's signature on a document several years earlier indicating that his family trust had agreed to secure a

$2 million loan from a Little Rock bank to keep Federal Express afloat. Ten days later while he was behind the wheel of his 1972 blue Ford LTD, Smith struck and killed a 53-year-old handyman who was leaving a Memphis bar around midnight. Oblivious, Smith drove on, only to be arrested by a police officer who happened to be following him and charged with leaving the scene of an accident.

Under pressure from his board, Smith agreed to step aside as chairman and chief executive of Federal Express, though he remained president and continued to run the business. Late one night Smith called Frock and Mike Fitzgerald, another of his top managers, and told them he was quitting. "There's just too much pressure, and I can't take it anymore," Smith said. Frock and Fitzgerald told Smith to meet them at Federal Express's office at the Memphis airport and persuaded him to change his mind. Toward dawn, Smith's mood brightened. "I could really go for a beer," he said. Fitzgerald produced a warm six-pack from the trunk of his car. Smith cooled it down with a blast from a fire extinguisher. "Just a little thing I learned in Nam," he said.

The following day, Federal Express's top executives rallied behind Smith and threatened to quit if the board fired him. Smith kept his job, and from then on, his luck turned. The district attorney in Memphis dropped the criminal charge against him. A Little Rock jury acquitted him of the forgery charges after Smith testified unabashedly that he had falsified the documents to save his company from going under. In July 1975, Federal Express turned its first monthly profit, and from then on, it operated in the black.

Soon, Federal Express needed bigger planes to keep up with all its orders. The Civil Aeronautics Board refused to grant its request, but tolerance for heavy-handed regulation was beginning to wane in Washington. Smith went to Capitol Hill, where he wooed legislators and swayed them with his argument that such antiquated rules unfairly limited the prospects of new companies like his. Smith acted as though he understood aviation law as well as anybody else, and he probably did. When a young general counsel of the House aviation committee tried to lecture him about how a new law should be crafted, Smith pulled a copy of the Civil Aeronautics Act of 1938 out of his own attorney's briefcase and waved it in the general counsel's face. "You don't know anything about this act," Smith snapped at him. Then he ripped the 250-page document in half and tossed it onto the table. "This is what I think of your argument," he said. Smith prevailed. In 1977, President Jimmy Carter signed a law deregulating the airfreight industry and freeing Federal Express to purchase DC-9s and Boeing 747s. Soon after, Federal Express went public, raising $18 million from investors in a stock offering.

The business press lionized Fred Smith and his upstart package delivery company. "Two tours in Vietnam and a six-year struggle to turn a college paper and a flock of purple airplanes into an airline have streaked Fred Smith's hair with gray at the age of 34," the Associated Press wrote. "But the still boyish-looking founder of Federal Express Corp., having made believers out of the doomsayers, shows no sign of retreating behind a stack of stock certificates."

However, Federal Express also attracted the attention of the USPS, which sent its overzealous inspectors into the company's Memphis hub. They opened packages in which they found items that fitted the postal service's new letter definition, such as receipts, catalogs, and even bumper stickers. Just as they had done with DHL, postal officials threatened Federal Express customers with fines and advised them to use the agency's competing Express Mail service instead.

Early on, Smith had been reluctant to join Larry Hillblom's crusade to break the postal service's monopoly, but now he was receptive. The two men struck up an unlikely friendship. Hillblom spent much of his time now in the South Pacific, where he pursued a hedonistic lifestyle. (After Hillblom's death in a plane crash in 1995, the *Wall Street Journal* and other publications reported that he bedded teenage girls, preferably virgins, and had sired a number of children who wanted a piece of his fortune.) He rarely visited Washington and when he did make an appearance, he refused to put on a suit and tie like a typical chief executive. He wore jeans and T-shirts just as he had done in college and usually had one of his girlfriends with him. Smith, on the other hand, was comfortable in Washington and willing to be the public face of the lobbying campaign. "He was just charismatic," says John Zorack, a lobbyist who worked for Federal Express and DHL during this period. "He could sell an issue like nobody I've ever known."

After its chaotic first few years, the USPS had begun to solve some of its problems. The clerks at the sorting machines learned the new system, and the percentage of letters arriving on time rose dramatically. The USPS adjusted the machines at the bulk mail centers so that packages could flow through them safely. In 1978, the board chose William Bolger, a 55-year-old former postal clerk and World War II bombardier from Waterbury, Connecticut, to be the postmaster general. Slim and gray haired, he was the first rank-and-file postal worker to hold the top position since Harry Truman had named Jesse Donaldson in 1947, and he came to the job with an intimate knowledge of the mail system, unlike most of his predecessors. "Everybody saw Bolger as the guy who can fix things," says Michael Coughlin, the assistant postmaster general of mail processing at the time. "Periodically, Bolger would pick up a pile of customer complaints, telephone the senders and see if he could personally help them."

Bolger had an idea to speed up mail processing with a nine-digit zip code, which would enable to the USPS's machines to sort letters so thoroughly that they would arrive at post offices in the order that letter carriers would deliver them. Eventually, the nine-digit code would become the standard for the mailing industry, but initially, Bolger's customers and their Congressional allies refused to support it, saying that nobody would be able to remember nine numbers. So Bolger offered sizable discounts to companies that pre-sorted their mail. It was a proposition that junk mailers found irresistible because it increased their profits.

Bolger was also determined to prevent private express from encroaching on his turf. "I'll resist, with every fiber of my being, any legislation to make it easier for private delivery systems to operate," he vowed. However, Bolger was about to learn the limits of a postmaster general's power under the new system. Before the reorganization, he could have exchanged local postmaster appointments for votes, but now he faced a hostile congress with little to offer. This was never more evident than when Bolger and his aides confronted Fred Smith and his allies in 1979 at hearings on the USPS's monopoly held by the House Subcommittee on Postal Operations and Services.

The USPS's general counsel Louis Cox tentatively defended the regulations. A tall, Harvard-educated attorney with gray hair and thick, black-framed glasses, Cox insisted that the postal service would lose billions of dollars a year if it was weakened.

The subcommittee's chairman, Charles Wilson, quickly grew impatient with Cox. "There are some interests, including many good USPS customers, charging that the postal service is expanding its monopoly," Wilson said. "Why?"

Cox professed astonishment. "I may say I have asked myself that same question," Cox said. "I don't really know the answer for sure."

When Wilson pressed Cox for a definition of a letter, the USPS general counsel responded with breathtaking opacity: "What is a letter? A letter is not just 'Dear so and so' in handwriting and so on," Cox mused. "A letter is quite an expansive conception."

"I am just telling you, Mr. Cox," Wilson said, "that if you don't become more realistic about the needs of business with their time-sensitive materials and have a more realistic approach to the interpretation of a letter, you are going to lose the whole doggone thing."

"I appreciate that," Cox replied.

"I'm trying to help you," Wilson insisted.

"I appreciate that, too, in every sense of the word 'appreciate,'" Cox said.

Cox argued that the idea of time sensitivity raised a myriad of legal questions. "We have seen bills introduced saying in somewhat more elaborate words that time sensitive mail, which is to say, mail that must be delivered by noon the next business day or within 12 hours or something of that kind, should be excepted," he said. "But if I postpone writing to someone I ought to write to until the stroke of midnight, as it were, then all of a sudden that letter of mine is, I guess, time sensitive."

"Obviously that is not what we are talking about," Wilson retorted.

"I know it isn't," Cox replied. "But if words of that kind are enacted into or put into our regulations, how are we going to enforce it?"

"That is what you went to Harvard for, for gosh sakes, to learn how to do these things," Wilson said.

"Even our best educational institutions are imperfect," Cox said. He insisted the USPS could provide rapid delivery for customers with Express Mail. No, it wasn't available everywhere in the country yet, but the USPS was working on that. Cox urged the subcommittee not to loosen its letter monopoly until the agency had a chance to fully test it.

Then it was Smith's turn to testify. He said he could provide a good definition of a time-sensitive message; it was one that customers would gladly pay Federal Express to transport rather than entrust it to the much cheaper, but shamefully inefficient U.S. Postal Service. He suggested that Cox had been less than candid when he claimed to be ignorant about why people were upset with the USPS's expansive definition of a letter. "They go in and use the private express statutes as an intimidating tool to create users for the Express Mail system,"

Smith said. "That is the reason you are hearing so much about it right now. We are absolutely convinced of it."

To hear Smith tell it, the USPS had only itself to blame for the rise of Federal Express and other private carriers that had materialized in recent years. "It is undeniably clear that the substantial increase in the number and importance of private delivery, express and courier services has coincided with a worsening decline in the quality of service rendered by the Postal Service," Smith said. He called on Congress to rein in the postal service and keep its inspectors out of the mailrooms of his customers. "Such practices amount to a raw abuse of government power," Smith said. "Such practices demand legislative action."

Executives from companies like Merrill Lynch, Bankers Trust, Prudential Insurance Company, and Aetna Life & Casualty testified that they too wanted the USPS to back off. "At a time when we are battling inflation and trying to keep insurance affordable, it is absurd for the Postal Service to attempt to extend the monopoly to items that are not, in any ordinary popular sense, letters," said Philip Shaughnessy, an Aetna vice president. "It is important to know that the great majority of the tons of material we ship each day is further distributed through the Post Office at first-class rates."

Hillblom didn't appear before the subcommittee but DHL's attorney Jim Campbell did. Early in his testimony, Campbell mentioned that DHL had offices in many Asian cities. Chairman Wilson interrupted him, "Let me stop you here," he said. "You say you operate in Hong Kong and Singapore?"

"Yes, sir."

"Good, we had hoped to visit those places in August to look into overseas private service, among others issues."

Wilson's subcommittee members must have exchanged surprised looks. Before the hearing, Campbell had learned that Wilson liked to take an annual government-paid trip to the Far East with his South Korean–born wife, but he hadn't found a reason this year.

Now Wilson had one. DHL and Federal Express were more than happy to arrange for dinners in August for the subcommittee members and their wives in Hong Kong, Singapore, and Seoul. Larry Hillblom showed up to make his case in this less formal setting. "When we went to Hong Kong, Larry was our host," says lobbyist John Zorack, who went along for the trip. "I had to laugh. We had a reception. Larry never wore anything but blue jeans and T-shirts. I said, 'Larry, you've got to at least dress up a little bit.' He went out and got a white shirt with embroidery on it. That was pretty high class for Larry."

Campbell, DHL's attorney, went along too and also has fond memories, "Son of a gun," he says. "We convinced Charlie Wilson and the subcommittee. He came back to Washington and basically told the postal service, You guys better wake up and get real or we're going to ram it down your throats. That's when the postal service caved in." That November, Bolger reluctantly announced the suspension of the USPS monopoly on what it described as overnight letters delivered by 10 AM. As a result, Federal Express started its much-publicized overnight letter business.

Bolger vowed to aggressively compete, but the postal service's Express Mail couldn't keep up with Federal Express. The USPS no longer had its own fleet of airplanes. Instead, it relied on commercial airlines to handle its overnight mail, and they took care of their passengers first and treated the mail like an afterthought. Federal Express guaranteed delivery by the following morning. The USPS could promise it only by 3 PM. Private carriers picked up packages and envelopes at the homes and offices of their customers; the USPS charged an extra $5.60 for pickup. By the mid-1980s, Federal Express was the largest overnight air express company in the United States, with $1.72 billion in sales. UPS, which had purchased jets and built its own hub in Louisville, Kentucky, was second with $675 million, followed by Purolator with $590 million. The USPS was in fourth place with $500 million.

Federal Express undermined the USPS in other ways too. Roger Frock recalls, "When the kids in our marketing department talked to customers about the postal service, in general, they said, 'The sleepy old Post Office. They do it at their own pace, and if it goes across the country it's going to take three to five days no matter what.'" As a result, Federal Express ran a television commercial in 1982 with two actors portraying a pair of overweight clerks who discuss their pensions while a customer desperate to mail a letter tries to get their attention. Finally, one of the clerks pulls the window shade down in the man's face, forcing him to go to a nearby Federal Express office. Bolger sent Fred Smith a furious letter demanding that Federal Express pull the spot; Federal Express refused. "We're just taking a commonly accepted attitude, such as the perception of postal workers, and having fun with it," Francis X. McGuire, a Federal Express spokesman, said. "I'm sorry to hear Mr. Bolger feels that way."

The American Postal Workers Union responded with a commercial celebrating the USPS and its employees. "One hundred and ten billion pieces of mail a year! Who in the world handles all that?" an announcer asked. But the USPS itself remained silent. "Our strategy was, 'Let it die. Let it go,'" says John Nolan, a former deputy postmaster general. "Unfortunately, it didn't die very fast. Some of those jokes hit us very hard."

The Federal Express campaign reflected the changing image of the postal worker in popular culture. In September 1982, the CBS sitcom *Cheers* debuted, featuring Cliff Clavin, a Boston letter carrier played by John Ratzenberger. The show's creators initially thought Cliff would appear only in the first season of *Cheers*, but the audience liked him so much that he became a permanent member of the ensemble. His uniform now hangs in the Smithsonian Institution's National Postal Museum. But unlike the streetwise postal workers who rescued Santa Claus in *Miracle on 34th Street*, Cliff seemed slightly damaged. His obsession with the postal service's rules was a running joke on *Cheers* along with the immense pride he took in his mundane job, but the audience laughed at Cliff rather than with him. He was lovable, but a bit pathetic.

In hindsight, this sad image of the postal worker seems to have been tailored for the Reagan era, when Americans became increasingly distrustful of federal institutions that had once been sacrosanct. Elected president in 1980, Ronald Reagan, a Republican from California, famously told an audience at a press conference the nine most terrifying words in the English language are: "I'm from the government and I'm here to help." His aides called for the privatization of Medicare, public housing, Amtrak, and the USPS. James Miller, a Reagan appointee who served as chairman of the Federal Trade Commission, became the chief evangelist of privatizing the postal service by abolishing the agency's monopoly so it would be forced to compete with private companies. Miller didn't seem worried by the old argument that private couriers could take the agency's most lucrative, urban routes and leave it with the money-losing rural ones. "Private enterprise will get the mail delivered just as it did in the Old West," he argued.

But Miller's vision of postal privatization was just the pipe dream shared by handful of libertarian ideologues. Reagan had to deal with a Democratic-controlled House of Representatives, whose leaders were allied with the postal workers' unions that were dead set against it. The USPS was also in a much stronger financial position than it had been in the 1970s. Bolger's presorting discounts had spawned the modern direct mail industry. Junk mailers started cross-referencing zip codes with census data, identifying the most desirable neighborhoods and blanketing residents with sales pitches.

In 1982, the USPS delivered 114 billion pieces of mail, or 494 per capita. Of that number, 62 billion were letters, but junk mail was becoming a bigger part of the mix. A decade earlier, it had been 25 percent of the mail. Now it accounted for 32 percent. The postal service's residential customers might have had mixed feelings about the growing number of ads in their mailboxes, but the USPS generated a surplus of $802 million and announced that it would stop taking a federal subsidy starting in 1983, two years ahead of schedule. After more than a decade of woes, the U.S. Postal Service finally had something to celebrate, but for how long?

10

Going Postal

It was still dark at 6:27 AM on Wednesday, August 20, 1986, when Mike Bigler pulled into the employee lot at the post office in Edmond, Oklahoma, where he worked as a letter carrier. He had purchased several boxes of doughnuts for his coworkers on his way to work, and he thought about asking Patrick Sherrill, another letter carrier who pulled up beside him in his blue Honda, to help carry the doughnuts, but Bigler changed his mind when he saw the dark look on Sherrill's face. He thought it was strange that Sherrill had his mailbag in the front seat covered by a sweater and raincoat. What did Sherrill need the extra clothes for on a day when the temperature was expected to reach 95 degrees?

Bigler shrugged and went inside. Sherrill was unusual; there was no other way to explain it. A 44-year-old former marine with a receding hairline and a mustache, Sherrill was constantly getting written up by his supervisors for being late for work, delivering mail to the wrong addresses, being rude to customers, and, once, for spraying a dog behind a five-foot fence with Mace. He muttered about taking revenge on his superiors. "I'm going to get even, and everybody's going to know," Sherrill told a fellow postal worker.

Over the next half hour, the Edmond post office filled up with 73 people. Some of the postal workers gathered in the break room for coffee and Bigler's doughnuts. Others stood at their workstations preparing the day's mail for delivery and chatting with each over the rock and roll from a local radio station that was playing through the intercom system and turned up louder than some would have liked.

Nobody noticed when Sherrill locked the rear doors and produced one of the semiautomatic pistols he was carrying in his sack. Without a word, he started firing at his coworkers. At first, people thought a prankster had set off firecrackers, until they heard screams and saw Sherrill's victims fall to the floor. A trained marksman who belonged to the Oklahoma Air National Guard shooting team, Sherrill pointed his weapon around the room, picking people off, only pausing for a few seconds at one point to put in earplugs.

Some postal workers, including some of the wounded, dived over the front counter and ran though the lobby doors into the parking lot. Two hid in the steel-reinforced vault used to store stamps. Many more lay on the floor playing dead, including Bigler, whom Sherrill shot in the back. "He wanted to slaughter us all," Bigler would later say.

In fifteen minutes, Sherrill killed 14 people and wounded six more before he sat in a supervisor's chair and shot himself in the head. When the police stormed the building, they found him dead on a floor littered with bodies, shell casings, and undelivered mail. It was the third-worst mass murder in American history and it had happened on the premises of the U.S. Postal Service.

The incident at the Edmond post office became a national story. "Mailman Slays 14, Self, in Oklahoma Massacre," the *Los Angeles Times* wrote. *Time* put it more succinctly: "Crazy Pat's Revenge." In the days that followed, the media reported that Sherrill had pointed a loaded handgun at an officer when he was in the Marines. He made lewd remarks and brushed up against women when he worked briefly at a low-level job at the Federal Aviation Administration in Oklahoma City. Sherrill had also previously worked at the Oklahoma City post office, where he would have been fired if he hadn't quit first. Soon after, the Edmond post office chose Sherrill over 22 other applicants because he was a veteran, which gave him extra points on the postal employment exam.

Four days after the shootings, Postmaster General Preston Tisch attended a memorial service for the slain workers at the Central State University football stadium. He told the audience of 3,500 people that there would be a moment of silence the following day at 4 PM at every post office. "At 40,000 post offices across the United States, our flag flies at half staff," Tisch said. "At 40,000 post offices, men and women weep." He maintained that the USPS had no idea what led Sherrill to slaughter his coworkers and would never know.

Not everybody agreed. The same day, Sherrill's friends and family buried his ashes a hundred miles away in Watonga, Oklahoma. On his grave, someone placed a bouquet of flowers from letter carriers in Irving, Texas, who had also sent a card with a disturbing message: "To those who understand what he went through as a carrier. No one will ever know how far he was pushed to do what he did."

The USPS found such talk absurd. Its spokespeople noted that there was little turnover at the postal service and a long list of applicants waiting for jobs. So how bad a place could it be to work? Supervisors blamed the unions for fomenting workplace tensions by using the grievance process to protect workers who were frequently absent or showed up on drugs. However, employees described the USPS as a Dickensian environment where managers drove them relentlessly to process ever growing amounts of mail and disciplined them for violating petty rules like whistling in the office and failing to hold letters at the proper angle. "These rules are set up to give them grounds for harassment," said Robert McLaughlin, a clerk in Des Moines who was suspended for seven days for the latter infraction.

It wouldn't be Preston Tisch's job to figure out what could make a letter carrier like Patrick Sherrill snap. A wealthy New York businessman, Tisch resigned in January 1988 after only 18 months on the job. It would be up to his successor, Anthony Frank.

*　*　*

Little more than a week after he had taken the oath of office on March 1, 1988, Anthony Frank found himself onstage at the University of Notre Dame with President Ronald Reagan for the unveiling of a 22-cent stamp honoring the school's legendary football coach Knute Rockne. Frank gave what he describes as a perfunctory speech. Then he listened as Reagan, who had famously played Notre Dame football star George Gipp in the 1940 movie *Knute Rockne—All American*, gave an autumnal speech that celebrated movies, sports, and his own presidency. When Reagan was finished, someone handed him a football. The 77-year-old president threw a perfect pass to a member of the university football team. "I've never forgotten this," Frank says in a telephone interview from his home in Carmel, California. "He took that football, and he passed it to the guy. How many people could do that? Pick one guy out of 17,000 and throw him a football?"

A tall, square-jawed Californian with dark, wavy hair, the 56-year-old became known as a dispenser of pithy sound bites himself. "He was an incredible spokesperson for the postal service," says William Henderson, a regional manager in North Carolina at the time. "He was very articulate, and very bright, and he had a way of synthesizing what the postal service was doing in a way that was very digestible for the average guy. He would say, 'We delivered enough mail today that if you had strung it piece to piece, it would have gone around the earth twice' and things like that."

The son of a wealthy German bank owner, Frank and his Jewish parents fled Germany to escape the Nazis when he was six years old, in 1938. The family settled in Los Angeles, where Frank's father became a broker for Merrill Lynch and a financial adviser to fellow German émigrés, such as author Thomas Mann and conductor Bruno Walter. After graduating from Dartmouth College, Frank worked in the financial industry himself, becoming president in 1971 of a small bank in northern California. He transformed it into First Nationwide, the country's sixth-largest savings and loan, and sold it to National Steel for $281 million in 1980. When National Steel needed cash, Frank engineered the sale of the bank for $493 million to the Ford Motor Company. Frank became wealthy enough that he no longer needed a paycheck. Public service appealed to him now. When a member of the USPS board of governors asked if he would be interested in the job of postmaster general, Frank said yes. "I think of myself as a professional manager," he told *Fortune*. "The Postal Service is the biggest management challenge in the U.S., maybe the world. For one thing, it is the most extraordinary anomaly; it's so big that nobody sees it."

Frank plunged into his new job. He delivered mail with carriers in Louisiana and later appeared as one in an episode of the television show, *Murder, She Wrote*. He visited post offices where the employees hadn't seen a postmaster general since the Depression. "People are hungry out in the field," Frank said. "Some of them can tell you the last time a postmaster was there. 'We had Jim Farley and I remember he said . . .' and I'm thinking, 'Good lord, Jim Farley!'" Frank wanted the postal service to purchase its own fleet of planes to compete better with Federal Express. He announced that the USPS would be opening "mini-post offices" in Sears, Roebuck department stores to boost stamp sales. He talked about reviving postal banking, which had been discontinued in 1966.

Frank was also determined to ramp up the USPS's automation program, which had been delayed yet again. In 1986, two postal inspectors had shown up unannounced at a USPS Board of Governors meeting and whispered something to Peter Voss, one of its members. Looking shaken, Voss stood up and followed the inspectors out of the room. The following day, he pleaded guilty to accepting kickbacks from a lobbying firm trying to win a $250 million contract for optical character readers for a Texas company. The incident paralyzed the USPS's automation efforts for a year and a half. When Frank arrived, only 38 percent of the mail was being processed by high-speed machines.

Meanwhile, the USPS's volume had risen to 160 billion items—or 656 per capita. Junk mail, which now made up 37 percent of the mail, continued to drive much of the growth, but the price of a first-class stamp climbed to 25 cents. Because of the slowdown of the automation program, the postal service had to hire more people to process all the extra mail. It had 833,486 employees now, and Frank predicted that if nothing changed, the USPS would have to add to another 125,000 people in the coming years. At some point, he warned, the system would become unaffordable, and the USPS would collapse.

As far as Frank was concerned, the economic benefits of automation couldn't be ignored. In one hour, 60 clerks could sort 36,000 letters by hand. It was a labor-intensive process that cost the agency $1,500. With mechanical letter-sorting machines, 17 workers could separate the same amount for only $540. But with optical character readers, the letters could be sorted by two workers at a cost of merely $108. The new machines also sprayed bar codes on letters, which made them fly through processing plants even faster. The optical character readers could now also read most handwritten addresses; the USPS had developed technology enabling it to decipher scrawls that would have stumped even the Dead Letter Office's Patti Lyle Collins in the previous century. The machines took pictures of letters and transmitted them to a remote facility where workers used algorithms to decipher the scribble. However, the optical character readers still couldn't read anything on a colored envelope, which meant that vast numbers of greeting cards still had to be sorted by hand.

Frank embarked on a $5 billion campaign to increase the number of these devices in postal facilities. At a meeting with his top aides, Frank came up with a slogan for it. He wanted to get 95 percent of the U.S. mail bar-coded by 1995. "95 in 95!" Frank said. This became his mantra, one that he preached to his managers, and large customers got further discounts if they bar-coded their own mail.

The changes at the USPS were long overdue, but they sharpened tensions between Frank and the postal workers' unions. Traditionally, letter carriers spent several hours in the morning sorting letters, cards, and magazines in the order in which they would be delivered. But now that the new machines did all of that for them, they had to spend more time on the street, which became a contentious point with the NALC. Even so, Frank maintained a good working relationship with the union's president Vincent Sombrotto. A charismatic, white-haired New Yorker, Sombrotto was one of the firebrands at Branch No. 36 who had instigated the 1970 wildcat strike, but when he was elected the union's president eight years later, he became a smooth Washington insider. "Vinnie was a piece of work," Frank says admiringly.

Occasionally, the two men lobbied members of Congress together. One time, they visited a senator from Minnesota who had also grown up in New York. "Vinnie stopped him in the middle of his sentence," Frank recalls. "He said: 'Seventy-Third Street.' The guy was speechless. He said, 'How did you know that?' Vinnie said, 'I grew up in New York. Each street had a different sound to it. I knew you were from Seventy-Third Street.' The senator was dumbstruck—as was I." Of course, there was always the possibility Sombrotto had looked the information up in advance. Either way, his conversational icebreaker had the desired effect.

Frank had a more fractious relationship with Moe Biller, now president of the 370,000-member APWU, which had become the largest postal workers' union. Another key participant in the 1970 strike, Biller remained an unabashed throwback to another period of labor history. "Biller always acted like he was still in the 1930s and his bosses were bashing him in the head," says Michael Coughlin, who served as deputy postmaster general under Frank. Biller's behavior was sometimes at odds with his rhetoric. Frank once bumped into him on an airplane. Frank was flying coach. Biller was in first class. "It was just a marvelous experience," Frank says.

Perhaps Biller had reason to be adversarial. The USPS would never replace carriers with machines, but the advanced optical character readers were a threat to the APWU and its members. Jaclynn Peon, a clerk who operated a mechanical letter-sorting machine in a processing plant in Garden City, New York, was devastated when the new devices arrived. She had mastered the old system; she and her coworkers had such good numbers that their managers rewarded them with an annual summer picnic and a Christmas party. "I loved Garden City," she says wistfully. "Everybody knew each other. It was wonderful."

But now Peon's skills were no longer needed there. Because of the no-layoff clause in postal workers' contracts, she could count on having a job somewhere at the USPS. She ended up at a much larger facility in Huntington Station, New York. "It felt like a prison," Peon says. "I'll tell you right now: I hated it." She had been used to her managers timing her activities in Garden City, but her new bosses timed her washroom breaks and confronted her when they felt she was taking too many. "You were questioned," she recalls. "'You are taking multiple trips to the bathroom. Is there a problem?'" Finally, Peon quit the USPS and became a nurse.

In Louisiana, 22 hand-sorting clerks were displaced by the machines in the suburbs of New Orleans and transferred into the city, where there were still pigeonholes to throw mail into. With the move, they forfeited their seniority rights and had to work the midnight shift. "They shuffled me away like an old piece of furniture," Alvin Coulon, a 27-year USPS veteran, told the *Washington Post*. These longtime clerks had once tossed 600 letters an hour. Now they practiced their ancient skill at a more leisurely pace. "We have to slow down," explained a clerk named C. J. Roux. "We don't want to work ourselves out of a job."

Moe Biller insisted his union wasn't against automation. "You might as well oppose the sun setting," he said. But Biller did everything he could to frustrate Frank's efforts and raise questions about his leadership. He called for his resignation when Frank tried to outsource the advanced letter-sorting operations. He organized a boycott of Sears when the USPS opened post offices in the department stores; Sears eventually backed out of the deal. When Frank appeared on *Late Night with David Letterman* and let the host tease him about the stodgy, unreliable postal service, Biller excoriated him for not defending the institution. "He just stood there like a potted plant," Biller scoffed.

The war between Frank and Biller grew more vituperative when a new wave of violence engulfed the postal service. Biller laid the blame at the management's feet. In June 1998, a clerk in Chelsea, Massachusetts, murdered a female coworker and took his own life. Six month later, a clerk in New Orleans killed a coworker with a shotgun and wounded two others. In August 1989, John Merlin Taylor, a 52-year old carrier in Escondido, California, murdered his wife while she slept and then went to work and killed two men with whom he had taken daily cigarette breaks. Frank and his wife flew to California and comforted the widows of the victims. "We did as good a job as we could in this calamity," Frank says. "The thing is, the guy who did the shooting had been named outstanding letter carrier just a few months earlier."

When the APWU blamed the slayings in Escondido on what it described as the postal service's militaristic management style, Frank was furious. "Obviously, this is a matter of great importance to me," he said. "But when you shoot your closest friends and your sleeping wife, is it fair to blame work on that? Is *that* the fault of the Postal Service?" By now, however, there was a pattern emerging in the slayings. Perhaps Frank had already noticed it. If so, he didn't say anything. Soon, he would.

On April 21, 1989, John Frezza was driving through Berkley, Michigan, a Detroit suburb, when a letter carrier behind the wheel of a white mail truck cut him off at a stop sign. The mailman jumped out of his truck. He looked a bit like Charles Bronson with his brown hair, his mustache, and his flat nose. He started swearing at Frezza. "You punks are all the same," he said. When Frezza tried to get his name, the carrier knocked him down. "Hey, what's going on?" Frezza asked. The letter carrier told Frezza he was lucky he hadn't knocked "his fucking teeth down his throat."

Frezza reported the altercation to the police. When the letter carrier's bosses at the post office in nearby Royal Oak found out about it, they suspended him for seven days and ordered him to undergo psychological counseling. His name was Thomas McIlvane, and he had frequently been in trouble since he was hired in 1983. His superiors hadn't wanted to hire him in the first place because he had a bad knee, but McIlvane knew how the system worked. He appealed the decision, and he got the job because he was a disabled veteran.

Like Patrick Sherrill, McIlvane had served in the Marines and been trained as a sharpshooter, but he had trouble controlling what he described as his "short fuse." In 1982, he was court-martialed for insubordination. The following year he drove a tank over an automobile in an apparent fit and still somehow received "a general discharge under honorable conditions." It wasn't as bad as a dishonorable discharge but it meant the Marines would never take him back and he couldn't join the reserves.

McIlvane didn't fare much better at the postal service. He kicked open swinging doors rather than pushing them. He was written up for arriving late at work and delivering mail to the wrong houses. He got into an argument with another carrier over a parking space. When a supervisor intervened, McIlvane told him, "Don't fuck with me."

Fortunately for McIlvane, he had a protector in Charlie Withers, the chief NALC steward in Royal Oak. A Vietnam War veteran with shoulder-length brown hair and a long mustache, Withers detested the management at Royal Oak and pushed back whenever possible, filing grievances on McIlvane's behalf. "He was a good letter carrier," Withers says. "I worked right next to him."

The relationship between labor and management at the Royal Oak post office became more difficult in 1990 when Daniel Presilla became its postmaster. Presilla came from Indianapolis, where he had been a high-level manger and earned praise for running a smooth bar coding operation. But he was also an autocrat. When injured employees in Indianapolis returned to work and requested light duty, Presilla made them spend their days in a glass-enclosed room on the processing floor reading postal manuals. So many postal workers in Indianapolis complained that the U.S. General Accounting Office investigated, but it found no evidence of widespread mistreatment of employees.

Presilla brought along several of his deputies including Chris Carlisle, who became Royal Oak's branch operations manager. He clearly wanted to clean house and seemed intent on starting with McIlvane, writing him up for small infractions. "They were targeting McIlvane," Withers says. "They were ganging up on him for all kinds of things that they weren't messing with other people about."

Carlisle sent McIlvane home for wearing shorts that were too short for work. When McIlvane returned to the office in long pants, he threw the shorts onto the branch manager's desk. Soon after, Carlisle showed the carriers a training film at the end of their shift. Eight carriers ended up filing their daily paperwork late, but McIlvane was the only one suspended. Carlisle told him to leave the building and said he would be in touch. "Yeah, and I'll be seeing you too," McIlvane replied.

Withers managed to get McIlvane a second chance, but when a supervisor called McIlvane at home and told him to come in to work, McIlvane spewed vulgarities at her. That clinched it. On July 31, 1990, Carlisle fired McIlvane. Withers filed a grievance contending the decision, and starting a process that could take more than a year to resolve. Always a believer in his troubled coworker, Withers told McIlvane that he had a strong case, but the union steward knew it would be difficult for him to wait for the outcome. Withers felt the need to warn Carlisle about it. "I'm not saying McIlvane is dangerous, but I don't want anybody to get hurt," Withers told him. "If I think he is going to go crazy, I'll come and tell you."

In the months that followed, McIlvane showed up several times at the post office and had to be escorted out of the building because he got into screaming matches with people. The human resources director was concerned enough to call postal inspectors in Detroit to see if they could do something about McIlvane. The inspectors gave him the brush-off. "We're not a babysitting service," one said.

Meanwhile, the grievance process dragged on. The USPS upheld McIlvane's firing and the union appealed, which meant the case was headed for arbitration. At times, McIlvane was optimistic, telling his roommate he planned to use his back pay to fix up his house. At other times, he spoke darkly about punishing his tormentors at Royal Oak. "They will not get away with this," he promised. McIlvane started calling some of his former supervisors and threatening them. "You better not turn your head or you will be dead—you fucking bitch," he told one woman.

During the summer of 1991, McIlvane lost his health insurance, which only unhinged him further. "If I lose the arbitration it will make Edmond, Oklahoma, look like a tea party," he told Paul Roznowski, president of NALC Local 3126, which represented Royal Oak. Another time McIlvane said he would make Edmond "look like Disneyland." He also spoke of murdering Carlisle. "If I lose this thing, I'm going to blow Carlisle's fucking brains out," he promised. The union people didn't warn the USPS about any of this because they worried that it would hurt his case.

On October 10, 1991, another postal worker went on a bloody rampage. Joseph Harris, who had recently been fired from his job as a clerk in Ridgewood, New Jersey, put on a ninja hood, black fatigues, and combat boots and snuck into the home of Carol Ott, his former supervisor. Harris shot her boyfriend in the head at he watched television and fatally slashed Ott with a samurai sword. Then he drove to the Ridgewood post office and killed two mail handlers as they arrived for work. When Harris surrendered there, he wore a gas mask and a bulletproof vest. Police relieved him of an Uzi, a machine gun, three hand grenades, some homemade bombs, and his blade. "I think Mr. Harris came prepared to die," said Joel Trella, chief of the Bergen County, New Jersey, police department. "He was armed quite heavily—more heavily than I've ever seen in my career."

Unnerved by the slayings in New Jersey, Carlisle appealed to the postal inspection service in Detroit. He sent a two-and-a-half-page letter to the inspectors, explaining that McIlvane's case was scheduled to go before an arbitrator on Monday, October 21. Carlisle feared that if McIlvane lost, he would seek revenge. The inspectors didn't reply. On the Friday before the hearing, Carlisle telephoned the Detroit office and pleaded with an inspector to be there in case McIlvane snapped. She reluctantly agreed. As it turned out, the two-day arbitration hearing was uneventful. McIlvane was agitated, getting up every 20 minutes or so to use the washroom. When nothing else out of the ordinary happened, the inspector decided not to return for the final day, much to Carlisle's exasperation.

When the hearings ended, employees at the Royal Oak post office braced themselves for a decision. Carlisle bought more life insurance and suggested that Withers do the same. "You know, McIlvane is going to lose and when he does, he'll kill you too," Carlisle told him. Another time, Carlisle stopped by Withers's workstation and inquired if he had purchased a bulletproof vest. Irritated, Withers responded, "If I were you I wouldn't bother because you'll get it in the head."

On November 8, the arbitrator ruled against McIlvane. The union called his house and left a message on his answering machine. A woman in the USPS personnel department called the Detroit inspectors and told them again about McIlvane's threats. An inspector promised to visit the post office and conduct an investigation. He said he would be in Royal Oak on November 14.

The morning of November 14 was unseasonably warm for late fall in Michigan. Charlie Withers arrived at the post office at 6:30 AM to take care of some union business. He still seethed about the loss of the McIlvane case. Chris Carlisle hurried over and said they needed to talk about something, but Withers waved him away. "Is this because of the McIlvane thing?" Carlisle asked. Withers said he had simply had enough of the "BS" that Carlisle and his people had heaped on the Royal Oak letter carriers. Later, Withers would wonder what Carlisle's last words to him might have been.

At 8:30 AM, Withers was upstairs taking to Leonard Brown, head of labor relations at Royal Oak, when they heard noises that sounded like popcorn popping. "It's a shooting!" Brown said. The two of them locked the office door, stuck a chair under the knob, and turned out the lights. It was McIlvane. He had entered the building through the rear loading docks with a sawed-off semiautomatic rifle hidden under his raincoat, along with two ammunition clips wrapped together with duct tape.

McIlvane went straight for Carlisle's office on the first floor and shot him before he could rise from his desk. Then he shot another supervisor who was sitting nearby. After that, McIlvane walked through the ground floor of the post office, firing at people randomly. "No, Tom, no!" one of his fellow carriers shouted. McIlvane shot Clark French, another NALC shop steward, as French ran out of the building. The bleeding postman escaped, but only because McIlvane let him go. He was headed upstairs to the second floor where there were more managers to kill.

At the top of the stairs, McIlvane tried the door of Leonard Brown's office, but he couldn't get it open. Inside, Brown and Withers heard him reload his rifle, dropping an ammunition clip on the hallway floor. McIlvane kicked open the door of the office next door and shot another labor relations specialist in the head. Then he proceeded down the hall to Postmaster Presilla's office. Presilla dialed 911. "He's trying to get in my door now!" Presilla told the dispatchers at the Royal Oak police department.

McIlvane furiously tried the knob, but it was no use. Presilla had barricaded himself inside. By now, McIlvane could probably hear the sirens of the police cars arriving outside. He had fired nearly 100 rounds, killing four people and wounding four more, but he wasn't done yet. He wandered into the stairwell and shot himself in the head. The police found him there, still breathing. They took him to Beaumont Hospital in Royal Oak, where he was pronounced dead at 12:33 AM the following day. The Royal Oak massacre wasn't the worst example of postal violence, but in some ways, it was the most tragic because both labor and management missed so many opportunities to prevent McIlvane's spree.

Moe Biller rushed to Royal Oak that afternoon to exploit the crisis. Speaking to traumatized workers in a garage next to the post office, Biller blamed the tragedy on the postal service's management. "It's clear that something is fundamentally wrong in the postal worker environment, and something must be done about it," Biller said. "Perhaps the saddest aspect of the Royal Oak situation is the fact that warning signs had been flashing there for months and months, but no one in management seemed to take them seriously." But Biller didn't mean McIlvane's threats or violent behavior. "I'm referring," he clarified, "to the chronic problems that had been reported concerning the management of the Royal Oak Facility."

Initially, the USPS insisted that there was nothing it could have done to prevent the tragedy in Royal Oak. "There is flat out no way to identify the character of an individual who would commit this sort of crime," a USPS spokesman insisted. The following day, Anthony Frank appeared in Michigan with a different message. He dismissed calls for the USPS to station police officers in post offices to protect the workers. "Let me be brutal," he said. "If we had a police officer at the back dock in this case, we would have had one more dead. These are public buildings. I don't think you can make them hermetically sealed. We can't make 40,000 post offices armed camps."

Instead, Frank announced that the USPS would review the hiring practices at every post office, conduct background checks of the agency's more than 800,000 employees, and create a 24-hour hotline that postal workers could use to report threats made by their fellow employees. In 10 days, employees inundated the line with stories of ex-workers who talked about killing their bosses and current ones who brought weapons to work and talked about using them on people there. Postal inspectors took 328 of the calls seriously enough to conduct investigations and arrested seven current and former workers for making threats.

On January 7, 1992, Frank tendered his resignation. He says he was eager to return to the West Coast, where his family was living, but he told colleagues privately at the time that he thought he could no longer be an effective leader. He had suffered too many defeats. Moe Biller had killed his plan for post offices in Sears. Private airlines with mail contracts had thwarted his proposal to create a new, USPS-owned airmail fleet. Frank had spent billions of dollars on automation, but he hadn't been able to get labor costs down.

The USPS had slipped back in the red, losing $1.5 billion the previous year. Frank had tried to erase the deficit by raising the price of a first-class stamp to 30 cents; the Postal Rate Commission would only approve a 29-cent stamp. Frank called the ruling "dumb" and said the only beneficiaries would be Chilean copper miners who would have to produce more raw material for pennies.

But Frank could take pride in his accomplishments too. The proportion of automatically processed letters was expected to reach 61 percent by the end of the year. In his final months, Frank shoved through another one of his signature achievements. Early on, he had talked about issuing a stamp honoring the late Elvis Presley. He didn't pursue it at the time. The idea was controversial because of Presley's drug problems. Now, however, Frank appeared on the talk show *Larry King Live* and announced that the USPS would create a 29-cent Elvis stamp. But first, he said, there would be a contest to see if the public preferred a stamp featuring Presley as a youthful sex symbol or a middle-aged crooner. The USPS received almost 1.2 million ballots. Young Elvis won by a three-to-one margin. "The U.S. Postal Service has finally found a way to be responsive to the public," wrote the *Chicago Tribune*.

Frank unveiled the Presley stamp at Graceland with the late singer's wife and daughter at his side. "It was great," he recalls. The Presley stamp became the most popular in the agency's history. On the first day, the USPS sold 300 million Presley stamps and had to quickly print 200 million more to satisfy the customers who were lining up in post offices across the country to purchase them. Best of all, the buyers kept four out of five of the stamps for posterity rather than using them to mail letters, which meant the King of Rock and Roll was immensely profitable for the postal service.

After he left the post office, Frank went public with what he really thought caused the shootings. In an interview with the *Washington Post*, Frank blamed the postal service's policy of giving preferential hiring treatment to disabled veterans like Patrick Sherrill and Thomas McIlvane. "When you mandate that—and the disability can be mental as well as physical—in a tiny, tiny minority of cases you're going to have people slip through who are basically unbalanced people trained to kill," Frank argued. "It's a lousy thing to say but I think it needs to be said." Frank also said he wished he had done more to change what he described as the postal service's "paramilitary character." He said that too many managers were former clerks and letter carriers who had taken abuse for years and became abusers themselves once they were in charge. Their attitude, he lamented, was, "I ate dirt for 20 years. Now it's your turn to eat dirt."

The Royal Oak massacre was a turning point for the USPS. In March 1992, it signed a joint statement on workplace violence with three of its four unions. The text, thumbtacked to bulletin boards in every post office and processing plant, stated that there was an "unacceptable level of stress in the workplace," but that nobody involved in the agency would tolerate harassment or threats of violence. The APWU was the only union that refused to sign the statement; Biller dismissed it as a publicity stunt. Actually, the statement was only the beginning of a lengthy process. The USPS drew up a list of personality traits that might indicate a potential killer, including a history of violent behavior, a fascination with semiautomatic weapons, an obsession with homicidal workplace incidents, a history of drug abuse, and an inability to take constructive criticism. In 1997, the USPS created teams around the country to look for employees with these traits. Nine more workers would go berserk and nine more employees would be killed, but by the end of the decade, the incidents had all but stopped.

Meanwhile, the raging postal worker became a cultural stereotype. In 1993, the *St. Petersburg Times* came up with the term "going postal" to describe what mailmen like McIlvane had done. The rampages inspired "Postal," a best-selling video game about a murderous postal worker. The APWU boycotted the game, but the publicity only seemed to fuel its sales. Newman, a maniacal letter carrier played by Wayne Knight, appeared on the popular NBC sitcom *Seinfeld* in 1992. In a 1993 episode entitled "The Old Man," Newman revealed his occupation. "I'm a United States postal worker."

"Aren't they the guys that always go crazy and come back with a gun and shoot everybody?" George Costanza asked with his usual lack of tact.

Newman's face darkened. "Sometimes," he replied.

"Why *is* that?" Jerry wondered.

"Because the mail never stops," Newman said, growing agitated. "It just keeps coming and coming, there's never a letup. It's relentless. Every day it piles up more and more and more! And you gotta get it out, but the more you get out, the more it keeps coming in. And then the bar code reader breaks and it's Publisher's Clearing House day."

As funny as Newman could be, such characterizations mortified real postal workers. It was bad enough when Federal Express ran advertisements depicting them as lazy; now a growing segment of Americans seemed to view them as lunatics. The USPS did everything it could to discourage use of the term "going postal." But people would continue to use it as a synonym for out-of-control behavior long after violence in post offices had dissipated and the USPS was overwhelmed by another crisis. This one would be more existential.

11

You've Got Mail!

It rained nearly every day in the Chiloé Archipelago off the coast of southern Chile where Gene Johnson served as a U.S. Peace Corps volunteer in 1962. He had left the United States a Democrat, but during his year in Chile he read *Atlas Shrugged* by the libertarian author Ayn Rand and became a Republican. When he came home, Johnson organized a group of Peace Corps veterans to campaign for Barry Goldwater, the party's presidential candidate in 1964. He could find only five of them, but they were an enthusiastic little group.

Johnson fared better in 1968 when Nixon ran for president. This time, Johnson worked as an advance man, and his candidate won the election. He and his wife decided to see what life was like in Washington, and with friends in Republican circles, Johnson found a job in 1971 at the U.S. Postal Service. "I was the last political appointee because they switched to a quasi-public operation," Johnson says with a laugh.

The USPS put Johnson in charge of a new department called Advanced Services, devoted to exploring futuristic mail services. Johnson tried fax mail, but it was too slow. "It took six minutes a page to send through the system," he says. "The technology was not there." He developed the Mailgram, which allowed people to have telegrams delivered by letter carriers, much like the system proposed by John Wanamaker seven decades earlier. In 1978, the USPS delivered 32 million Mailgrams, but that barely registered at an agency that transported 97 billion pieces of mail that year.

Johnson needed to come up with something much bigger. The USPS was losing vast amounts of money at the time, and its future looked even worse. The previous year, a congressionally appointed committee led by Gaylord Freeman, the former chairman of First National Bank of Chicago, had predicted that the USPS would lose 23 percent of its first-class mail by 1985 as people began paying their bills electronically and chatting with each other on networked computers. Freeman urged the USPS to start providing electronic mail if it wanted to survive the technological onslaught. "Unless the Postal Service really makes a commitment, which it has not made, to electronic message transfer, they face a really bleak future," he warned.

Fortunately, Johnson was working on just such a project. It was called Electronic Computer Originated Mail, or E-COM for short. The postal service's big customers, like banks and insurance companies, prepared most of their mail on computers. Rather than printing it out and mailing it themselves, Johnson wanted them to transmit it electronically to the USPS's Sperry Rand Univac 1108 computer system in Middletown, Virginia. From there, the postal service would send it to post offices around the country where clerks would print out the letters, seal them in envelopes, and pass them on to letter carriers who would deliver these missives to people's homes and businesses. "There was billions of billions of billions of pieces that were computer-generated and could be sent directly from the computer into the Postal Service and sent out to the post offices for printing and delivering," Johnson says.

E-COM wasn't terribly fast—the USPS promised two-day delivery of the messages and hoped to reduce that to one day—but it was quicker than sending a letter across the country the old-fashioned way, which took three days. Johnson's superiors were enthusiastic about the plan. Postmaster General William Bolger said the USPS could charge 15 cents for these messages, the same as a first-class letter. "If you had the volume to support it we could do it for 10 or 11 cents," Bolger added.

Almost immediately, there were howls from the private sector. Companies like AT&T complained that E-COM was just a step away from the kind of computer-to-computer e-mail that it hoped one day to provide. AT&T didn't want to have to compete with the postal service, a government agency with its own police force. What if the USPS decided to enforce its monopoly in this new medium?

The USPS insisted it had no plans to get into e-mail, but it didn't matter. The Postal Rate Commission, which had to approve the proposal, subjected E-COM to a contentious 15-month review. "I spent 20 days on the witness stand," Johnson recalls. "They asked me eight thousand questions." In the end, the PRC rejected the USPS's E-COM plan and offered its own instead. It refused to let the postal service create its own electronic network between post offices. Instead, the PRC wanted to open up the system to outside telecommunication companies and let them transmit E-COM messages. The USPS would just stuff the letters into envelopes and mailboxes.

Johnson was dumbfounded. The PRC's ruling might have pleased the postal service's critics, but it made E-COM more cumbersome to use and much more expensive. The USPS would now have to charge 26 cents for a single E-COM letter. Johnson didn't see how it could survive now.

Even so, the postal service signed up customers like Merrill Lynch, Shell Oil, the AFL-CIO, the Equitable Life Assurance Society, Hallmark Cards, and the Moral Majority, then a prominent lobbying group for the Christian right. On January 4, 1982, William Bolger sent the first official E-COM from a terminal in Washington: "We are very proud of this milestone in the history of the Postal Service and pleased to share this occasion with you through this message."

The USPS sent only three million E-COM messages in the first year and 15 million in the next. In 1984, the number reached 23 million, but that wasn't enough to make money. The *Washington Post* reported that E-COM's biggest customer was Automotive Incentive, a direct mail car sales company in a Detroit suburb. It spewed out electronically generated junk mail: "This is your PER-SONAL INVITATION to ATTEND the GREATEST AUTOMOTIVE INVENTORY REDUCTION SALE in the HISTORY OF MANASSAS. The Manassas Dealers involved MUST SELL 500 vehicles immediately!!"

In 1985, the USPS canceled the service, having lost $40 million on it. "A lot of people blamed it on the postal service, but it was really the Postal Rate Commission that screwed it up," says Johnson, who had departed by then to work for International Telephone & Telegraph. "It just got so bastardized it didn't work at all." (A decade later, Johnson and another former USPS executive founded a company called Mail2000, which followed virtually the same business model as E-COM. They ended up selling it to UPS for $100 million.)

The failure of E-COM would haunt the USPS, which largely avoided electronic mail through the rest of the decade. It was clearly a risk for the postal service to dabble in this technology, and there didn't seem to be a pressing need. The dire predictions of the decline of first-class mail hadn't come true. Instead of vanishing in the 1980s, first-class mail rose from 48 billion pieces in 1980 to 89 billion pieces in 1990 during the bountiful Reagan years.

Yes, first-class mail was becoming a slightly smaller percentage of the overall volume, thanks to the junk mail revolution, but during this period, the postal service's biggest problem was finding better ways to move hard copy mail, not worrying about the arrival of the electronic kind, which now seemed like something that wouldn't happen for years to come. "Rightly or wrongly, I didn't spend much time on electronic mail," says former postmaster general Anthony Frank. "I spent more time trying to get the public and business to use bar codes."

By the early 1990s, the situation had changed. A British scientist had invented the World Wide Web and people had begun to talk about "surfing the Internet." America Online started mailing people disks that they could stick into their computers to set up e-mail accounts using dial-up connections. Soon, it had a million members.

E-mail was described as something life-changing and even addictive. "I'd rather give up my telephone than my e-mail," wrote *Newsday* technology columnist Josh Quittner.

Frank's successor Marvin Runyon paid close attention to it all. Appointed in 1992, the 67-year-old Runyon had long silver hair and sideburns. He commuted home on the weekends to his house on a hillside outside Nashville, with a mirrored exercise room equipped with $40,000 worth of Nautilus equipment. After reading the New Age health guru Deepak Chopra, Runyon told a reporter he thought he could live to the age of 120. (He died in 2004 of lung disease, missing the target by 41 years.)

Runyon had made a name for himself as chairman of the Tennessee Valley Authority (TVA), a public corporation on which the Kappel Commission had modeled the organizational structure of the postal service. As the TVA's chief executive, Runyon earned the nickname, "Carvin' Marvin," for slashing 11,000 jobs as part of a turnaround. He had to travel with bodyguards after that, but his knife-wielding impressed some people. In 1992, Bert Mackie, a member of the USPS's board of governors, read a profile of Runyon in an airline magazine on a flight back from Washington to his home in Oklahoma and decided that "Carvin' Marvin" was just what the postal service needed.

The USPS delivered 171 billion pieces of mail in 1993, Runyon's first full year. While junk mail rose by a healthy five percent that first year, the growth of first-class mail was slowing compared with the 1980s. This was troubling because first-class mail paid for nearly three-quarters of the agency's costs. The USPS made $49 billion that year, but it lost $1.2 billion.

Runyon lived up to his nickname. In his first few weeks, he offered early buyouts to 30,000 middle managers. However, the unions demanded the same buyout for their members, and in the end, 47,828 employees departed, many of them carriers and clerks whose loss forced the USPS to pay a considerable amount of overtime to deliver all that mail promptly. "We needed a surgeon and we got

Freddy Krueger," said Vince Palladino, president of the National Association of Postal Supervisors.

But Runyon also wanted to bring in more money. Post offices started selling T-shirts, neckties, and coffee mugs decorated with the USPS logo and images of stamps. In search of another philatelic hit, Runyon approved a stamp honoring Bugs Bunny, a first for the postal service, which had never issued a stamp with a cartoon character before. Some serious collectors were aghast. "It's impossible for me to see that this is anything but a crass commercial campaign that takes away from the higher purpose of the stamp program," said Kathleen Wunderly, educational director for the American Philatelic Society. Bugs Bunny didn't top Elvis Presley, but he performed well for the USPS. The postal service printed 265 million of the 32-cent Bugs Bunny stamps and had to produce 100 million more to meet the demand.

Runyon also wanted the postal service to extend its reach to the Internet. In 1993, he hired the USPS's first chief president of technology applications to create products for the digital age. His name was Robert Reisner.

A baby-faced 46-year-old with an undergraduate degree from Yale University and an MBA from Harvard, Reisner was working as a consultant on the privatization of a government-owned telephone company in the former Soviet Union when he got a call from a head-hunter working for the USPS. From his office in Washington, he had figured out how to hook the phone system up to an old Sputnik satellite so users could make international calls. "It was pretty wild," Reisner recalls. His next step was to move to Russia and run the company, which didn't excite him as much. The postal service's job offer intrigued him, and he took it.

Some of Reisner's new colleagues greeted him skeptically. "You know why we hired you, don't you?" the head of the engineering department asked him. "So we can fire you."

"Really?" Reisner replied.

"Yeah, we can't do that with someone who's been with us for 25 years. They don't want to *do* these things. They just want to talk about them."

That was nothing compared with the disbelief Reisner encountered from the technology industry. Some laughed outright at the idea of the lumbering USPS trying to compete with nimble start-ups, but it didn't bother Reisner. "I don't think we're going to convince the net culture that we're cool," he said. "But we're not going to go away."

Some of his early efforts were awkward. Reisner helped the USPS launch its first website in 1994. "The Postal Service is on the information superhighway," the agency declared in a quaintly worded press release. "We have linked to the Internet World Wide Web, or Web for short. . . . Web users can view vast amounts of information in a user-friendly format and can jump to related information with just the click of a mouse button." Visitors to the site could look up zip codes and take a postal history quiz, but they couldn't buy stamps online yet.

Reisner worked with Time Warner on a short-lived experiment enabling the company's cable television customers in Orlando, Florida, to use their remote controls to shop for groceries that the USPS would deliver. Time Warner lost millions of dollars and ended up canceling it. Reisner oversaw an effort to put 10,000 Internet-connected kiosks in post offices so that customers without computers could access the Web, but the devices sat unused in dingy lobbies. "It's like a pay phone," Reisner laments. "If you put it behind a pillar, nobody uses it. So you have to put kiosks in the right place, and it sounds silly, but you have to have someone plug it in, and you have to have a barker to show people that they can get things on it." Presumably, the USPS couldn't count on its window clerks to step in; it was difficult enough just to get them to smile at customers.

However, Reisner developed practical ideas like a digital postmark that would certify e-mail just as the traditional postmark did with paper envelopes. He hoped it would enable law firms to file court documents online. The USPS also started a service allowing customers to create flyers and catalogs on their home computers and e-mail them to the USPS, which delivered them as hard copy. As far as Reisner was concerned, these things all fit the agency's mission to bind the nation together by enabling citizens to correspond with each other. "I gave some speeches and talked about how the postal service has changed its technology many times," he recalls. "We need to understand that we're moving into an era in which correspondence isn't going to flip from paper to electronic. It's going to flip back and forth and we need to have an agile service."

The USPS also tried to defend itself against the inevitable spread of electronic bill payment by purchasing, from American Express in New York, a company that opened envelopes with checks, scanned them with optical character readers, and sent them electronically to banks. "The core technology was ours. We bloody well invented it," says Cathy Rogerson, the postal service's head of new business at the time. "Reading a check is just like reading an envelope. There's nobody better at that than the postal service."

But others felt just as strongly that the USPS was straying from its mission. "This thing doesn't need reinventing," said Robert Setrakian, a USPS board member who clashed with Runyon. "Its mission is hard copy delivery, and all it needs to do is to be sure it gets there." Edward Gleiman, chairman of the Postal Rate Commission, warned of another disaster like E-COM if the USPS wasn't reined in. "It is at a crossroads with no signpost," he testified at a congressional hearing. "Do we want the postal service to limit its focus to its historical mission—the delivery of hard copy mail? Do we want it to become a lean mean collection processing and delivery machine, which probably means little growth and eventual downsizing? Or do we want it to attempt to compete in new technologies and enter fields heretofore foreign to it? If it pursues new, competitive markets, will it be more or less likely to perform successfully?" Gleiman obviously didn't think so.

After a rocky beginning, Runyon restored the USPS to financial health. The agency enjoyed three years of budget surpluses starting in 1995. In the third year, the USPS delivered 190 billion pieces of mail, meaning that the average person received 712 items. First-class mail was barely 50 percent of the volume now; junk mail was 40 percent. But at least the postal service was no longer awash in red ink.

Meanwhile, the dot-com boom was now in full swing. America Online, now known as AOL, had 13 million members in 1998 and inspired a hit romantic comedy entitled "You've Got Mail," about two bookstore owners who fall in love while exchanging e-mail. New Web-based companies materialized, offering other digital postal services. Evite, iRSVP, and TimeDance provided online invitations. Internet users could sign up for e-card services offered by various online companies, and send digital postcards and Valentine's Day and Christmas salutations.

Reisner was now the postal service's vice president of strategy, and he was more convinced than ever that the USPS needed to be part of this revolution. But it seemed as though everywhere he turned, somebody was telling him to forget about it. The banking industry was adamantly opposed to the USPS's check scanning project. The technology industry wanted the postal service to stay away from the Internet. "Silicon Valley had a pretty strong lobby," Reisner says. "It was arguing that the postal service shouldn't do it." Federal Express and UPS joined the campaign to rein in the postal service, arguing that it was using money from its monopoly business of delivering letters to enter new markets where it didn't belong.

Still, Reisner was stunned when the Government Accountability Office audited the USPS's new services and issued a report in 1998, saying they had lost $84.7 million in three years. Reisner still gets upset talking about this. He says his projects were still in their infancy, and it wasn't fair for anybody to expect them to be profitable yet. What's more, the ruling came in a year when the USPS made $60 billion and had a surplus of

$550 million. "You're telling me that we shouldn't have spent $84 million trying to better understand a technology that is going to ultimately cannibalize our core products?" Reisner asks.

The same year, Runyon resigned and, soon after, he joined the board of Stamps.com, a successful startup that allowed customers to purchase stamps online and print them from their computers. Its investors included Microsoft co-founder Paul Allen. This might have seemed like a natural business for the USPS, but it feared that private companies would complain that it was abusing its monopoly privileges.

The Board of Governors didn't want to bring in another head-strong outsider like Runyon so it elevated William Henderson, USPS's chief operating officer. Henderson must have seemed like a safe choice. An affable 50-year old who had a priestly forehead and wore bowties, Henderson was a lifelong USPS employee and a second generation one at that. His father had been a railway mail clerk in North Carolina. "He was very devoted," Henderson says. "Those were the days when the trains would come along and pick up mailbags, and he would come home raving mad if a postmaster forgot to leave his out."

Henderson had distinguished himself in the 1990s as the post-master of Greensboro, North Carolina where he promised customers that they wouldn't have to wait in line at post offices for more than five minutes. He also sent supervisors out to bring them their mail if it was delivered to the wrong address; Henderson says it didn't happen very often. "The carriers are pretty damn accurate," he says. "We did have a carrier who was dyslexic and transposing numbers, but there was no rampant issue."

As it turned out, Henderson was more enamored with the Internet than his predecessor. He could see that online shopping was boosting the USPS's package business. So Henderson struck up a relationship with Jeff Bezos, chief executive of Amazon.com. The USPS promoted Amazon in its television ads and talked about building a distribution center across the street from its Seattle headquarters, but UPS was able to move faster and grabbed the site instead.

Henderson had a plan for every American to get a free e-mail address with the suffix .us tied to the physical address. "It would have been a great opportunity for the postal service," Henderson says. "If we could control millions of mailboxes in the United States effectively, we can certainly control e-mail addresses." (The USPS also briefly entertained the idea of giving its customers e-mail addresses composed of their first initials, their nine-digit zip code, and the last two numbers of their street address. Here's how it would have worked for President Bill Clinton. His address at the White House was 1600 Pennsylvania Avenue, Washington, DC 20500-0003. That would have made his e-mail bc20500000300@usps.com.)

Technology lobbyists and their allies in Congress vehemently objected. Representative Christopher Cox, a California Republican, introduced an amendment prohibiting the USPS from using the suffix .us. "The U.S. Postal Service won't become the U.S. Portal Service," his office said. There was a similar uproar when the USPS started an online bill-paying venture with a company called Check-Free. The Computer and Communications Industry Association, a lobbying group representing companies such as Yahoo and Netscape, said the private sector should handle this. "We don't need a big, heavy, stifling competitor, subsidized by public funds, trying to compete in some of the most dynamic areas of our economy," said Ed Black, the association's president. "They could have a big negative impact."

Ultimately, Henderson decided that the only way for the postal service to survive and prosper in the Internet era was to give up its letter monopoly and become a private company. "It was my belief that the monopoly was worthless," he says. "It was really an impediment to making changes." At this point, he says, nobody could process letters as efficiently as the USPS, which was now feeding two-thirds of them through optical character readers. There was an example to follow overseas. Germany had decided to privatize Deutsche Post, its government-operated postal service. But rather than simply stripping the Deutsche Post of its letter monopoly, the German government allowed it to use cash flow from its traditional mail business to finance its transformation. Two years earlier, Deutsche Post purchased 51 percent of DHL, which enabled it to become a global delivery service. Then in 2000, it conducted its first public stock offering, selling 30 percent of its shares and raising $5.6 billion. (Two years later, Deutsche Post would spend $568 million for an additional 25 percent of DHL.)

At Henderson's request, Reisner drew up a privatization plan referred to as "the endgame strategy." Reisner began talking to Gary Gensler, the Treasury Department's undersecretary for domestic finance, about how it might work. In 2000, Henderson and Reisner met with Elaine Kamarck, a senior staff member in the Clinton administration. Kamarck listened as Reisner talked about the USPS's challenges and raised the possibility of privatization. Then she reminded them that Vice President Al Gore was running for president. "Well, we would have to ask our union friends," she said. "You know, they are critical to the upcoming campaign." Soon after, Gensler called Reisner and told him there would be no more discussions about privatization. "We're putting this on the back burner," Gensler said.

It was always clear to Henderson that the postal workers' union had more political influence with the Clinton White House than he did. One time, Henderson was eating lunch in Washington with the NALC's president Vincent Sombrotto. The labor leader interrupted their conversation to take a call from Clinton himself. "I mean, I couldn't really remember [Clinton] ever calling me," Henderson says.

After three years, Henderson resigned as postmaster general in 2001. "I had gone to the White House," Henderson says. " I had talked to Congress. The customers weren't receptive either. They just wanted us to deliver mail." (In 2006, he took a job as chief operating officer of Netflix, another Internet company that was a heavy user of the mail.) Reisner also departed that year and went back to the consulting business. Sometimes, he advised foreign posts about how to create new kinds of services in the age of the Internet. Unlike in America, people in European countries and Canada didn't think that the government was intrinsically bad and the private sector was inherently good. So the postal services in these countries encountered less resistance as they moved away from solely delivering paper-based mail. They were eager to get ideas from Reisner who had held a high position at the world's largest mail delivery operation.

The USPS would now take the approach that Reisner's critics had advised. There would be no more risky digital initiatives. The postal service would focus on delivering the mail and forget about the Internet. It would also have to reduce its costs. In 2001 the USPS lost money, first-class mail started to decline and the GAO put it on its list of high-risk federal agencies, fearing that it might not be able to cover the health care costs of retired letter carriers and clerks in the coming decades. The GAO estimated that these expenses could be as high as $32 billion. That year, the USPS appointed Jack Potter, a hefty former letter carrier from the Bronx with a sonorous New York accent, as its new postmaster general. It would be up to him to streamline hard copy delivery and balance the budget.

Potter's job was complicated by the terrorist attacks on September 11, 2001. That morning, he was at a board meeting at the USPS headquarters in L'Enfant Plaza. His secretary summoned him to take an emergency telephone call in his office. When he returned, Potter told the board that two planes had hit the World Trade Center in New York. Fifteen minutes later, everyone in the room watched through the window in disbelief as a third hit the Pentagon. The FAA grounded all planes. From an emergency command center in the basement, Potter and his aides hastily arranged for a fleet of trucks to keep the mail moving.

That afternoon, people in Brooklyn who had watched the Twin Towers fall were relieved by the sight of letter carriers stoically making their rounds, which gave them the sense that the country was still functioning. Potter himself emerged in October as an unlikely hero after a wave of anthrax attacks unnerved the nation again. A reporter at the *National Enquirer* in Tampa, Florida, received an anthrax-laced letter and died. Similar letters were sent to U.S. Senator Thomas Daschle and NBC news anchor Tom Brokaw. Two mail clerks who worked in a processing plant in the Brentwood neighborhood in Washington, D.C., died of anthrax inhalation.

Rather than tell the public that they had nothing to fear when they went to the mailbox, Potter admitted he wasn't sure. "The chances are very, very slim," he said. "Again, people should do things that are safe and when they handle mail, they should wash their hands." Potter also worked closely with union leaders to assure workers, who were provided with gloves and facemasks, that everything would be OK. "It was Potter and Vince Sombrotto," says George Gould, the NALC's legislative director at the time. "You know, there was a lot of fear and if they hadn't shown that kind of leadership, it would've been a disaster. They went around the country together and talked to groups of letter carriers and other postal employees and just let them know that they had a plan and they were going to work together and not let it happen again." William Burrus, who succeeded Moe Biller as the APWU's president that year, feels similarly: "I give Potter credit. He steered the institution through it."

Because of 9/11 and an economic recession, the USPS's total volume fell in 2002 to 203 billion pieces, down nearly five billion from the year before. But it rose again to 206 billion pieces in 2004 as the American economy recovered and the real estate market took off. Banks flooded people's homes with subprime mortgage offers and credit-card solicitations. In 2005, junk mail surpassed first class for the first time in history. It was a dubious milestone. For every piece of first-class mail that vanished, the USPS needed three junk items to make up the difference.

Still, Potter could boast that the USPS was delivering twice as much mail as it had twenty years earlier with the same number of employees. He introduced the Forever Stamp, which people would always be able to use to mail a letter no matter how much rates climbed. The Internet might have been hurting first-class mail growth, but it was rejuvenating the postal service's package business. Potter appeared before 15,000 cheering eBay users in Las Vegas to express his gratitude. "I have one message today for the entire eBay community," Potter said. "We, the Postal Service, we love you. We love every buyer, every seller, every power seller."

It appeared that Congress might finally do something to help the USPS too. For years, the USPS had complained that it was supposed to operate like a business, but it had to submit every proposed stamp price increase to the Postal Rate Commission for approval, a process that would drag on for months. The USPS couldn't offer discounts to the large companies as UPS and FedEx did, hindering its ability to compete with them.

In 2006, the Republican-controlled Congress passed the Postal Accountability and Enhancement Act, which granted some of Potter's wishes. It shifted the $27 billion in pension liabilities for workers with military service to the Department of Defense. It allowed the USPS to raise its rates without the commission's approval as long as they didn't exceed the Consumer Price Index, and it allowed the postal service to negotiate special deals for packages that didn't fall under its monopoly.

However, the new law strictly limited the USPS's mission to "the delivery of letters, printed matter, or mailable packages." In other words, the postal service was now legally forbidden to sell neckties in post offices, buy a check processing company, or create an e-mail service. The law also required the USPS to make annual payments of more than $5 billion a year for the next decade to build a fund to pay for the health care of its future retirees, which the GAO had estimated could cost as much as $32 billion. For some former postal service executives, it was a surreal moment. Essentially, Congress was making the postal service pay in advance for costs that it wouldn't have to make for decades. But in the age of the Internet, the USPS's future was uncertain, so the elected officials wanted to make sure it had the money in the bank no matter what.

Potter sounded ecstatic when President George W. Bush signed the bill. "We're planning for the future right now," he said. "Today, the postal service is operating in the black." But privately, Potter was grim. "I called Jack and said, 'Is this a good thing?'" William Henderson remembers, "and he said, 'No.'"

The USPS had no trouble making the payment that year as it delivered 213 billion pieces of mail, its historic peak. Then the economy collapsed, and the postal service lost more than a fifth of its volume in four years. The great migration to electronic bill paying finally occurred as companies and businesses tried to save money in the recession, which also ravaged the junk mail industry. In such a climate, the yearly health care prepayment became unaffordable, and it contributed heavily to the $20 billion in financial losses that the USPS suffered during this period. And the postal service wasn't alone. Hallmark shuttered greeting card plants and shed employees. Shares of Pitney Bowes, the postage-meter manufacturer, plunged. It seemed as if everybody in the mailing business was in pain.

At a press conference in Washington on March 2, 2010, a weary-looking Potter unveiled a plan to close rural post offices and end Saturday delivery. "We need to rethink everything and every approach to move the postal service forward," he said, trying to sound optimistic. "There are no sacred cows." But Potter didn't have the stomach to carry out these reforms. Six month later, he announced his retirement.

Could anybody fix the USPS? Its own studies indicated that the lost mail would never return. That year, the postal service's volume fell to 171 billion pieces, roughly what it had been in 1993. By 2020, the USPS predicted, it would decline to as little as 151 billion. Meanwhile, the number of addresses it had to service was steadily growing at a rate of one million a year as Americans built new homes and office buildings. That meant letter carriers were visiting more and more doorsteps with mailbags over their shoulders that were becoming lighter and lighter.

12

"Thank God for Amazon"

Cliff Island is 10 miles from Portland, Maine, in Casco Bay, but it feels farther away. The trip by ferry can take an hour and a half because the crew stops at several other islands along the way, dropping off passengers, groceries, and the mail. Once you arrive, it's hard to avoid the Cliff Island post office, which is just beyond the town dock, on the first floor of the recreation center. For 14 years, Anna Dyer, a soft-spoken woman with glasses and graying hair, was the island postmaster and a local institution. She knew everything about the island's nearly 60 year-round residents and quite a bit about the 250 summer people. She knew that the older people didn't like it when the USPS put Elvis Presley on a stamp. "He's a druggie," one woman complained. "It's outrageous that he's on a stamp."

"That's fine," Dyer answered, "but you know, everybody has their own ideas about that."

She had to enforce the USPS's rules, which became more rigid after 9/11 and the anthrax scare. There was no door-to-door delivery on Cliff Island, so everybody needed a post office box. Now Dyer had to ask people who wanted one for their IDs, even though she had known most of the islanders all her life. One woman refused to show her driver's license. "I've known you since you were a baby," she told Dyer. Dyer apologized, but insisted on seeing it anyway. "It was a tough transition for the community," she says. "Back in the day, it was a little bit looser."

Over time, Dyer came to know many people's secrets too. They came in for their mail and ended up talking about their problems. "I always thought I was the island psychiatrist," she says. "I think it was because people felt comfortable with me. They knew that things they said would never go further."

As time went on, Dyer had a complaint of her own. People were still coming in to check their mailboxes and confide in her, but they weren't buying anything. "People are using the computer to pay bills or they have auto-pay," she says. "There were days at the post office where I never sold a stamp." It was painful for Dyer. She loved using the mail, sending everybody on the island birthday cards, Halloween cards, Valentine's Day cards, and Christmas cards, carefully selecting the right stamps for the recipients. Dyer even had a pen pal in Scotland, with whom she had been exchanging letters since 1959. Her Scottish friend wanted to switch to e-mail now, but Dyer couldn't bring herself to do that.

Dyer felt the effects of the disappearing mail in other ways too. When she took over the post office in 1998, the USPS's district office in Portland was full of managers. But so many left because of budget cuts that it became difficult for Dyer to get anyone on the phone when she had a problem. So Dyer kept in touch with the other island postmasters in Casco Bay. If one of them had a problem with the office computer or the credit card machine, they would solve it together.

In July 2011, Dyer took the ferry into Portland with her husband, Bruce, who had a dentist's appointment. While Anna waited in the reception area, she checked her cell phone messages. Her supervisor had left one, saying that the Cliff Island post office was on a list of 3,700 that the USPS might close. Dyer had figured something like this would happen one day. Still, she was shocked. Cliff Island needed daily mail delivery. Without it, she feared, the island would become a more remote and less desirable place to live.

Dyer telephoned the other island postmasters to see what they had heard and found that their post offices were on the closure list too. Patrick Donahoe, the new postmaster general, said he was doing this to save the USPS, although many people would accuse him of trying to destroy it.

"Are you a fan of the Allman Brothers?" Donahoe asked. "They used to sing that song 'One Way Out.' There's a way out." It was early April 2011, and he sat in a blue leather chair in his wood-paneled office, surrounded by postal artifacts. There was a portrait of Benjamin Franklin on loan from the Smithsonian Institution and a bronze statue of a Pony Express rider. An automotive enthusiast, Donahoe had decorated his office with framed images of hot rod stamps.

A tall, broad-shouldered native of Pittsburgh with curly brown hair, Donahoe was surprisingly upbeat for someone in charge of an agency on the verge of bankruptcy. He conceded that letters were disappearing, but junk mail was coming back as the economy recovered from the recession, and packages continued to rise with the expanding e-commerce market.

Donahoe had a plan to shrink the USPS so it could survive on the remaining mail stream. He wanted to end Saturday delivery, which he said would save $3 billion dollars a year. Donahoe hoped to close money-losing post offices and shutter processing plants that were no longer needed. He was also negotiating new union contracts enabling the USPS to hire new workers at lower salaries. "Crisis, unfortunately, opens doors that ordinarily wouldn't be open to us," he said.

Donahoe was no stranger to anybody in the world of mail. He had spent his entire adult life in the postal service. In 1976, Donahoe was a 20-year-old student at the University of Pittsburgh. He had an after-school job at a W. T. Grant department store that paid $2.25 an hour. His uncle, a letter carrier, told him he could do better. "You ought to take the postal test," he told Donahoe. "The pay is $4.76 an hour." Donahoe breezed through the exam and started working afternoons at Pittsburgh's central sorting plant. He told himself he would stay until he graduated from college. "I just never left," he says, chuckling. "That's the story of a lot of people here."

The enormity of the postal service fascinated Donahoe. Every evening, trucks arrived at the plant with one million pieces of mail from Pittsburgh and the surrounding cities in western Pennsylvania. Donahoe and his coworkers sorted it by zip code and loaded it onto another fleet so it would be delivered all over the world. He felt a sense of achievement every night when it was done. Donahoe soon became a manager, overseeing men who operated 16 mechanical letter-sorting machines. When a postal worker died in a vehicular accident, Donahoe was charged with getting thousands of mail trucks inspected so it wouldn't happen again. As he put it, he was "trying to get things organized in a world that's not terribly organized."

Over the years, Donahoe became known as a crisis manager who could parachute into a dysfunctional district and get it running smoothly. In 1993, the USPS put him in charge of the Capitol district in Washington, D.C., where five out of ten letters arrived late. Clerks were rude to customers. Employees told congressional investigators that a high percentage of their coworkers were either drunk or stoned on the job. Donahoe discovered that the optical character readers were overriding bar codes and sending letters to the wrong addresses. "You had mail going all over the place for years!" Donahoe says. "People were like, 'Well, there's nothing we can do about it.' I was like, 'Ah, yes, there is!'" He had the clerks play role-playing games with each other so they would learn to be more polite to stamp buyers. When Donahoe departed in 1997, the district's on-time delivery rate had reached nine out of ten letters. He says the district's customer satisfaction scores had risen from "the mid-50s to up to the 90s."

When he became chief operating officer in 2001, Donahoe oversaw the cleanup of anthrax-contaminated facilities and the placement of biohazard detection systems. He also unveiled a plan to cut costs by $1 billon a year, which made his senior vice presidents gasp. There was only one way to get there. Eighty percent of every dollar spent by the USPS went to employees' salaries and benefits. Donahoe had to reduce the number of employees through attrition. Remarkably some plant managers still let clerks sort mail by hand because they didn't want them to lose their jobs. Donahoe put a stop to that. "It was like, push that volume into machines," he says. In 2000, the USPS had 901,238 employees. By the end of the decade, there were 671,687.

It would be up to Donahoe to sell his remedies to the American public and, more important, to their elected officials. He faced a divided Congress. Democrats controlled the U.S. Senate. Their party received the vast amount of contributions from postal workers' unions in the 2010 midterm election, so they were eager to support legislation that protected jobs. Senator Thomas Carper, a Democrat from Delaware, introduced a bill in May 2011 that would have relieved the postal service of its annual prefunding payment, sparing it the need to make painful cuts. "If we do nothing, we face a future without the valuable services that the postal service provides," Carper said.

The Republican majority in the House of Representatives, which had been elected the previous year, was less charitably inclined. Darrell Issa, a congressman from Southern California, was now chairman of the House Oversight and Government Reform Committee, which had jurisdiction over the USPS. He argued that anything that relieved the postal service of its $48 billion future health care obligation would be a taxpayer-funded "bailout." Instead, Issa wanted to treat the USPS's pending default as a bankruptcy. He proposed legislation to create a commission that would take over the agency's finances, nullify its union contracts, and lay off large numbers of employees. He advocated closing two post offices in every congressional district, although he sounded nervous about it. "Let's hope there's not one—or three—in mine," Issa said at a hearing. (A spokesman for Issa said he was trying to "introduce a bit of levity" into the proceedings and was fully in favor of closing post offices.)

Meanwhile, the White House seemed determined not to get involved. Two years earlier, President Barack Obama had offhandedly expressed impatience with the perennially troubled USPS at a rally for his health care proposal in Portsmouth, New Hampshire. "UPS and FedEx are doing just fine," he joked. "It's the post office that's always having problems." The NALC responded with an angry letter accusing the president of giving the agency "a kick in the chest." Now Obama remained silent, even though the White House quietly inserted language in its federal budget proposal absolving the USPS of all but $1.5 billion of the mandatory 2011 payment. That would enable it to muddle through for another year.

That July, Donahoe announced a list of 3,700 post offices under consideration for closing and said he hoped to make a final decision by the end of the year. He said the plan would save the USPS $500 million a year and argued that it didn't need as many post offices at a time when more than 35 percent of the postal service's stamp sales came from grocery stores, drugstores, office supply stores, ATMs, and the agency's own website, adding that the postal service would allow local store owners to sell stamps and accept packages in affected towns to soften the blow.

Many of the post offices on Donahoe's list were in forgotten towns with evocative names like Odd, West Virginia and Sleetmute, Alaska. Their residents may have purchased fewer stamps, but they couldn't imagine losing their local post office. People in small towns tended to think of their post office as a community center, a place where they mingle with their neighbors. In many parts of rural America, it was one of few places still open on the main street.

On a snowy Friday in November 2011, I drove to Redfield, New York, an hour north of Syracuse. Redfield had 550 residents and a post office on the closure list, and not much else. The hotel where people once held wedding receptions had closed after a fire several years before and never reopened. People driving through Redfield stopped at the nearby convenience store only to see a sign indicating that it was no longer in business. Locals said the owner had suffered a stroke the previous year and no one else had wanted to sell cigarettes and lottery tickets. There was a bar with a Budweiser sign outside welcoming hunters, but other than that, only the post office on the town square showed signs of life.

The following day, the sun came out and townspeople converged on the post office to check their P.O. boxes and mail packages. In Redfield, at least, the Saturday morning trip into town to get the mail was still a ritual. The recurring theme from the residents was that Redfield was dying and, without the post office, most people would leave. There was no cell phone service in the town. If people wanted to pay their bills on the Internet, they had to use slow dial-up connections. In the 1960s, rural Americans worried that their towns would lose their names to the zip code. These days, the people of Redfield feared losing their zip code if the post office closed.

The U.S. Postal Service assured Redfield's citizens that they would get home delivery if the post office was shut down, but that didn't make anybody happy. Redfield typically gets several feet of snow in the winter, and it buries people's mailboxes. So nearly everybody had a P.O. box. "This morning, there were 10 inches of new snow," said Tanya Yerdon, the town supervisor. "I go out and plow and the last thing I want to worry about is hitting the damn mailbox."

Similar complaints, large and small, were heard in the other towns with endangered post offices. In South Bethlehem, Pennsylvania, angry residents protested the proposed closing of their local post office at a meeting with USPS officials. "We are adamantly opposed to it," said Dana Grubb, president of the local historical society. In many towns, residents circulated petitions. "We're not going to take this lying down," said Philip Lack, a retired college professor in

Orchard, Iowa. "Besides the social aspect, there is also a community bulletin board where people can see what's going on. It's just a nice thing to have in town." In Breaks, Virginia, Keith Mullins, a retired coal miner, decried the USPS's plan. "We ain't started carrying no picket signs or throwing rocks yet," he said. "Maybe in the future."

In December, twenty Democratic senators wrote to Donahoe asking him to delay his ruling for five months. Shortly afterward, Senator Max Baucus, a Montana Democrat and chairman of the Senate Finance Committee, invited Donahoe to visit Ingomar, a town in his state with an endangered post office. In April, Baucus paraded Donahoe though the tiny post office, trailed by the local press corps. Then Baucus and Donahoe spoke to 150 anxious people in the school gymnasium. Donahoe listened patiently as the silver-haired senator played to the crowd. "It doesn't make sense for the financial problems of the postal service to be solved on the backs of the rural communities of America," Baucus said. He noted that the USPS operated 50 post offices in the nation's capital and wondered why Donahoe didn't close some of those instead.

Donahoe tried to explain the Internet had devastated the postal service's most profitable business. "We've lost about 27 percent of our first-class mail," he said.

But most of his listeners didn't seem interested in the postal service's problems. "I need you to really consider what we are saying," said a woman from a town with no Internet service. "People need their rural post offices."

Another woman said the USPS needed to start selling merchandise in post offices again as it had in the 1990s. "You used to sell teacups and T-shirts," she said. "That was awesome."

"We've had some issues with people not wanting us to do that," Donahoe said.

Baucus made Donahoe promise in front of the crowd that he wouldn't make a final decision on his post office closing plan without consulting the Senate first. By then, it was an academic point anyway. The following month, Donahoe scrapped his closure plan and announced another to reduce window hours in 13,000 rural post offices, in some cases to as few as two hours a day. Ultimately, he said the USPS would save the same amount of money, but the capitulation showed how weak the postmaster general was politically.

Donahoe's proposal to end Saturday delivery of letters, but not packages, didn't fare any better. Polls showed that at least 70 percent of Americans didn't mind giving up Saturday delivery if it helped the financially troubled USPS. However, the greeting card and junk mail lobbies opposed it. So did letter carriers who feared their jobs were at risk. Donahoe tried to explain his thinking in Buffalo to 2,500 rural letter carriers gathered for their annual convention in August 2012. "Right now, 70% of Americans pay bills online," Donahoe said. "If you go back to the year 2000, only 5% paid their bills online. That's a lot of 45-cent stamps, billions of them, which we are no longer selling." But the rural carriers booed Donahoe when he brought up five-day delivery. Then they gave a standing ovation to a local congressman who had called for the postmaster general's resignation because the USPS was targeting a local mail processing plant for possible closure.

The same summer, Fredric Rolando, president of the NALC, used the issue to rally his members at their convention in Minneapolis. He lamented that the USPS was "insolvent," that Congress was "deadlocked and dysfunctional . . . especially when it came to postal issues," and that the White House was "like a deer frozen in the headlights." Worst of all, Rolando said, Donahoe had joined with House Republicans in a plan to "dismantle the postal service." "If we let nature take its course, we won't be fighting five-day delivery," Rolando warned. "We'll be fighting three-day delivery or worse. And we won't be fighting for a better contract. We'll be fighting for any kind of contract."

In August 2012, the USPS defaulted on its $5.6 annual retiree health care prepayment. One might have anticipated that this would have a sobering effect on the debate about the USPS's future. After all, an enormous federal agency, the second-largest civilian employer after Wal-Mart, had just effectively declared bankruptcy. Perhaps now Donahoe's pleas for help would get a fair hearing in Washington.

Instead, critics of Donahoe's plan redoubled their efforts. Lobbyists for Hallmark Cards worked the halls of Congress and pushed members to oppose his plan to eliminate Saturday delivery. Maynard Benjamin, CEO of the Envelope Manufacturers Association, joined the battle. "The least-used delivery day is Tuesday, and mail builds up on Thursdays and Fridays," he said. "Why did they throw Saturday under the bus?"

In the spring of 2013, the NALC organized rallies around the country to save Saturday delivery. In Perth Amboy, New Jersey, 1,200 letter carriers and their supporters dressed in red-white-and-blue T-shirts emblazoned with the slogan "Delivering for America," and chanted "USA for six days!" As *Newsweek* had put it in the late 1940s, "postmanitis" was still contagious. Several congressmen spoke at the event. "You are the ones [who] for 200 years have gone to every home in America six days a week tying this country together, building communities, making sure that everybody stays in touch, not skimming the cream off the top and just talking to the big money folks or expensive businesses—no, everybody," said U.S. Representative Rush Holt, a New Jersey Democrat. "That's what sets you apart."

At a rally in Raleigh, North Carolina, Craig Schadewald, vice president of the state's NALC chapter, shouted, "Neither rain, nor snow, nor the postmaster general's misguided plan will stay these supporters from protecting six-day delivery." Meanwhile, in Roanoke, Virginia, 91-year-old James Rademacher came out on a snowy day to join local union members at a protest. "If they open the door here for eliminating one day, we're in trouble," he said. He added that he could have been home watching college basketball, but as a former letter carrier, he had to stand up for six-day delivery. "It's in my blood," Rademacher said. "That's why I'm here. I believe in this."

In March 2013, Republicans from rural districts joined forces with liberal Democrats and reaffirmed six-day delivery in the annual appropriations bill, dooming Donahoe's cost-cutting plan. It didn't seem to matter that around the world, postal services were making similar cuts in the face of declining mail volumes. New Zealand announced it would move to three-day delivery in cities and five days in rural areas to avoid a financial crisis. Canada said it would end home delivery in urban areas over the coming five years. Australia Post asked its customers if they would be willing to pay the equivalent of $26 a year for five-day delivery. If not, the Australian postal service wondered if they would accept three-day delivery instead. It decided to stick with free six-day delivery, but the questionnaire suggested that delivery changes were inevitable in a time of dwindling mail.

Meanwhile, many foreign postal services were closing their post offices and moving their operations into local stores. "At the end of this year, we will only have 30 post offices left in Norway," said Norway Post's chief executive officer Dag Mejdell in a 2014 interview. "The rest are 1,400 postal shops, which are basically retailers that run small postal operations, where you can buy your stamps and pick up your parcels. That has helped. We used to have 35 mail [processing plants] in Norway. Now we have nine."

At the same time, foreign postal services were using the savings to develop the kind of digital services that the USPS had tried to introduce in the 1990s only to be slapped down. Itella, the Finnish postal service, keeps a digital archive of its users' mail for seven years and helps them pay bills online securely. Swiss Post lets customers choose if they want their mail delivered at home in hard copy or scanned and sent to their preferred Internet-connected device. They can also decline junk mail deliveries.

Sweden's PostNord has developed an app that enables users to send physical postcards from their smartphones. It has also developed technology allowing them to send letters without stamps. PostNord texts them a numerical code that they can jot down on envelopes instead. "The customers are all on these digital interfaces now," says Anders Åsberg, PostNord's head of marketing and development. "That's where the growth is going to be in the future."

But for Donahoe making any of these changes seemed impossible. In November 2013, he unveiled a plan to open post offices in stores owned by Staples, the office supply chain. "Staples is open seven days a week, they're open nine o'clock at night," he said. "They like the foot traffic." However, Donahoe soon found himself in another labor battle, this time with the APWU. Two months earlier, the union had elected Mark Dimondstein, a former aide to Moe Biller, as its new president. During the election, Dimondstein sued the APWU to get its e-mail lists because he complained it was too expensive to send voters letters. He won the case.

After his electoral victory, Dimondstein called for a boycott of Staples. "This is a direct assault on our jobs and on *public* postal services," he said. Union members picketed stores, prompting the American Federation of Teachers to tell its members not to buy back-to-school supplies there. It was too much for Staples; the company canceled its plan for the in-store post offices. The APWU may no longer have had as many members as in Biller's heyday, but it was still the largest postal workers' union, with nearly 200,000 members, and it could make life difficult for Donahoe.

Donahoe remained surprisingly ebullient for someone with a myriad of problems. In 2013, the total mail volume fell to 158 billion pieces, roughly the same as it had been a quarter of a century ago, and the USPS defaulted for the second year in a row on its annual $5.6 billion retiree health care prepayment. Congress was still deadlocked on postal reform; there wasn't much Donahoe could do about that. "We talk to the White House people," he said. "I've met the president, but I've not talked to him about it. Believe me, he has much bigger issues than the postal service."

There was one reason for the postmaster general to be hopeful. Thanks to the rise of online shopping, package volume rose that year by six percent to three billion items. It seemed as though the dying institution still had a pulse. "There's a little saying that we have," Donahoe said. "The Internet giveth and the Internet taketh away. We've lost a substantial part of our letter business, but e-commerce has been great for us."

The USPS was already delivering smaller parcels for UPS and FedEx. Then in November 2014, Donahoe announced that the USPS would deliver packages on Sundays for Amazon.com, ending the century old ban on Sunday mail delivery. The postal service could manage this because of its new labor contracts, which required new employees to work early mornings, evenings and Sundays when veterans would have been automatically entitled to overtime. In another era, the unions surely would have resisted, but now they conceded that the USPS needed more freedom in the digital age. "We did this with the idea that we were going to have some non-traditional deliveries—evening deliveries, Sunday deliveries," says Jim Sauber, the NALC's chief of staff.

That Christmas, UPS and FedEx were overwhelmed by Amazon orders and delivered many of them late, much to the displeasure of the e-commerce giant. The USPS, on the other hand, had a smooth holiday season because of its new Sunday workforce. "We did get a rush of packages at the end, and our people came through," Donahoe said. "As a matter of fact, we delivered over 100,000 packages on Christmas day."

Since then, the unlikely relationship between the futuristic retailer and America's oldest federal agency has only grown closer. In 2014, Amazon built a network of more than 15 sorting centers where it separates packages and then trucks them directly to post offices; the government's carriers then take them the last mile. Amazon plans to build more of these plants around the country, weaving its operations more intimately into those of the USPS. The postal service won't say how many packages it carries for Amazon; Amazon doesn't even respond to calls to its press office about this. But David Vernon, an analyst at Bernstein Research who tracks the shipping industry, estimates that in 2014, the USPS handled 40 percent of Amazon's packages—almost 150 million—more than either UPS or FedEx.

In October 2014, the USPS started another service with Amazon that harked back to its failed partnership with Time Warner in the 1990s. In cities such as San Francisco and New York, letter carriers arrive on doorsteps as early as 3 AM with groceries for Amazon customers who ordered them the night before. "I never thought I would order groceries and have them delivered to my house, but people do it," Donahoe says. "It's amazing."

A visit to the Franklin Delano Roosevelt Post Office in Manhattan shows how Amazon is reshaping the postal service. When the FDR Post Office was completed in 1968, the four-story building on Third Avenue was a post office and a processing center filled with clerks sorting letters, first at pigeonhole cases and later using machines equipped with an optical character reader. The clerks worked three shifts, but as the mail volume dropped, the USPS shut down the building's processing operation, leaving much of the cavernous building vacant. For a time, it even thought about renting out the space to a big box retailer like Staples. What else could it have done with all that empty space in the heart of Manhattan?

Now the upper floors of FDR Post Office have been converted into package handling operation. Jesse Garrett, a postal service supervisor who oversees Sunday delivery in Manhattan, enjoys seeing the building come back to life. A third-generation postal worker from Oklahoma, the 32-year-old Garrett came to New York City to be a record producer and instead ended up taking a job delivering parcels for the USPS in 2007. "It was down, down, down, bad, bad, bad," Garrett recalls. "People used to pay bills with first-class mail, and they don't do that anymore. The post office's number one product was going away."

Garrett became a supervisor, and in 2013, the USPS put him in charge of Sunday delivery at the FDR Post Office. "All of a sudden, we became the premiere package delivery company, in large part, due to our partnership with Amazon and our willingness to go to seven days," he says. "Every day, you hear, 'Thank God for Amazon.'"

Garrett has assembled a team of recently hired carriers to handle new kinds of delivery from Sunday to same-day to groceries. One is a former Bank of America employee laid off during the financial crisis. Another is an ex-exotic dancer searching for more than tips. Then there is Shante Sapp, a 29-year-old former nurse who wanted a more stable income and soon found herself driving a van in the USPS's Internet-fueled package delivery service. She has seen only growth at the postal service. "Nobody is really delivering letters anymore," Sapp says. "It's mostly junk mail. If you have to send something important, you mail it. but otherwise, that's all being done electronically now. But parcels are picking up."

There's a bleaker aspect to the embrace of Amazon by both the USPS's management and its unions. For the unions, it's an endorsement of a company that has long had a fraught relationship with its own rank and file. Amazon warehouse employees in some cases make only $12 an hour, a pittance compared to a veteran postal worker.

For the postal service's managers, it means increasingly tying their business to a fiercely competitive company led by Jeff Bezos, whose loyalty in the long term is dubious. Amazon already has its own trucks and drivers; it is testing same-day delivery and crowd-sourced delivery, along with its much-publicized experiment with drones. "Amazon will drop us in a heartbeat if they find a better way," says the NALC's Sauber. "We can't just put all our eggs in one basket. We want to become a utility for all retailers, big and small. We want to be a merchant selling to both sides."

It will only get more challenging for the USPS. It isn't just battling with FedEx and UPS for customers. Google and eBay are offering same-day delivery to people who shop on their sites. Uber is picking up and dropping off packages for its users. Start-ups like Deliv and Roadie have their own versions of crowdsourced delivery.

The USPS must compete with such fast-moving rivals at a time when it has virtually no money to invest in upgrading its operations. It desperately needs to replace its 190,000 mail trucks, the world's largest fleet. Most of them are more than 25 years old, and they are configured to carry letters rather than packages. They also lack basic safety features like seat-belt reminders and anti-lock brakes. But it has been estimated that it would cost as much as $5 billion to purchase new ones. The USPS doesn't have that kind of money.

In November 2014, a year after the announcement of the Amazon deal, Donahoe announced his resignation. Before he departed, he made a farewell speech to a handful of journalists at the National Press Club in Washington. It was an icy January morning, and many reporters didn't bother taking off their coats. "It's a tough day for a letter carrier, especially going up and down steps," Donahoe said. "Keep them in our thoughts today as they are out there making sure the mail gets delivered."

Donahoe read his prepared remarks, repeating many of the reforms for which he had failed to win support in Congress. The reporters looked disinterested, checking their e-mail or their Twitter feeds on their laptops. The only one who seemed excited to be there was a writer for *Direct Marketing News* a junk mail trade publication. He had a buzz cut and an earring and boasted that his publication's readers were "paying the bills" for the USPS.

As usual, Donahoe was buoyant, but his frustration showed during the question-and-answer period. One writer asked why the postal service didn't put banks in post offices again. "We don't know anything about banking," Donahoe said.

"You don't know anything about groceries either," the reporter persisted.

"We know a lot about delivery," Donahoe said. "We're the best delivery company in the world. We know more about delivery than anyone else."

A woman asked Donahoe why he was closing mail processing plants when postal workers' union officials and their congressional allies objected to it. "When I was a kid starting out in Pittsburgh in 1976, every night Bell Telephone would bring in mail," Donahoe said. "Remember Bell Telephone? How about Mellon Bank? They would bring mail in. Or Duquesne Power and Light? They are still in business. But every night, in every facility across the country, people would bring in commercial mail. We would sort it and deliver it overnight."

Donahoe said those days were done. He explained that he was hired to work an afternoon shift that no longer exists throughout the country because there is so little mail. "The bottom line is this," Donahoe said. "With the exception of the holidays and your birthday, think about your own mailbox. When was the last time you got a piece of mail that had a stamp on it? You don't get it."

The questions kept coming and Donahoe's answer remained the same. "If I take a survey, I'll bet a lot of people in here don't pay any bills by mail," he said. "I hate to say it, but that's what's happening." The room was silent. The reporters looked uncomfortable. Did the outgoing postmaster general just say they were destroying the US Postal Service?

Donahoe had groomed a successor whom he said would be just right for the job. "Who is he?" a senator asked.

"His name is Megan," Donahoe replied.

On April 7, 2015, Megan Brennan, the nation's first female postmaster general, appeared onstage at the Warner Theatre in Washington, D.C., with first lady Michelle Obama, talk show host Oprah Winfrey,

and poet Nikki Giovanni. They were there to unveil a new Forever stamp honoring the late author Maya Angelou. A former letter
carrier from Pottsville, Pennsylvania, Brennan was dressed for the
occasion in a bright fuchsia jacket and a dark skirt, and she had come
with a prepared speech. "Today," she said, "Dr. Angelou receives the
Postal Service's highest honor, the commemoration of her image on
a United States postage stamp, and yet her life, so meaningful and
varied, can hardly be contained within the four corners of a stamp."

Predictably, Winfrey stole the show, channeling the honoree:
"She would have called me up and she would have said 'Babe, *ha ha
ha*! They're going to have a *stamp* with my name and face on it! How
incredible is that?'"

Unfortunately, the tribute was marred by the *Washington Post*'s
discovery that Angelou hadn't actually written the inspirational
quote on the stamp. The USPS had used the words of a children's
book author that have sometimes been mistaken for Angelou's own.
"It seemed to many that the folks at the Postal Service had simply
believed too readily what they read on the Internet," the *New Yorker*
wrote. It was too late. The USPS had already printed 80 million of
the stamps. It was an awkward beginning for Brennan, but it's the
USPS. "It delivers more than 40 percent of the world's mail like
clockwork six days a week, but then something like this happens and
people say the USPS can't do anything right."

The Angelou stamp was the least of Brennan's troubles. Packages continued to rise, but first-class mail continued to fall and even
junk mail was weakening. In Washington, few people seemed to care
or even notice. The only presidential candidate in the 2016 election
who talked about the postal service was Bernie Sanders, the 74-year-
old senator from Vermont and self-proclaimed "Democratic socialist" who had vigorously opposed any of the USPS's transformation
efforts. "We have people in Congress and wealthy corporate interests
who want nothing else but to privatize and destroy the United States
Postal Service," Sanders told a cheering crowd of APWU members

at an event in Las Vegas. "But we are not going to allow them to do that!"

Sanders, who was facing former secretary of state Hillary Clinton in the Democratic primary, extolled the postal service as an engine of democracy in words that would have resonated with John Wanamaker. "The strength of the postal service, as you all know, and what many people sometimes take for granted, is that the postal service provides *universal* services, six days a week, to every corner of America, no matter how small, no matter how remote," Sanders said in his distinctive Brooklyn accent. "In other words, if you are a big business, you get your mail six days a week. If you are a low-income person on a dirt road in a small town in Vermont, you get your mail six days a week." Sanders didn't bother to mention that Americans are getting mostly junk mail now.

Even people who admired Sanders's passionate defense of the USPS found it archaic in today's world. "The goals are laudable," said Gene Del Polito, president of the Association of Postal Commerce, the country's leading group of junk mailers. "But the mail doesn't hold the place it once held in society. How are we going to pay for it without cuts?"

Daphne Carmel, founder of Deliv, a Silicon Valley same-day package carrier, has an idea. "Amazon should just buy the postal service," she says

In her early months on the job, Megan Brennan was doing her best to keep her sense of humor. She comes from a family of postal workers. Her brother Brian is a letter carrier in Pennsylvania, and he kids his big sister about the monthly videos in which she addresses her employees. "Do I have to watch these?" he asked her.

"Yes, you must," Brennan told him. "It's a condition of your employment."

Epilogue

In late 2015, Evan Kalish had visited 6,557 post offices. He had 29,084 more to go, but it was getting harder for him to travel. He had a job working in the shipping department at a clinical genome testing company. He had a girlfriend, too; her name was Amy. Not long after they had become an item, Kalish drove her from Queens to upstate New York, where she had spent her childhood. It was a long trip; Kalish wanted to break it up with some post office stops. "You can have four," Amy told him.

"Make it six," Kalish said.

"Fine," Amy agreed.

Evan and Amy found some off Route 17 along the Susquehanna River. They stumbled across one that had been closed after a flood a few years before and never reopened. There was another that looked like it had been abandoned years ago; it was like a ghost post office. There wasn't even a mailbox in front of it now, just a faded community bulletin board that reminded them of when the building was the center of the town's life. They also found a post office with two lovely murals from the New Deal. "I see why you like this," Amy told him. "It's really cool."

Evan was elated. He couldn't drag Amy along on one of those marathon days when he visited thirty post offices, but she was good for five or six as long as Evan reciprocated by doing something she enjoyed, like going to a party. "I'm more of an introverted person,"

Kalish said. "Group events? I find them draining. Going to post offices is my way of recharging."

Amy got a kick out of the attention her boyfriend received for his unusual hobby. He talked about it on NPR. *Time* magazine called to inquire about his quest. The Association of United States Postal Lessors, a lobbying group for landlords who have post offices in their buildings, invited Kalish to speak at its annual conventions in Las Vegas and New Orleans. The events could be gloomy; it's not the greatest time to have the federal agency as a tenant. The landlords grumbled that the USPS was pressuring them to lower their rents because stamp sales were down. Kalish did his best to cheer them up with stories and pictures from his journeys. He also got to see a lot of great post offices on these trips.

Still, it bothered Kalish that he wasn't making more progress, and he hoped to increase his count in 2016. He had visited post offices in 49 states, but he daydreamed of sending letters from United States post offices in Puerto Rico and the Virgin Islands. He was seriously thinking about traveling to Alaska and hiring a bush pilot to take him to post offices that could only be reached by plane.

Meanwhile, Kalish squeezed in visits whenever he could. He was relieved to find that post offices in small towns were still open, but he couldn't always get inside because the USPS had reduced their hours so dramatically. He felt as though he was witnessing the disappearance of a fundamental aspect of American life; it was just vanishing more slowly than he had expected four years earlier when Patrick Donahoe announced his closure plan. "A lot of post offices in small towns are open three or four hours a day," Kalish lamented. "It's more of a crapshoot when I'm passing through."

On a Monday afternoon, he was driving home from a wedding in Cleveland on I-80. He hoped to push through to Queens without stopping, but he missed a turn and ended up on I-76. Kalish didn't realize his mistake for 20 minutes, and by then, he was deep in southern Ohio. He was furious with himself until he remembered there were post offices in the area that he hadn't been to yet.

He pulled off the highway and found four. One was a jewel from the New Deal. The postmaster took Kalish into her office. She opened her file cabinet and showed him old photographs of the building. Kalish knew he wouldn't get home to Queens until late. He had to go to work the next morning, but so what? When he passed through Ohio again, would this post office be open? He couldn't take the chance.

Acknowledgments

You never know where a story will take you, and it was in that adventurous spirit that I volunteered in early 2011 when Josh Tyrangiel, former editor in chief of *Bloomberg Businessweek*, said offhandedly that he was interested in a story about the U.S. Postal Service. I didn't know the first thing about the USPS, but Josh knows a good story. This was no exception but it wasn't easy. I spent three months reporting and going through several drafts before I got it right.

The story was entitled "The End of Mail," and when it was published that May, it got more of a response than anything else I'd ever written. Whether they love it or hate it, people *care* about the postal service. It was clear that there was a bigger story to tell. I struggled with a book proposal for too long. My agent Adam Eaglin came along at just the right time and connected me with Jamison Stoltz, senior editor at Grove Atlantic. Jamison was enthusiastic about this project when we met in 2013, and his feeling about it has never waned, which has been enormously helpful, along with all his suggestions on how to make this a better book.

The USPS is a big topic. You need people to guide you as you try to figure it out. Jim Campbell, one of the world's most respected experts on the mail delivery, was kind enough early on to send me four disks holding all of the annual reports of the postmaster generals to Congress dating back to 1824 and a wealth of other historical documents. I can't thank him enough for doing that. Sue Brennan, senior media relations representative at the USPS, helped me find my way around inside the USPS. She couldn't have been more supportive. I'm also grateful to Jenny Lynch, the postal service's historian. Sue and Jenny functioned as a tag team, answering my questions about the colonial post and antebellum mail delivery the same day.

I spent a lot of time talking to USPS executives including U.S. Postmaster General Megan Brennan and her predecessors Patrick Donahoe, William Henderson, Anthony Frank, Paul Carlin, and Benjamin Franklin Bailar. They were so gracious, answering my dumb questions and telling me fascinating things. So were former deputy postmaster generals Michael Coughlin and John Nolan and many more former officials, whose stories I tried to bring to life in this book.

I got to know people at postal workers' unions too. Jim Sauber, chief of staff at the National Letter Carriers Association, helped me understand the views of his members. I visited the Walter Reuther Library at Wayne State University, where Mike Smith was kind enough to provide me with his insightful interviews with former NALC presidents James Rademacher and Vincent Sombrotto, which I drew heavily on to write my chapters about the 1970 postal workers' strike. Mike put me in touch with Jim Rademacher himself. Jim and I had a lengthy conversation in 2013. He is 92 years old and just as passionate about the postal service as ever. I'm grateful to him for sharing his stories. I also talked several times to Mark Dimonstein, president of the American Postal Workers Union, and also relied on documents and press clippings from the late APWU president Moe Biller's papers at the Taminent Library and Robert F. Wagner Labor Archives at New York University.

I had some fine researchers. Christine Bednarz clicked with the subject matter and spent hours at the Library of Congress, the USPS library, the Smithsonian National Postal Museum, and the Historical Society of Philadelphia gathering material. In the final stages, my friend Danielle Muoio retrieved articles for me and did important interviews when I was in the midst of rewrites.

Then there is my family. I dedicate this book to them not simply because I think they are the greatest. They put in a lot of work on it. My wife, Eileen, read most of these chapters early on and told me hard truths about them. I didn't always want hear them at the time, but she was invariably right, though it took me a while to accept it sometimes. We've been married for 28 years; sometimes it's like that. Our daughter Faith transcribed taped interviews and seemed to instantly grasp arcane postal matters.

Our son Colin was more steeped in this project than anyone besides the author. Like his father, he became something of a postal expert. He found old newspaper clips and did research reports on the Pony Express and the rise of private carriers like Federal Express and DHL. He transcribed countless interviews quickly and accurately and read most of these chapters, helping me strengthen them. Colin and I traveled together to Detroit and Washington, D.C., to do research. It was great fun to go to these places, get the work done, and then hang out. When can we do it again?

As I was writing, three of my talented editors at *Bloomberg Businessweek*—Bryant Urstadt, Nick Summers, and Jim Aley—read chapters and helped me improve them as they have done with many of my articles. And all my colleagues at the magazine were supportive in their own way from editor in chief Ellen Pollock on down. It's a pleasure to come to work every day with such a great group.

Notes

Prologue

xi **"I really got into it," he says:** Author interview with Evan Kalish.

xi **There were 36,723 post offices in the United States:** USPS, *Annual Report 2008: Connecting People and Business*, 27, http://www.prc.gov/docs/62/62761/annual_report-2008.pdf.

xiii **Six days a week, its 300,000 letter carriers deliver 513 million pieces of mail:** *Postal Facts 2015*, 12, https://about.usps.com/who-we-are/postal-facts/postalfacts2015.pdf.

xiii **the postal service has what it refers to as "shirt pocket" routes:** Author interview with Patrick Donahoe, former U.S. postmaster general.

xiv **In 2011, Oxford Strategic Consulting, an English firm, studied the postal services in developed countries:** "Delivering the Future: How the G20's Postal Services Meet the Challenges of the 21st Century," Oxford Strategic Consulting, Executive Summary (December 15, 2011), 4.

xiv **"Nobody aims to be a postal worker," says Orlando Gonzalez, a letter carrier and union organizer in New York:** Author interview with Gonzalez.

xiv **Long before Abraham Lincoln was president of the United States, he was the postmaster of New Salem, Illinois:** *The United States Postal Service: An American History, 1775–2006* , USPS, November 2012, 9, https://about.usps.com/publications/pub100.pdf.

xvi **"Why are they the way they are?"** *Washington Post* **columnist Mary McGrory asked in 1988:** Mary McGrory, *The Best of Mary McGrory: A Half-Century of Washington Commentary*, ed. Phil Gailey (Kansas City, MO: Andrews McMeel Publishing, 2006), 270.

xvi **"We are so diverse that only extraordinary means could have held us together when so many forces seemed designed to tear us apart,"** Lawrence

O'Brien, Lyndon Johnson's postmaster general, said in an eloquent 1966 speech: "Address by Postmaster General Lawrence F. O'Brien Before the Magazine Publishers Association and the American Society of Magazine Editors," U.S. Postal Service Library, April 3, 1967.

xvii By its own calculations, it owed nearly $73 billion in mid-2015: USPS, Form 10-Q, March 31, 2015, 4, https://about.usps.com/who-we-are/financials/financial-conditions-results-reports/fy2015-q2.pdf.

xvii "It is the one of the biggest businesses in the country," President Harry Truman said in 1951. "And without it, the rest of the country would not be able to do business at all": "Address Before the National Association of Postmasters," Harry S. Truman Library & Museum, September 17, 1951, http://trumanlibrary.org/publicpapers/index.php/index.php?pid=442&st=&st1.

Chapter 1

1 The placard above the door on Second Street in Philadelphia said "The Sign of the Bible": Walter L. Ferree, "Andrew Bradford: A Pioneer Printer of Pennsylvania," *Pennsylvania History: A Journal of Mid-Atlantic Studies* 21, no. 3 (July 1954): 214, https://journals.psu.edu/phj/article/view/22356.

1 He had arrived the previous day after fleeing Boston: Benjamin Franklin, *The Autobiography of Benjamin Franklin* (New York: Pocket Books, 1940), 31.

1 Bradford also operated a general store: Ferree, "Andrew Bradford," 217.

2 He ran a general store on the premises: Carl Van Doren, *Benjamin Franklin* (New York: Penguin Books, 1991), 128.

3 "I accepted it readily": Franklin, *The Autobiography of Benjamin Franklin*, 117.

3 "He suffered greatly from his neglect": Ibid.

3 13 American post offices: *The United States Postal Service: An American History*, 5.

4 The mail arrived once a week in Philadelphia, New York, and Boston: Ruth Lapham Butler, *Doctor Franklin: Postmaster General* (Garden City, NY: Doubleday, Doran & Company), 37.

4 "I would only add that, as I have respect for Mr. Benger": "From Benjamin Franklin to Peter Collinson, 21 May 1751," Founders Online, National Archives, http://founders.archives.gov/documents/Franklin/01-04-02-0042.

5 Archaeologists have determined that by 1900 BC: Carl H. Scheele, *A Short History of the Mail Service* (Washington, DC: Smithsonian Institution Press, 1970), 8.

5 Two centuries later, the Egyptian pharaohs created a network: Ibid., 10.

5 King Darius of Persia: Ibid., 3.

6   Many have assumed that this is the motto of the U.S. Postal Service, but the USPS doesn't have one: "Postal Service Mission and 'Motto,'" USPS, October 1999, https://about.usps.com/who-we-are/postal-history/mission-motto.pdf.

6   The Romans improved on the Persian system: Alvin F. Harlow, *Old Post Bags* (New York: D. Appleton, 1928), 18.

7   The Muslim caliphs established mail routes: John Freeman, *The Tyranny of E-Mail* (New York: Scribner, 2009), 26.

7   And when Marco Polo visited China in the late thirteenth century: Harlow, *Old Post Bags*, 48.

7   By 1297, the University of Paris had created one: Ibid., 32.

8   In 1516, King Henry VIII of England called for the creation: Royal Mail Group, www.royalmail heritage.com.

8   In 1635, King Charles I of England opened the Royal Mail to the public: Royal Mail Group, http://500years.royalmailgroup.com/gallery/opening-the-postal-service-to-everyone/.

9   The British government formalized the system in 1639, designating a tavern owned by Richard Fairbanks as the first colonial post office: *The United States Postal Service: An American History*, 4.

9   In 1673, New York's governor Francis Lovelace established a monthly post between New York and Boston on a trail known as "the King's Highway": Ibid., 4.

9   Neale was an odd choice: Mike Atherton, *Gambling* (London: Hodder & Stoughton, 2006).

9   Virginia and Maryland refused: Scheele, *A Short History of the Mail Service*, 48.

10   "This is to give notice that all persons in town and country": Wesley Everett Rich, *The History of the United States Post Office to the Year 1829* (Cambridge, MA: Harvard University Press, 1924), 27.

10   Franklin set a bad example: Walter Isaacson, *Benjamin Franklin: An American Life* (New York: Simon & Schuster, 2003), 157.

11   they could split an annual salary of £600: Van Doren, *Benjamin Franklin*, 211.

11   So, even before their appointments officially went into effect: Butler, *Doctor Franklin*, 46.

11   They cut the time it took for a letter to travel from Philadelphia to New York: Ibid., 50.

11   Franklin created the Dead Letter Office: Van Doren, *Benjamin Franklin*, 213.

11   Franklin and Hunter borrowed £900: Isaacson, *Benjamin Franklin*, 157.

11   **In 1760, the colonial post generated its first surplus:** *The United States Postal Service: An American History*, 5.

12   **he longed to run the colonial post by himself:** Isaacson, *Benjamin Franklin*, 207.

12   **They decided to have riders carry mail at night:** Ibid.

12   **American postmasters requested a shipment of bugles:** Butler, *Doctor Franklin*, 132.

13   **"It is the practice in many other instances to allow the non-residence of American officers":** Benjamin Franklin, *Memoirs of Benjamin Franklin*, vol. 1 (New York: Derby & Jackson, 1859), 270.

13   **"If I should lose the post office":** "From Benjamin Franklin to Deborah Franklin, 22 June 1767," Founders Online, National Archives, http://founders. archives.gov/documents/Franklin/01-14-02-0113.

13   **"In this they are not likely to succeed, I being deficient in that Christian Virtue of Resignation":** "To Jane Mecom, 30 December 1770," Founders Online, National Archives, http://founders.archives.gov/documents/ Franklin/01-17-02-0186.

14   **As far as he was concerned, he had transformed the colonial post:** Albert Henry Smyth, ed., *The Writings of Benjamin Franklin*, vol. 4 (London: The Macmillan Company, 1906), 192.

14   **"How safe the correspondence of your Assembly committees along the continent will be":** Ibid.

14   **"The people never liked the institution":** Ward L. Miner, *William Goddard, Newspaperman* (Durham, NC: Duke University Press, 1962), 128.

15   **"As he had frequently threatened to resign his office":** Ibid., 149.

16   **"When the English ministry formerly thought fit to deprive me of the office":** Albert Henry Smyth, ed., *The Writings of Benjamin Franklin*, vol. 9 (London: The Macmillan Company, 1906), 693.

16   **"The most single-minded politicians could never long forget that there was a philosopher among them":** Van Doren, *Benjamin Franklin*, 745.

16   **It operated 75 post offices and transported 265,545 letters on 1,875 miles of post roads:** Pliny Miles, *Postal Reform: Its Urgent Necessity and Practicability* (New York: Stringer & Townsend, 1855), 26, http://babel.hathitrust.org/cgi/pt? id=hvd.32044081924474;view=1up;seq=1.

17   **"The Western settlers (I speak now from my own observation) stand as it were upon a pivot.... The touch of a feather, would turn them any way":** "Letter to Benjamin Harrison," October 10, 1784, TeachingAmericanHistory.org, http://teachingamericanhistory.org/library/document/letter-to-benjamin-harrison-3/.

18 "It is easy to see what hand could be made of the post offices, if ever they are under the direction of an improper person": Gales and Seaton, eds., *Annals of Congress (The Debates and Proceedings in the Congress of the United States, 1834–1856)*, http://press-pubs.uchicago.edu/founders/print_documents/a1_8_7s3.htm.

18 "Wherever information is freely circulated, there slavery cannot exist": Richard R. John, *Spreading the News: The American Postal System from Franklin to Morse* (Cambridge, MA: Harvard University Press, 1995), 35.

19 By the turn of the century, there were 903 post offices and 20,817 miles of post roads in the United States: Miles, *Postal Reform*, 26.

19 "I view it as a source of boundless patronage to the executive, jobbing to members of Congress and their friends, and a boundless abyss of public money": Thomas Jefferson, *The Works of Thomas Jefferson*, vol. 8, ed. Paul Leicester Ford (New York and London: G. P. Putnam's Sons, 1904), http://press-pubs. uchicago.edu/founders/documents/a1_8_7s4.html.

20 "To write from Portland (Maine) to Savanna and receive an answer back": Francis C. Huebner, "Our Postal System," *Records of the Columbia Historical Society, Washington, D.C.* 9 (1906): 141, http://www.jstor.org/stable/40066939?seq= 1#page_scan_tab_contents.

20 "The most active and intelligent [blacks] are employed as post-riders": Deanna Boyd and Kendra Chen, "The History and Experience of African Americans in America's Postal Service," National Postal Museum, http://postalmuseum.si.edu/ AfricanAmericanhistory/p1.html.

Chapter 2

23 this was twice as many as Great Britain: John, *Spreading the News*, 5.

23 The American Post Office used private contractors to transport mail by horseback, stagecoach, steamboat, and three-wheeled sulky on 116,000 miles of post roads, and often generated a yearly surplus: Miles, *Postal Reform*, 26.

23 Theodorus Bailey, the city's postmaster, padded downstairs every morning in his bathrobe: John, *Spreading the News*, 162.

24 the General Post Office, which employed 8,764 postmasters whose ranks outnumbered the country's 6,332 soldiers: *The United States Postal Service: An American History*, 11.

24 "Mr. McLean, will you accept a seat upon the bench of the Supreme Court?": Ben Perley Poore, *Perley's Reminiscences of Sixty Years in the National Metropolis* (Philadelphia, Chicago, Kansas City: Hubbard Brothers, 1886), 98.

24 "General Jackson, I have come here to talk to you about my office": Ibid., 111.

25 "large masses of newspapers, pamphlets, tracts and almanacs, containing exaggerated, and in some instances, false accounts": *Report of the Postmaster General*, Post Office Department, December 1, 1835, 397.

27 One day in 1838, William Harnden, a frail high-strung 26-year-old with dark hair and extravagant sideburns, wandered into the Reading Room: Alvin F. Harlow, *Old Waybills: The Romance of the Express Companies* (New York and London: D. Appleton-Century Company, 1934), 13.

27 "I immediately advised him to travel between the two cities": "An American Enterprise," *Harper's New Monthly Magazine*, August 1875.

27 "IMPORTANT TO MERCHANTS, BROKERS, BOOK-SELLERS AND ALL BUSINESS MEN": Harlow, *Old Waybills*, 18.

27 "I can't make it go": Ibid., 19.

28 Everything seemed to be going Harnden's way until January 13, 1840, when he dispatched his younger brother, Adolphus, to Boston: Ibid., 20.

29 "Receive nothing mailable," he warned one of his associates: Ibid., 37.

29 "making a deep hole in the coffers of Uncle Sam": *Report of the Postmaster General*, Post Office Department, 1841.

29 "Mr. H. deservedly enjoys the highest confidence": Ibid.

29 "These private expresses will only be found to operate upon the great and profitable thoroughfares": *Annual Report of the Postmaster General*, 1843, 447.

30 "His hand?" Harnden fumed: Harlow, *Old Waybills*, 23.

30 "Because the king's business required haste": Ibid., 31.

31 "If *you* choose to run an express to the Rocky Mountains": Henry Wells, *Sketch of the Rise, Progress, and Present Conditions of the Express System* (Albany, NY: Van Benthuysen's Steam Printing House, 1861), 10.

31 "It may amuse you to hear that the oyster was a powerful agent": Harlow, *Old Waybills*, 35.

31 Wells started a letter delivery service in 1844: Richard R. John Jr., "Private Mail Delivery in the United States During the Nineteenth Century: A Sketch," *Business and Economic History*, vol. 15 (paper presented at the thirty-second annual meeting of the Business History Conference, 1986), 141.

33 "Zounds, sir," Hobbie replied: Ibid., 144.

33 "Intemperance is filling our alms-houses with paupers": Hugh Davis, *Joshua Leavitt, Evangelical Abolitionist* (Baton Rouge: Louisiana State University Press, 1990), 55.

34 **"So long as the church sanctions and sustains it, slavery is impregnable"**: Ibid., 125.

34 **"Horrible!" Leavitt wrote:** Ibid., 145.

34 **"Of all the wild and visionary schemes which I have ever heard of, this is the most extraordinary"**: Chris West, *A History of Britain in Thirty-Six Postage Stamps* (New York: Picador, 2013), 5.

35 **That year, the Royal Mail handled 169 million letters, more than twice as many as the year before:** Miles, *Postal Reform*, 27.

35 **"It is the complete leveler. . . . The poorest peasant, the factory-girl, the match-vender, the beggar, even, enjoy the benefits of the cheap postage"**: Joshua Leavitt, "The Moral and Social Benefits of Cheap Postage," *Hunt's Merchants' Magazine*, December 1849, 10.

35 **"Give us the British system of postage, and slavery is dead!"**: Davis, *Evangelical Abolitionist*, 158.

35 **"The mode of managing and conducting the post office in the Kingdom of Great Britain is not only different from, but much less expensive"**: *Report of the Postmaster General*, Post Office Department, 1844.

36 **"The operations of the system, as it exists, have become odious"**: *The Congressional Globe Containing Sketches of the Debates and Proceedings of the First Session of the Twenty-Eighth Congress*, vol. 13, ed. Blair and Rives (Washington, DC: Congressional Globe, 1844), 195.

36 **"Find the proper rate"**: Ibid., 196.

36 **"This is a bill for the benefit of cities, to the injury of the country"**: Ibid., 340.

37–38 **"No American citizen can hesitate to lend his aid to accomplish a measure which is fraught with so many blessings to every portion of our community"**: "An Address of the Directors of the New York Cheap Postage Association to the People of the United States" in *The American Postal Network, 1792–1914*, vol. 3, ed. Richard R. John (London and Brookfield, VT: Pickering & Chatto, 2012), 325.

38 **"Maybe the letters will come pouring upon you in such multitudes that you'll wish for the old rate of postage"**: David M. Henkin, *The Postal Age: The Emergence of Modern Communications in Nineteenth-Century America* (Chicago: University of Chicago Press, 2006), 34.

38 **"It is a very good plan for you to correspond with your relatives in Wisconsin"**: Ibid., 94.

39 **By 1854, the number of American post offices had risen to 23,584:** Miles, *Postal Reform*, 26.

40   "There were knocks on the doors, taps on the windows, and beseeching calls at all corners of the house": Bayard Taylor, *Eldorado, or Adventures in the Path of Empire* (New York: G. P. Putnam, 1861), 209.

40   "Those who were near the goal frequently sold out their places to impatient candidates": Ibid., 212.

41   "We have to request a more strict observance of stamping letters": Philip L. Fradkin, *Stagecoach: Wells Fargo and the American West* (New York: Simon & Schuster, 2002), 25.

41   "I am called sanguine at home": Ibid., 15.

42   "Remember boys . . . nothing on God's earth must stop the United States Mail": Mary A. Helmich, "The Butterfield Overland Mail Company," Interpretation and Education Division, California State Parks, 2008, http://www.parks.ca.gov/?page_id=25444.

42   "Our heavy wagon bounded along crags as if it would be shaken to pieces": "Overland Mail to California in the 1850s," USPS, https://about.usps.com/who-we-are/postal-history/overland-mail.htm.

42   "Had I not just come out over the route, I would be perfectly willing to go back": Helmich, "The Butterfield Overland Mail Company."

Chapter 3

46   In February 1861, six southern states—South Carolina, Florida, Alabama, Mississippi, Georgia, and Louisiana—declared themselves a new nation and seized nearly 9,000 post offices: *Report of the Postmaster General*, United States Post Office Department, 1863.

47   "They left him at 2 this morning": Rita Lloyd Moroney, *Montgomery Blair, Postmaster General* (Washington, DC: United States Post Office Department, 1963), 15.

47   "I have troubles enough": Ibid., 15.

49   "It is impractical," Medill said: George A. Armstrong, "The First Railway Postal Car," *The World To-Day: A Monthly Record of Human Progress*, vol. 14, from December 1, 1907 to June 1, 1908, 308.

51   "A mail bag is an epitome of human life": J. Holbrook, *Ten Years Among the Mail Bags or Notes from the Diary of a Special Agent of the Post Office Department* (Philadelphia: H. Cowperthait & Co., 1855), 15.

51   "no obscene book, pamphlet, picture, print, or other publication": Helen Lefkowitz Horowitz, *Rereading Sex: Battles over Sexual Knowledge and Suppression in Nineteenth-Century America* (New York: Alfred A. Knopf, 2002), 313.

54 "**From Maine to California, we believe the new order of Protestant Jesuits called the YMCA is dubbed with the well-merited title of the American Inquisition**": Heywood Broun and Margaret Leech, *Anthony Comstock, Roundsman of the Lord* (New York: Albert & Charles Boni, 1927), 126.

55 "**All were very much excited and declared themselves ready to give me any law I might ask for**": Ibid.

55 "**They were brazen**": Ibid., 134.

55 "**The Devil seemed determined to claim me as his servant**": Ibid., 140.

56 "**I do not want any fat office created, whereby the Government is taxed or for some politician to have in a year or two**": Ibid., 137.

57 "**The mail of the United States is the great thoroughfare of communication leading up into all our homes, schools and colleges**": Anthony Comstock, *Frauds Exposed; or, How the People Are Deceived and Robbed, and Youth Corrupted* (New York: J. Howard Brown, 1880), 391.

58 "**a religion-monomaniac**": Ezra Heywood, *Cupid's Yokes: Or, the Binding Forces of Conjugal Life* (Princeton, MA: Co-Operative Publishing, 1876),12.

59 "**The fresh air was never more refreshing,**" Comstock wrote: Anthony Comstock, *Traps for the Young* (New York: Funk & Wagnalls, 1883), 164.

59 "**I have a warrant for your arrest for sending obscene matter through the mail,**" Comstock informed him: Ibid.

59–60 "**In Boston . . . as I had momentarily left the chair in which I was presiding over a public convention**": Martin Henry Blatt, *Free Love and Anarchism: The Biography of Ezra Heywood* (Urbana: University of Illinois Press, 1989), 114.

61 "**Two plainer violations of the Bill of Rights—two meaner outrages upon liberty, decency, and morality—have never been perpetrated among our people!**": T. B. Wakeman, *The Unanswered Argument Against the Constitutionality of the So-Called Comstock Postal Laws* (New York: The National Defense Association, 1880), 28.

61 "**I found it crowded with long-haired men and short-haired women**": Comstock, *Frauds Exposed*, 424.

62 "**Heywood is certainly a champion jackass,**" the poet wrote: Blatt, *Free Love and Anarchism*, 143

62 "**The court is robust enough to stand anything in that book**": Ibid., 144.

63 "**Europeans love to hear of such things**": Broun and Leech, *Anthony Comstock, Roundsman of the Lord*, 229.

63 "**George Bernard Shaw? . . . Who is he?**": Ibid., 230.

63 "**When the Constitution of the United States authorized Congress to establish post offices and post roads, it was not intended that the**

authority should go beyond this": Margaret Sanger, "Should Women Know?" *The Spur*, February 1915, 58, in *The Public Writings and Speeches of Margaret Sanger*, https://www.nyu.edu/projects/sanger/webedition/app/documents/show.php?sangerDoc=305121.xml.

Chapter 4

65 "Wanamaker is in no sense a leader of the party": Richard White, "The Bullmoose and the Bear: Theodore Roosevelt and John Wanamaker Struggle over the Spoils," *Pennsylvania History: A Journal of Mid-Atlantic Studies* 71, no. 1 (January 9, 2004): http://journals.psu.edu/phj/article/view/25850.

65 "Would he ever have been thought of for a place in the Cabinet if he had not contributed or raised this money?": "The Week," *The Nation*, 1889.

66 "Harrison still speaks to me": Herbert Adams Gibbons, *John Wanamaker* (New York and London: Harper & Brothers, 1926), 332.

68 "The idea clung to my mind that I could accomplish more": Joseph H. Appel, *The Business Biography of John Wanamaker, Founder and Builder* (New York: The Macmillan Company, 1930), 39.

68 "You are making a mistake": Ibid., 40.

69 "Any article that does not fit well": Ibid., 52.

69 "How about the top of the page?" Wanamaker responded: Gibbons, *John Wanamaker*, 102.

71 "We raised so much money the Democrats never knew anything about it": Ibid., 259.

71 "My Dear Sir, we did not have the pleasure of meeting during the campaign": Ibid., 264.

71 "General Harrison sent for me": Philadelphia Citizens, *John Wanamaker, The Record of a Citizens' Celebration to Mark His Sixty Years Career as Merchant, April 1861—April 1921* (Philadelphia: Printed for the Committee, 1921), 37.

72 "The whole range of domestic life finds a full expression here": Marshall Henry Cushing, *The Story of Our Post Office* (Boston: A. M. Thayer & Company, 1893), 253.

73 "One of the most valuable of the acquirements which are Mrs. Collins' possession is the knowledge of the city locality of almost every street in this and most other countries": Alice Graham McCollin, "The 'Blind Reader' at Washington," *Ladies' Home Journal*, September 1893.

74 "We feel rather proud if we quicken a mail between New York and Chicago by three hours": Cushing, *The Story of Our Post Office*, 999.

75 **"I made no recommendation in my message warranting you to proceed as you have"**: "Jay Gould Kicks, He Gets Harrison to Check Wanamaker's Postal Telegraph Scheme," *New York Times*, April 13, 1890.

78 **"The free delivery is a success in the broadest sense of the word"**: *Report of the Postmaster General of the United States* (Washington, DC: Government Printing Office, 1891), 123.

78 **"It is evident, then—indeed, we have proved it"**: Cushing, *The Story of Our Post Office*, 1004.

78 **"Bring the post office to the farmers' doors"**: Charles H. Greathouse, "Free Delivery of Rural Mail," *Yearbook of Agriculture—1900*, 1901.

78 **"The United States mail is a great civilizer"**: Letter from the Postmaster General, in Response to Senate Resolution of January 13, 1892, Relative to the Extension of Free-Delivery System to Rural Districts.

79 **"I am glad to know this," Wanamaker responded**: Gibbons, *John Wanamaker*, 282.

80 **"The footprint of the mail carrier is the signpost of civilization"**: Ibid., 320.

80 **"There was nothing to be done this past year except to trudge along the old roads"**: *Report of the Postmaster General of the United States* (Washington, DC: Government Printing Office, 1892), 3.

80 **"The old system is really colonial"**: Ibid., 12.

81 **"One man has a lard pail hung out on a fence post"**: *Annual Reports of the Post-Office Department for the Fiscal Year Ended June 20, 1897* (Washington, DC: Government Printing Office, 1897), 123.

81 **"That saves us time and anxiety"**: Greathouse, "Free Delivery of Rural Mail," 524.

82 **"I live three and a half miles from the Tempe post office"**: *Annual Reports of the Post-Office Department for the Fiscal Year Ended June 20, 1897*, 112.

82 **the world's only reindeer route**: "Carrying the Mail Within the Arctic Circle," *Chicago Tribune*, September 12, 1909.

83 **"It brings the men who live on the soil into close relations with the active business world"**: Theodore Roosevelt, "Second Annual Message," December 2, 1902, http://www.presidency.ucsb.edu/ws/?pid=29543.

84 **"The cost of living and the prices of many things would not have been as high the last twenty years if Parcel Post, postal savings and cheapened telegraph service had been granted"**: *Golden Book of the Wanamaker Stores: Jubilee Year, 1861–1911* (Privately printed, 1911).

86 **"Why weren't the Wrights a little earlier with their flying machine?"**: Gibbons, *John Wanamaker*, 310.

Chapter 5

87 **Postmaster General Albert Burleson, a dour 54-year-old Texan referred to by his fellow cabinet members as "the cardinal":** Adrian Anderson, "President Wilson's Politician: Albert Sidney Burleson of Texas," *The Southwestern Historical Quarterly* 77, no. 3 (January 1974): 247.

89 **"What's the matter?":** Captain Benjamin B. Lipsner, *The Airmail: Jennies to Jets* (Chicago: Wilcox & Follett, 1951), 17.

91 **In 1957, however, one of them turned up:** Ted Johnson, "The 150th Anniversary of the Balloon *Jupiter* Airmail Flight," Smithsonian National Postal Museum, 2009, http://postalmuseum.si.edu/collections/object-spotlight/balloon-jupiter.html.

91 **"The Post Office Department has been up in the air long enough, and now let us get down to terra firma":** Henry Ladd Smith, *Airways: The History of Commercial Aviation in the United States* (Washington, DC: Smithsonian, 1991), 55.

92 **"I had the bait gourd," Burleson said:** Anderson, "President Wilson's Politician: Albert Sidney Burleson of Texas," 352.

92 **The typeface for the famous quotation from Herodotus above the entryway is now believed to have been chosen by Ira Schnapp:** Todd Klein, "Ira Schnapp and the Farley Post Office," http://kleinletters.com/Blog/ira-schnapp-and-the-farley-post-office/.

93 **he was a segregationist who transferred black clerks in Washington to the Dead Letter Office:** Boyd and Chen, "The History and Experience of African Americans in America's Postal Service."

93 **(During the war, Burleson did take them over with disastrous results):** Richard B. Kielbowicz, "Postal Enterprise: Postal Office Innovations with Congressional Constraints, 1789–1970," prepared for the Postal Rate Commission, May 30, 2000, 62.

94 **"Pupils talked about him in whispers":** Moses Koenigsberg, *King News: An Autobiography* (Philadelphia: F. A. Stokes, 1941), 35.

94 **"He has suffered starvation, and has been well nigh crazed with thirst":** "Through Mexico on a Cycle, Otto Praeger Returns Safe from His Venturesome Trip," *New York Times*, July 7, 1892.

95 **"You know, we have a lot of it in the winter months":** Otto Praeger, "Moss from a Rolling Stone," unpublished memoir.

96 **"One instant, the plane became a tremendous elevator":** Barry Rosenberg and Catherine Macaulay, *Mavericks of the Sky: The First Daring Pilots of the U.S. Air Mail* (New York: William Morrow, 2006), 78.

97 **"I am afraid that the officers who are flying these routes are laboring under the attitude of mind that this aerial mail service is merely for the**

NOTES

purpose of carrying a handful of mail": William M. Leary, *Aerial Pioneers: The U.S. Air Mail Service, 1918–1927* (Washington, DC: Smithsonian Institution Press, 1985), 44.

97 "I've covered as much as 300 to 400 miles a day, only stopping for gasoline and oil or necessary repairs": Ibid., 52.

98 "There is no guess work about it": Rosenberg and Macaulay, *Mavericks of the Sky*, 109.

98 they called Hell's Stretch: Ibid., 195.

99 "What do you mean follow?" he asked: Lipsner, *The Airmail: Jennies to Jets*, 106.

102 "The metropolis was wonderful—lights twinkling everywhere": Ibid.

102 "You made a great flight": Rosenberg and Macaulay, *Mavericks of the Sky*, 129.

102 "START THE MAIL SHIP WITHOUT A MINUTE'S DELAY": Leary, *Aerial Pioneers*, 63.

103 "All that remains of New York to Chicago air mail service, which began life fresh and full of vigor yesterday morning, is a trail of broken or lost airplanes": Ibid., 70.

103 "The Areo mail of this country is doomed to failure": Ibid., 76.

103 "Max Miller was the best pilot who ever sat in a plane": Ibid., 124.

104 "When he said, 'By Golly, that's what we'll do,' there was no appeal": Ibid., 116.

104 "Commercial aviation has arrived": Ibid., 95.

104 "a maze of canyons, deep narrow [gorges], and sharp crest ridges": Ibid., 129.

106 "I felt as if I had a thousand friends on the ground": Rosenberg and Macaulay, *Mavericks of the Sky*, 236.

107 "By this time I was flying over territory that was absolutely strange": Ibid., 238.

108 "I feel fine," he told a reporter: "Knight's Story of Trip; Pilot Tells of Flight in Dark Through Snow and Fog," *New York Times*, February 24, 1921.

109 "I wish everyone could have the pleasure and excitement of those first hesitant probes across the dark plains": Dean C. Smith, *By the Seat of My Pants: A Pilot's Progress from 1917 to 1930* (Boston: Little, Brown, 1961).

109 "The U.S. Post Office runs what is far and away the most efficiently organized and efficiently managed Civil Aviation undertaking in the world": Leary, *Aerial Pioneers*, 203.

110 "There is a revolutionary fact abroad in the land: aircraft have gone to work": J. Parker Van Zandt, "On the Trail of the Air Mail," *National Geographic Magazine*, January 1926.

112 "Someone has got to solve this problem, or we are going to have a collapse of the passenger-carrying industry in this country": F. Robert van der Linden, *Airlines and Air Mail: The Post Office and the Birth of the Commercial Aviation Industry* (Lexington: University Press of Kentucky, 2002), 122.

Chapter 6

113 "Don't go, Wilbur," he said. "Wait until the others have gone": Katherine Crane, *Mr. Carr of State: Forty-Seven Years in the Department of State* (New York: St. Martin's Press, 1960), 308.

114–15 When the *St. Louis Times* mentioned Tiffany in an article about the growing popularity of stamp collecting and wrote of his collection of 13,000 stamps, it withheld his name: Alvin F. Harlow, *Paper Chase: The Amenities of Stamp Collecting* (New York: Henry Holt and Company, 1940), 46.

115 The *American Journal of Philately* called it "the meanest looking stamp we have ever seen": Ibid., 4.

116 like the postmaster of Newport, Rhode Island, who refused to fill a dealer's order for stamped envelopes. "If you want them for business purposes, I'll get them for you," the postmaster said. "But if it's for collectors, I can't bother with them": Ibid., 199.

117 "Do you know you can learn history and geography and the strange customs of strange places just by studying stamps?": Richard Logan, "We Need Another Captain Tim," *American Philatelist*, February 2010, 150–51.

117 Colonel Ned Green, a one-legged sybaritic millionaire, traveled to stamp dealers in a chauffeured limousine and stored his purchases in a New York apartment: Stanley M. Bierman, *The World's Greatest Stamp Collectors* (Sidney, OH: Linn's Stamp News, 1990), 114–30.

119 "From the view point of the collector per se, the victory of Governor Roosevelt at the polls this November would be the most desirable ever in philatelic history": Robert. L. D. Davidson, "APS: The First Century," *American Philatelist*, August 1986, 740, http://stamps.org/userfiles/file/history/FirstCentury/1011-History.pd.

119 the Hoover campaign wrote to the society to tell it that the incumbent had "a high opinion of philately": Ibid.

120 "Some people have memories for figures, some for books," he said: S. J. Woolf, "Farley, 50, Tells How to Win Friends," *New York Times Magazine*, May 29, 1938.

120   "Jim Farley passes fall like snowflakes on the deserving and the grateful": Alva Johnson, "Big Jim," *New Yorker*, November 28, 1931.

120   "I do not see how Mr. Roosevelt can escape becoming the next presidential nominee": James A. Farley, *Behind the Ballots: The Personal History of a Politician* (New York: Harcourt, Brace, 1938), 62.

120   "Get ready to move to Washington": Ibid., 188.

121   "I virtually had to slip back and forth to the office like a man dodging a sheriff's writ": Ibid., 228.

121   "Dear Jim, have we a Democratic postmaster appointed at Newberry, South Carolina?": James A. Farley Papers, Library of Congress.

122   For Farley, it was "like a fantastic tale from the Arabian Nights": Farley, *Behind the Ballots*, 285.

122   Roosevelt also had to read a lot of mail: Jonathan Alter, *The Defining Moment: FDR's Hundred Days and the Triumph of Hope* (New York: Simon & Schuster, 2006), 220.

123   "By all means, authorize the stamp immediately before those ardent ladies reach the White House," Roosevelt joked: Brian C. Baur, *Franklin D. Roosevelt and the Stamps of the United States 1933–45* (Sidney, OH: Linn's Stamp News, 1993), 112.

123   he had a complete collection of "original Roosevelts": Farley, *Behind the Ballots*, 338.

124   "The summary, autocratic and dictatorial manner of canceling the air mail contracts without a hearing is worthy of fascism, Hitlerism or Sovietism at their best": Virginia Van Der Veer Hamilton, *Hugo Black: The Alabama Years* (Tuscaloosa: University of Alabama Press, 1982), 228.

124   "The continuation of deaths in the Army Air Corps must stop," he said: Arthur M. Schlesinger Jr., *The Age of Roosevelt*, vol. 2, *The Coming of the New Deal, 1933–1935* (Boston: Houghton Mifflin, 1958), 453.

124   Farley pointed out that the Post Office got a better deal; its yearly airmail costs fell from $19.4 million in 1933 to less than $8 million in 1934: Farley, *Behind the Ballots*, 268.

125   "I do not think that this should be continued, even if such sheets are regarded merely as samples and not available for postage in the regular way": Baur, *Franklin D. Roosevelt and the Stamps of the United States*, 73.

125   Farley had already given a sheet of Mother's Day stamps to William Wallace Atterbury, president of the Pennsylvania Railroad: Ralph L. Sloat, *Farley's Follies* (Federalsville, MD: Bureau Issues Association, 1979), 57.

125 "When that Mother's Day stamp came out, I think Mrs. Roosevelt got one of the sheets and another got loose": Ibid., 13.

126 "The real question at issue is not whether certain philatelists or stamp dealers have been injured, but whether Mr. Farley or any official of the United States has used his official position to show favors and bestow valuable gifts upon a special group of people": Ibid., 32.

126 "It was the biggest turnout since the opening day of Congress": Ibid., 30.

126 The *Washington Post* called it "the greatest stamp rush in history": Baur, *Franklin D. Roosevelt and the Stamps of the United States*, 77.

126 "To Hon. James A. Farley, Master Salesman of the World": Sloat, *Farley's Follies*, 101.

128 "As long as the critics felt that I should be purer than the pure Anthony Comstock in regard to souvenir stamps, I had no wish to disappoint them": Farley, *Behind the Ballots*, 263.

128 "The United States has become the stamp-collecting wonder of the world," wrote the *New York Times*: "Insatiable Is the Collector," *New York Times*, March 24, 1935.

129 "Hitler to the contrary notwithstanding, art can know no dictation": "Kent's Eskimo Letter," *Washington Post*, September 18, 1937.

130 "The mural is a picture which, to speak frankly, depicts a group of fat women, scantily clad, disporting themselves on a beach": Marlene Park and Gerald E. Markowitz, *Democratic Vistas: Post Offices and Public Art in the New Deal* (Philadelphia: Temple University Press, 1984), 25.

130 "The only trouble with the pictures is that they are so good they call for more of the same": Ibid., 27.

131 "I never knew anyone to take as much interest in the public buildings of the neighborhood as my husband": Eleanor Roosevelt, "My Day," May 31, 1938, http://www.gwu.edu/~erpapers/myday/displaydoc.cfm?_y=1938&_f=md054967.

131 "I think you'll find, my boy, they are exactly one inch across," he replied: Bernice L. Thomas, *The Stamp of FDR: New Deal Post Offices in the Hudson Valley* (Fleischmanns, NY: Purple Mountain Press, 2002), 59.

131 "We are seeking to follow the type of architecture which is good in the sense that it does not of necessity follow the whims of the moment": Franklin D. Roosevelt, "Address at the Dedication of the New Post Office in Rhinebeck, New York," May 1, 1939, http://www.presidency.ucsb.edu/ws/?pid=15756.

132 "Someone once asked me if I thought I had 50,000 friends," Farley said: S. J. Woolf, "Farley, 50, Tells How to Win Friends."

133 **"Jim Farley has done more favors and made more friends than any politician in American history":** Joseph Alsop and Robert Kintner, 'Farley and the Future," *Life*, September 19, 1930.

133 **"I've got as good a chance to be president as anybody in the world":** "Roosevelt or Farley in 1940? Jim Farley Goes to Sound Out the Country," *Life*, May 22, 1939.

133 **"This is going to be a huge job, but I feel sure it will be worth it," he wrote:** Daniel Scroop, *Mr. Democrat: Jim Farley, the New Deal and the Making of Modern American Politics* (Ann Arbor: University of Michigan Press, 2006), 162.

133 **"Jim, I don't want to run and I'm going to tell the convention":** James A. Farley, *Jim Farley's Story: The Roosevelt Years* (New York: McGraw-Hill Book Company, 1948), 249.

134 **"I should like to see any of you any time. . . . Only don't crowd in at the same time":** Remarks of Hon. James A. Farley to the officials and employees of the Post Office Department in farewell, August 30, 1940, U.S. Postal Service Library.

134 **"Let's get this straight. . . . I am the postmaster general, despite the fact that a lot of people think Jim Farley still has the job":** "Postal Employees Hear F. C. Walker; He Reminds 1,200 Here That He Is Postmaster General, Even If Few Believe It," *New York Times*, April 24, 1944.

134–35 **"They're mighty fine designs":** Baur, *Franklin D. Roosevelt and the Stamps of the United States*, 292.

135 **"It might tell those suffering victims in Europe that we are struggling for their own regeneration":** Ibid.

135 **"An air-mail sack weighs about 70 pounds," Walker said:** Everett Smith, "Walker Praises Mail as Morale Builder," *Christian Science Monitor*, September 24, 1942.

136 **"It seemed like it was the only way to stay out of trouble":** Nate Sullivan, "The 'Vargas Girl' Trials: The Struggle Between Esquire Magazine and the U.S. Post Office and the Appropriation of the Pin-Up as a Cultural Symbol" (thesis, University of Nebraska at Kearny, 2013).

136 **"sole dictator over the nation's reading matter":** Laurence Burd, "Lashes Walker 'I Am' Complex in Esquire Ban," *Chicago Daily Tribune*, January 1, 1944.

137 **"The design has to be as simple as possible," Roosevelt said:** Baur, *Franklin D. Roosevelt and the Stamps of the United States*, 319.

137 **"Yes," Roosevelt said, brightening. "I certainly did":** Ibid., 317.

138–39 **"Before man reaches the moon," Summerfield said, "mail will be delivered within hours from New York to California, to England, to India or to Australia by guided missile": "Missile Mail," U.S. Postal Service historian, July 2008, https://about.usps.com/who-we-are/postal-history/missile-mail.pdf.

Chapter 7

141 **In the fall of 1963, when people went to their local post office to purchase stamps, many encountered a wide-eyed, orange-faced figurine:** Smithsonian Postal Museum, "Flashing Across the Country: Mr. Zip and the ZIP Code Promotional Campaign," http://postalmuseum.si.edu/zipcodecampaign/p4.html.

141 **The acerbic Washington columnist Drew Pearson once received a letter addressed to "S.O.B., Washington":** J. Edward Day, *My Appointed Round: 929 Days as Postmaster General* (New York: Holt, Rinehart and Winston, 1965), 47.

142 **The Post Office wanted Mr. Zip to become as familiar as Smokey the Bear:** Smithsonian Postal Museum, "Flashing Across the Country: Mr. Zip and the Zip Code Promotional Campaign."

143 **"I'm tired of the image of the American Letter Carrier being held up for public ridicule":** Ibid.

143 **"Even if they're not using it, . . . they're talking about it":** Ibid.

144 **Harry Semrow, the postmaster of Chicago, was known in the city as "the world's happiest postmaster":** "Biggest 'Thank You' Party: Chicago Postmaster Hosts Night for 13,000 Workers," *Ebony*, February 1964.

144 **Some even called him "the swingingest postmaster we've ever had":** Ronald M. Chizever, "They're Wild About Harry Semrow," *Chicago Daily News*, May 8, 1964.

144 **A handsome six-foot-four conservatory-trained pianist:** Ibid.

144 **Semrow's Chicago post office was the largest mail processing facility in the world:** Charles Remsberg, "The Day the Mails Stopped," *Saturday Review*, December 17, 1966.

145 **"We were really in a bind," said Clairborne Bolton, Semrow's assistant director of operations:** Associated Press, "Zip Code Plays Santa Claus Part," December 22, 1964.

146 **"We had mail coming out of our ears," McGee lamented:** *The United States Postal Service: An American History*, 38.

146 **The magazine *Saturday Review* called it "the most incredible snarl in the mail movement since the inauguration of the U.S. postal system—and, in the view of some experts, a nightmarish preview of mail service horrors that lie ahead":** Remsberg, "The Day the Mails Stopped."

147 **"There's no doubt they slow things down," a union leader claimed:** Ibid.

147 "The conditions that produced chaos and the mail logjam are not confined to Chicago," O'Brien said. "We are trying to move our mail through facilities largely unchanged since the days of Jim Farley": *The United States Postal Service: An American History*, 38.

148 "Larry, Jack is a man of destiny": Lawrence F. O'Brien, *No Final Victories: A Life in Politics—From John F. Kennedy to Watergate* (Garden City, NY: Doubleday, 1974), 50.

148 *Time* magazine put him on the cover in September 1961, calling him "one of the most important of New Frontiersmen": "White House and Congress: Power, Patronage and Persuasion," *Time*, September 1, 1961.

149 "I need you more than you need me—and more than Jack Kennedy needed you": O'Brien, *No Final Victories*, 163.

149 "Well, what do you think about this?" Johnson told her. "Your brother's got two jobs now": Ibid., 201.

149 "I want you to meet your new boss, the postmaster general": Ibid., 203.

150 "Time is running out and trouble is spreading," *Fortune* wrote. A *Reader's Digest* article bore the headline, "Crisis in the Post Office." *U.S. News and World Report* asked, "Can Anything Be Done About U.S. Mail Service?": "A New Design for the Postal Service," Address by Postmaster General Lawrence F. O'Brien Before the Magazine Publishers Association and the American Society of Magazine Editors, April 3, 1967.

151 "If we had run the telephone system in this way, the carrier pigeon business would still have a great future, and I would sell my shares in AT&T—if I had any": Ibid.

152 "A.T.&T is a pure meritocracy, run by men who started at the bottom and worked up, step by step, winning the nod of many bosses along the way," *Time* magazine wrote: "The Bell Is Ringing," *Time*, May 29, 1964.

153 "How do I manage this operation? My friend, I don't manage it, I administer it": *Towards Postal Excellence: The Report of the President's Commission on Postal Organization*, June 1968.

153–54 "If I could, I'd make it a private enterprise and I would create a private corporation to run the postal service and the country would be better off financially," Kappel later said. "I can't get from here to there": Sarah F. Ryan, "Understanding Postal Privatization: Corporations, Unions and 'The Public Interest'" (thesis, Rutgers University, 1999).

154 Marvin Watson, the new postmaster general, told people that the Kappel Commission's plan was "going nowhere": Author interview with Kappel Commission staff member William Sullivan.

155 **"Mr. President," Blount said, "if you want to reform the Post Office, I'd be delighted to do it. If you want a postmaster general like the rest of them, I'm not interested":** Winton M. Blount, *Doing It My Way* (Lyme, CT: Greenwich Publishing Group, 1996), 96.

156 **"That son of a bitch takes away all the job opportunity Republicans have been crying for [for] a generation," said H. R. Gross, a Republican congressman from Iowa:** Ibid., 100.

156 **"We called together all of the Republicans in a private off-the-cuff discussion," says Paul Carlin, Blount's legislative aide:** interview with author.

157 **"Larry, why don't you stand here to my right?" Nixon said:** O'Brien, *No Final Victories*, 211.

157 **"The volume of mail continues to increase," Blount told a Senate committee:** Hearings Before the Committee on Post Office and Civil Service, United States Senate, 1969.

157 **"If we don't pass postal reform and get Blount out of town, he's going to kill us with those grits," complained one of Blount's guests:** Blount, *Doing It My Way*, 102.

157 **"He wouldn't budge on anything," Kappel later said:** David Whitman, "Selling the Reorganization of the Postal Service," Kennedy School of Government, 1984.

158 **Rademacher had attacked Blount's public relations campaign, calling it "one of the smoothest and most massive attempts at public brainwashing since the German glory days of Joseph Paul Goebbels":** "Hearings Before the Committee on Post Office and Civil Service, United States Senate, Ninety-First Congress" (Washington, DC: U.S. Government Printing Office, 1969), 800.

Chapter 8

159 **"We're expecting our first child. . . . Could you possibly take a day or two off so I could get some money?":** Author interview with James Rademacher.

160 **"That's how much they care about you if you treat them right," he says. "Not every carrier treats them right, of course, but the majority do":** Ibid.

161 **Years later, one of the union's press officers would describe Rademacher as "a modern-day Moses":** Joseph Young, "Postal Union Boss Called a 'Modern-Day Moses,'" *Washington Star*, April 5, 1971.

162 **"It has been suggested by the city carriers that we cast our lot with them," said one of their leaders:** Lester F. Miller, *The National Rural Letter Carriers Association: A Centennial Portrait* (Cherbo, 2003).

164 **"Congress suffers from a strange occupational ailment," the magazine wrote:** M. Brady Mikusko and F. John Miller, *Carriers in a Common Cause: A History*

of Letter Carriers and the NALC (Washington, DC: Research and Education Dept., National Association of Letter Carriers, 2014), 51.

165 **"Fifty million tired taxpayers have been hit in the mailbox with this ruling," protested Senator Alexander Wiley:** Laurence Burd, "Order for Mail Slash Called Pressure Move," *Chicago Daily Tribune*, April 20, 1950.

165 **"When we are angry (and we have had many occasions to be angry in recent years), we say so in no uncertain terms":** William C. Doherty, *Mailman, U.S.A.* (New York: David McKay Company, 1960), 209.

165 **"I suppose [segregation] has been debated endlessly in all democratic forms of government since long before the War Between the States or the Civil War," he said. "*It is just one of those things*":** Philip F. Rubio, *There's Always Work at the Post Office: African American Postal Workers and the Fight for Jobs, Justice, and Equality* (Chapel Hill: University of North Carolina Press, 2010).

166 **"Dear Mr. Baker, this is where I got the information to call him a sadist. I quoted Funk & Wagnall's. Yours very truly":** James Rademacher, Oral History, Walther P. Reuther Library of Labor and Urban Affairs, Wayne State University.

166 **"They just hated me," Rademacher laughs:** Ibid.

167 **"That's it," he said. "You don't want a union? Go . . . now . . . get out!":** Ibid.

168 **"Why then, there will be little old AT&T ready and willing, oh so willing, to pick up the pieces and inherit the entire communications complex of the United States of America":** *Evening Star*, July 25, 1969.

168 **"The time has come," Rademacher predicted, "when responsible union leaders can no longer control the troops":** "Postal Crisis Warning Given," *Washington Daily News*, June 10, 1969.

168 **The top salary of a letter carrier was $6,000—or the equivalent in today's dollars of $38,000 a year:** Mikusko and Miller, *Carriers in a Common Cause*, 66.

169 **So he sent carriers out after work in 400 cities to retrace their routes and deliver stamped postcards with the message: "SOS: Save our Service! Notify President Nixon right now to sign a pay bill":** Author interview with Rademacher.

169 **"We got your message," Colson said. "We'd like to discuss this with you. When can you come over?":** Rademacher, Oral History.

170 **"Cool it," he told them. "We're making progress":** Ibid.

170 **New York's Branch No. 36, the NALC's biggest branch, which represented 7,200 letter carriers in Manhattan and the Bronx:** Mikusko and Miller, *Carriers in a Common Cause*, 68.

171 **It was 1,555 in favor of a strike and 1,055 opposed:** "The Day the Mail Stopped," *Newsweek*, March 30, 1970.

171 **"Well, we voted," he declared, banging his gavel. "That's it. This is a democratic union":** Vincent Sombrotto, Oral History, Walther P. Reuther Library of Labor and Urban Affairs, Wayne State University.

171 **"Your brothers and sisters across the river in Brooklyn are with you 100 percent," Leventhal said. "We're shoulder to shoulder":** Ibid.

172 **"This is a letter carriers' strike," one yelled. "What I want to know is whether the clerks are going to cross our picket line":** Ibid.

172 **"But I'm sure as good union members, they will respect any picket line":** John Walsh and Garth Mangum, *Labor Struggle in the Post Office: From Selective Lobbying to Collective Bargaining* (Armonk, NY: M. E. Sharpe, 1992), 21.

172 **"What am I going to do?" Johnson asked:** Author interview with James Rademacher.

172 **"The Post Office will use every means in its command to punish, fine, and imprison leaders of the walkout," Blount warned:** Ibid.

173 **"Our members are so militant, so upset they will stay out 'til hell freezes over," said Henry S. Zych, president of the Chicago NALC branch:** "Mail Strike Here!" *Chicago Tribune*, March 21, 1970.

173 **"President Nixon comes face to face today with his most pressing domestic crisis in a showdown forced not by students, restless blacks, or the new left, but by the most solid and dependable corner of middle America—the mailman":** "The Politics of a Strike: Crisis Tied to Maneuvering over Postal Reform," *Washington Post*, March 22, 1970.

173 **"We'd like to meet with you as soon as possible to try to settle whatever the problem is," Shultz said:** Author interview with Rademacher.

174 **Some of its members waved signs that said, "Dump the Rat" and "Impeach Rat-emacher":** "The Day the Mail Stopped."

174 **"That's the greatest compliment they ever paid me":** Sombrotto, Oral History.

174 **"We're from the SDS":** Strikers Reject Young Radicals' Aid," *New York Times*, March 24, 1970.

175 **"I'm with you guys," another SDS member assured them. "You know, if we weren't spending all that money in Vietnam we could all get good salaries":** Ibid.

176 **"A modern economy is sustained by an endless flow of carefully directed paper," *Newsweek* observed:** "The Day the Mail Stopped."

176 **"It was all I could lug," Purcell said:** "How a Brokerage Firm Manages to Operate During Postal Tie-Up: Salesman Becomes a Courier; Brink's, Bank Wires Help; Some Dividends Are Delayed," *Wall Street Journal*, March 24, 1970.

176 **The Post Office told businessmen they could also entrust letters to the porters on Amtrak trains:** "Air of Confusion Reigns at Post Office Center," *New York Times*, March 21, 1970.

177 **"You can't do that!" the man shouted:** "The Day the Mail Stopped."

177 **"Yes, but this is different," the man said:** Ibid.

177 **"Get back to work," he commanded:** Ibid.

177 **"Essential services must be maintained," Nixon said:** "Emergency Cited: President Says Issue Is Survival of Rule, Based Upon Law," *New York Times*, March 24, 1970.

178 **"I'm a little embarrassed," admitted Arthur Solomon:** "Stamp Business Here Hurt, Too," *New York Times*, March 25, 1970.

178 **"We know that people are hired temporarily at Christmas time":** "The General and His Brief Campaign," *New York Times*, March 26, 1970.

178 **"We would exchange verses from *Don Quixote* and *Rime of the Ancient Mariner* and other classics":** Author interview with William Burrus.

178 **"I never expected to be doing this," he said:** "New York Mountain of Mail Attacked by 600 Servicemen," *New York Times*, March 24, 1970.

179 **"This is a letter carriers' strike," he said. "I'm not getting off TV":** Rademacher, Oral History.

180 **"We got eight percent in addition to six percent":** Author interview with Rademacher.

180 **"We are going to have chaos and it's going to be widespread in the postal system if we don't change the system," he warned:** "Blount Sees Walkout if Postal Reform Lags," *Washington Post*, April 28, 1970.

180 **"One of the first things that this administration, that is only two years old, wants to do is get out of the stranglehold that Congress has on us":** "Rademacher Urges Postal Reform Move," *Midland Daily News*, May 23, 1970.

181 **"I think what distinguishes the present Postmaster General is that he is probably the first who holds this office who instead of fighting to stay in the President's Cabinet has fought to get out," Nixon said:** Richard Nixon, "Remarks on Signing the Postal Reorganization Act," August 12, 1970, http://www.presidency.ucsb.edu/ws/?pid=2623.

Chapter 9

183 **In 1971, its managers presided over an organization with 728,911 employees and a $9 billion annual budget:** *Annual Report of the Postmaster General, July 1, 1970–June 30, 1971*, United States Postal Service.

183   **In 1971 it delivered 50 billion letters, which accounted for 57 percent of its total volume:** Ibid.

183   **These machines weren't as fast as the optical character readers, but they could process 36,000 letters an hour:** Edward Edelson, "How Science Will Speed Your Mail," *Popular Science*, March 1971.

184   **"These days, it seems, just about everybody has some personal horror story to tell about the U.S. Postal Service":** Irwin Ross, "What the Postal Service Can't Deliver," *Fortune*, 1973.

185   **Between 1971 and 1975, the postal service signed three collective bargaining agreements that raised the experienced postal worker's annual salary:** "Postal Pact Seen Costing $1 Billion Annual by 1978," *Wall Street Journal*, July 22, 1975.

185   **"I don't consider it generous," Filbey said. "It is the best the Postal Service could do under the present circumstance":** Ibid.

185–86   **"I thought it was a mistake when they made the change and put it into a separate agency way out of the cabinet," Farley said:** WCBS interview, May 29, 1975, U.S. Postal Service Library.

186   **"It is clear now that turning the United States Post Office into an autonomous public corporation in 1971 has failed to realize the hopes of its proponents":** "Delivering the Bad News," *New York Times*, April 21, 1977.

186   **"Consider a corporation whose volume is stagnating":** "Managing the Mail," *Washington Post*, April 25, 1977.

186   **Hillblom mocked their sit-ins, saying they would never achieve anything unless they adopted Mao Tse-tung's:** James D. Scurlock, *King Larry: The Life and Ruins of a Billionaire Genius* (New York: Scribner, 2012), 10.

187   **All they had between them was $500 in cash and a credit card:** Mary A. Fischer, "Where's Poppa?" *GQ*, August 1998.

188   **Hillblom flew to Hong Kong and hired Henry Litton:** Scurlock, *King Larry*, 52.

188   **The press agent invited Hong Kong's postmaster to debate Henry Litton at a posh downtown hotel:** Ibid.

188   **"They were thugs," says James Campbell, a former DHL attorney. "They were selling protection":** Author interview with Campbell.

189   **The U.S. Postal Service had issued new regulations in 1974, defining a letter broadly as "a message directed to a specific person or address and recorded in or on a tangible object":** James I. Campbell Jr., *The Rise of Global Delivery Services* (Washington, DC: J. Campbell Press, 2001), 20.

189   Smith's father suffered a heart attack in 1948, when Fred was four years old: Vance H. Trimble, *Overnight Success: Federal Express and Frederick Smith, Its Renegade Creator* (New York: Crown, 1993), 58–62.

189   As a boy, Smith suffered from Perthes' disease: Jennifer L. O'Shea, "10 Things You Didn't Know About Fred Smith," *U.S. New and World Report*, July 24, 2008.

190   Smith ultimately got around that by purchasing small, French-built Falcons: Roger Frock, *Changing How the World Does Business: FedEx's Incredible Journey to Success—The Inside Story* (San Francisco: Berrett-Koehler, 2006), 32.

191   "They needed service primarily in the northeast where they were having some problems getting mail moved rapidly on an overnight basis," says Roger Frock, a former Federal Express senior vice president: Author interview with Frock.

191   He was crushed when the planes arrived around midnight with only six items, including a birthday present Smith had purchased for an employee and a bag of dirty laundry: Trimble, *Overnight Success*, 152.

191   "You mean you took our last $5,000?" Roger Frock said. "How could you do that?": Frock, *Changing How the World Does Business*, 101.

191   But shortly after, he told his board that he was about to be indicted: Trimble, *Overnight Success*, 185.

192   Ten days later while he was behind the wheel of his 1972 blue Ford LTD, Smith struck and killed a 53-year-old handyman who was leaving a Memphis bar around midnight: Ibid., 186.

192   "There's just too much pressure, and I can't take it anymore," Smith said: Ibid., 191.

192   "I could really go for a beer right now," he said: Frock, *Changing How the World Does Business*, 149.

192   The district attorney in Memphis dropped the criminal charge against him: Trimble, *Overnight Success*, 206.

192   A Little Rock jury acquitted him of the forgery charges after Smith testified unabashedly that he had falsified the documents to save his company from going under: Ibid., 207.

193   "You don't know anything about this act," Smith snapped at him: Frock, *Changing How the World Does Business*.

193   "Two tours in Vietnam and a six-year struggle to turn a college paper and a flock of purple airplanes into an airline have streaked Fred Smith's hair with gray at the age of 34," the Associated Press wrote: "His Air Freight Line Success Beats Odds," *Chicago Tribune*, October 1, 1978.

194   "He was just charismatic," says John Zorack, a lobbyist: Author interview with Zorack.

194   **"Everybody saw Bolger as the guy who can fix things," says Michael Coughlin:** Author interview with Coughlin.

195   **"I'll resist, with every fiber of my being, any legislation to make it easier for private delivery systems to operate," he vowed:** "U.S. Postal Service: A Monopoly Trying to Beat the Competition," *Nation's Business*, May 1979.

195   **"There are some interests, including many good USPS customers, charging that the postal service is expanding its monopoly," Wilson said:** "Private Express Statutes Hearings Before the Subcommittee on Postal Operations and Services of the Committee on Post Office and Civil Service," U.S House of Representatives, 1978, 20.

197   **"At a time when we are battling inflation and trying to keep insurance affordable, it is absurd for the Postal Service to attempt to extend the monopoly to items that are not, in any ordinary popular sense, letters," said Philip Shaughnessy:** Ibid., 74.

197   **"Let me stop you here," he said. "You say you operate in Hong Kong and Singapore?":** Ibid., 201.

198   **"I had to laugh. We had a reception. Larry never wore anything but blue jeans and T-shirts":** Author interview with Zorack.

198   **the USPS charged an extra $5.60 for pickup:** "For Post Office Overnight Mail Service Is Absolutely Positively Not So Easy," *Wall Street Journal*, June 12, 1985.

199   **"When the kids in our marketing department talked to customers about the postal service, in general, they said, 'The sleepy old Post Office'":** Author interview with Frock.

199   **"We're just taking a commonly accepted attitude, such as the perception of postal workers, and having fun with it," Francis X. McGuire, a Federal Express spokesman, said:** Ernest Holsendolph, "A Postal Service Retort," *New York Times*, May 12, 1982.

199   **"Our strategy was, 'Let it die. Let it go,'" says John Nolan, a former deputy postmaster general:** Author interview with Nolan.

200   **"Private enterprise will get the mail delivered just as it did in the Old West," he argued:** "Reagan Official Urges End to Postal Service," Associated Press, August 28, 1985.

Chapter 10

202   **He had purchased several boxes of doughnuts for his coworkers on his way to work:** Michael H. Bigler, "Former Postman Remembers 'Fateful Day,'" *Edmond Sun*, April 19, 1987.

202 **"I'm going to get even, and everybody's going to know":** *Report of the United States Postal Service Commission on a Safe and Secure Workplace* (New York: National Center on Addiction and Substance Abuse at Columbia University, August 2000), 153.

203 **"He wanted to slaughter us all," Bigler would later say:** Tim Talley, "Survivors Recall 1st 'Postal' Massacre," Associated Press, August 19, 2006.

204 **the Edmond Post Office chose Sherrill over 22 other applicants because he was a veteran:** Ed Kelley, "Killer Quit City Post Office to Avoid Being Fired," *Newsweek*, February 20, 1987.

204 **"At 40,000 post offices across the United States, our flag flies at half staff," Tisch said:** "Oklahoma Town Conducts Memorial for Victims," Associated Press, August 25, 1986.

204 **"To those who understand what he went through as a carrier. No one will ever know how far he was pushed to do what he did":** Ibid.

204 **"These rules are set up to give them grounds for harassment," said Robert McLaughlin, a clerk in Des Moines:** "Right and Wrong Ways of the Postal Service," United Press International, December 12, 1980.

205 **"I've never forgotten this," Frank says in a telephone interview from his home in Carmel, California:** Author interview with Anthony Frank.

205 **"He was an incredible spokesperson for the Postal Service," says William Henderson, a regional manager in North Carolina at the time:** Author interview with Henderson.

206 **sold it to National Steel for $281 million in 1980:** Steven Greenhouse, "Slim, Profitable National Steel," *New York Times*, September 23, 1983.

206 **"I think of myself as a professional manager," he told *Fortune*:** Colin Leinster, "Can This Man Really Deliver?" *Fortune*, August 14, 1989.

206 **"People are hungry out in the field," Frank said:** Jacqueline Trescott, "The Man in the Postmaster's Hot Seat," *Washington Post*, December 18, 1989.

206 **The following day, he pleaded guilty to accepting kickbacks from a lobbying firm trying to win a $250 million contract for optical character readers for a Texas company:** "Wide Postal Probe Set in Wake of Fraud," Associated Press, June 4, 1986.

207 **"95 in 95!" Frank said:** Author interview with Michael Coughlin.

208 **"Vinnie was a piece of work," Frank says admiringly:** Author interview with Frank.

208 **"Biller always acted like he was still in the 1930s and his bosses were bashing him in the head":** Author interview with Coughlin.

209 **"I loved Garden City," she says wistfully. "Everybody knew each other. It was wonderful":** Interview with Jaclyn Peon.

209 **"They shuffled me away like an old piece of furniture":** Dana Priest and Judith Havemann, "U.S. Postal Service Mixes Technology with Antiquity," *Washington Post*, December 24, 1989.

210 **"He just stood there like a potted plant," Biller scoffed:** "Pushing the Envelope at the Post Office," *Businessweek*, November 24, 1991.

210 **"We did as good a job as we could in this calamity," Frank says:** Interview with Frank.

210 **"Obviously, this is a matter of great importance to me," he said:** Michael Granberry, "Postal Chief Scolds Critics Who Link Job Stress, Killings," *Los Angeles Times*, August 18, 1989.

211 **"You punks are all the same," he said:** *A Post Office Tragedy: The Shooting at Royal Oak*, Report of the Committee on Post Office and Civil Service, House of Representatives, Investigation into the Events of the Shooting on Thursday, November 14, 1991, at the U.S. Post Office at Royal Oak, Michigan.

211 **When a supervisor intervened, McIlvane told him, "Don't fuck with me":** Ibid.

212 **"He was a good letter carrier," Withers says. "I worked right next to him":** Interview with Charlie Withers.

212 **"Yeah, and I'll be seeing you too," McIlvane replied:** *A Post Office Tragedy*.

213 **"I'm not saying McIlvane is dangerous, but I don't want anybody to get hurt," Withers told him:** Ibid.

213 **"You better not turn your head or you will be dead—you fucking bitch," he told one woman:** Ibid.

213 **"If I lose the arbitration it will make Edmond, Oklahoma, look like a tea party," he told Paul Roznowski:** Ibid.

214 **"I think Mr. Harris came prepared to die," said Joel Trella, chief of the Bergen County, New Jersey, police department:** Robert Hanley, "4 Slain in 2 New Jersey Attacks and Former Postal Clerk Is Held," *New York Times*, October 11, 1991.

214 **"You know, McIlvane is going to lose and when he does, he'll kill you too," Carlisle told him:** Charlie Withers, *The Tainted Eagle: The Truth Behind the Tragedy* (Self-published, 2009), 81.

215 **"Is this because of the McIlvane thing?" Carlisle asked:** Charlie Withers, *The Tainted Eagle*, 18.

216 **"He's trying to get in my door now!" Presilla told the dispatchers:** *A Post Office Tragedy*.

216 **"I'm referring," he clarified, "to the chronic problems that had been reported concerning the management of the Royal Oak Facility":** *Divisional/ Regional Summary, Royal Oak Michigan Tragedy, November 14, 1991,* U.S. Postal Service, 3.

217 **"Let me be brutal," he said:** Bill Kole, "Shooting Aftermath: Postal Service to Review Backgrounds of All Workers," Associated Press, November 15, 1991.

217 **Frank called the ruling "dumb":** "Pushing the Envelope at the Post Office."

217 **The proportion of automatically processed letters was expected to reach 61 percent by the end of the year:** *Annual Report of the Postmaster General, Fiscal Year 1991,* U.S. Postal Service, 19.

218 **"The U.S. Postal Service has finally found a way to be responsive to the public," wrote the *Chicago Tribune*:** "A Young Elvis for the Ages," *Chicago Tribune,* June 8, 1992.

218 **"It was great," he recalls:** Author interview with Frank.

218 **"When you mandate that—and the disability can be mental as well as physical—in a tiny, tiny minority of cases you're going to have people slip through who are basically unbalanced people trained to kill":** Felicity Barringer, "Does Postal System Fuel Workers Anger?" *New York Times,* May 8, 1993.

219 **In 1993, the *St. Petersburg Times* came up with the term "going postal":** Karl Vick, "Violence at Work Tied to Loss of Esteem," *St. Petersburg Times,* December 17, 1993.

Chapter 11

221 **It rained nearly every day in the Chiloé Archipelago off the coast of southern Chile where Gene Johnson served as a U.S. Peace Corps volunteer in 1962:** Mike Petriella, *The Break Equation* (Charleston, SC: Advantage, 2011), 80.

221 **"I was the last political appointee because they switched to a quasi-public operation":** Author interview with Gene Johnson.

221 **"It took six minutes a page to send through the system," he says:** Ibid.

221 **In 1978, the USPS delivered 32 million Mailgrams, but that barely registered at an agency that transported 97 billion pieces of mail that year:** *Annual Report of the Postmaster General Fiscal 1978,* U.S. Postal Service, 24.

222 **a congressionally appointed commission . . . predicted that the USPS would lose 23 percent of its first-class mail by 1985:** *Report of the Commission on Postal Service,* vol. 1, April 1977.

222 **"Unless the Postal Service really makes a commitment, which it has not made, to electronic message transfer, they face a really bleak future," he warned:** "Postal Service Reform," *CQ Almanac 1977.*

222   It was called Electronic Computer Originated Mail, or E-COM for short: Patricia Koza, "Computers Are Going into Mail Business," United Press International, December 10, 1981.

222   "There was billions of billions of billions of pieces that . . . could be sent directly from the computer into the Postal Service . . . ," Johnson says: Author interview with Johnson.

222   Postmaster General William Bolger said the USPS could charge 15 cents for these messages: "Postal Service Is Beginning Tests of Electronic Mail Transmission," *New York Times*, November 22, 1978.

223   "I spent 20 days on the witness stand," Johnson recalls: Author interview with Johnson.

224   "This is your PERSONAL INVITATION to ATTEND the GREATEST AUTOMOTIVE INVENTORY REDUCTION SALE in the HISTORY OF MANASSAS": Michael Isikoff, "Critics Want to Stamp Out 'E-COM' Mail," *Washington Post*, December 4, 1983.

224   "A lot of people blamed it on the postal service, but it was really the Postal Rate Commission that screwed it up," says Johnson: Author interview with Johnson.

224   "Rightly or wrongly, I didn't spend much time on electronic mail," says former postmaster general Anthony Frank: Author interview with Frank.

225   "I'd rather give up my telephone than my e-mail," wrote *Newsday* technology columnist Josh Quittner: "Computers in the '90s: An Express Love Letter About E-Mail," *Newsday*, April 5, 1994.

225   he offered early buyouts to 30,000 middle managers. However, the unions demanded the same buyout for their members, and in the end, 47,828 employees departed: Bill McAllister, "Can Marvin Runyon Deliver?" *Washington Post*, July 10, 1994.

225–26   "We needed a surgeon and we got Freddy Kruger," said Vince Palladino, president of the National Association of Postal Supervisors: Ibid.

226   "It's impossible for me to see that this is anything but a crass commercial campaign that takes away from the higher purpose of the stamp program," said Kathleen Wunderley: Jeff Wilson, "Bugs Bunny, First Cartoon U.S. Postage Stamps, Gets Collectors Licking," Associated Press, May 23, 1997.

226   "It was pretty wild," Reisner recalls: Author interview with Robert Reisner.

226   "You know why we hired you, don't you?": Ibid.

227   "I don't think we're going to convince the net culture that we're cool": Stephen Lynch, "Postal Service Set to Make 'Snailmail' Cyber-Ready," *Orange County Register*, April 23, 1996.

227 **"It's like a pay phone," Reisner laments:** Author interview with Reisner.

228 **"I gave some speeches and talked about how the postal service has changed its technology many times":** Ibid.

228 **"The core technology was ours. We bloody well invented it":** Author interview with Cathy Rogerson.

228 **"This thing doesn't need reinventing," said Robert Setrakian, a USPS board member:** Bill McAllister, "Time for Clinton to Put His Stamp on the Postal Service," *Washington Post*, December 31, 1994.

228 **"It is at a crossroads with no signpost," he testified:** Hearings Before the Subcommittee on the Postal Service of the Committee on Government Reform and Oversight, House of Representatives, 1995.

229 **America Online, now known as AOL, had 13 million members in 1998:** Company press release, http://www.timewarner.com/newsroom/press-releases/1998/08/27/aol-surpasses-13-million-member-mark.

229 **"Silicon Valley had a pretty strong lobby," Reisner says:** Author interview with Reisner.

230 **"You're telling me that we shouldn't have spent $84 million trying to better understand a technology that is going to ultimately cannibalize our core products?" Reisner asks:** Author interview with Reisner.

230 **"He was very devoted":** Author interview with William Henderson.

231 **His address at the White House was 1600 Pennsylvania Avenue, Washington, DC 20500-0003. That would have made his e-mail bc20500000300@usps.com:** "E-Mail Going Postal? USPS to Test Electronic Service," Associated Press, August 1, 2000.

231 **"The U.S. Postal Service won't become the U.S. Portal Service," his office said:** Bob Woods, "Action on '.us' Delayed, as Is NTIA Reauthorization," *Newsbytes*, August 5, 1999.

231 **"We don't need a big, heavy, stifling competitor, subsidized by public funds, trying to compete in some of the most dynamic areas of our economy":** Frank James, "E-Commerce Giants Get Jittery over U.S. Postal Service," *Chicago Tribune*, November 8, 2000.

231 **"It was my belief that the monopoly was worthless," he says:** Author interview with Henderson.

232 **Deutsche Post purchased 51 percent of DHL ... (Two year later, Deutsche Post would spend $568 million for an additional 25 percent....):** "EU Approves Deutsche Post Buy," *Journal of Commerce*, October 22, 2002.

232 **"Well, we would have to ask our union friends," she said:** Author interview with Reisner.

232 **"We're putting this on the back burner," Gensler said:** Ibid.

232 **"I mean, I couldn't really remember [Clinton] ever calling me," Henderson says:** Author interview with Henderson.

232 **"I had gone to the White House," Henderson says. "I had talked to Congress. The customers weren't receptive either. They just wanted us to deliver mail":** Ibid.

233 **Potter told the board that two planes had hit the World Trade Center in New York:** Author interview with Patrick Donahoe.

234 **"It was Potter and Vince Sombrotto," says George Gould, the NALC's legislative director at the time:** Author interview with Gould.

234 **"I give Potter credit. He steered the institution through it":** Author interview with William Burrus.

234 **For every piece of first-class mail that vanished, the USPS needed three junk items to make up the difference:** "The End of Mail," *Bloomberg Businessweek*, May 30, 2011, http://www.bloomberg.com/bw/magazine/content/11_23/b4231060885070.htm.

235 **"I have one message today for the entire eBay community," Potter said:** Katie Hafner, "Postal Service Finds a Friend in the Internet," *New York Times*, August 2, 2006.

235 **the new law strictly limited the USPS's mission to "the delivery of letters, printed matter, or mailable packages":** Kevin R. Kosar, "The Postal Accountability and Enhancement Act: Overview and Issues for Congress," *Congressional Research Service*, December 14, 2009.

236 **"We're planning for the future right now," he said:** Leonard, *The End of Mail*.

236 **"I called Jack and said, 'Is this a good thing?'":** William Henderson remembers. Author interview with Henderson.

236 **Hallmark shuttered greeting card plants and shed employees:** Jennifer Peltz and Sarah Skidmore, "Even in Holiday Cards, a Message of Tough Times," Associated Press, December 19, 2008.

Chapter 12

237 **"He's a druggie," one woman complained. "It's outrageous that he's on a stamp":** Author interview with Anna Dyer.

239 **"Are you a fan of the Allman Brothers?":** Ibid.

240 **"You ought to take the postal test," he told Donahoe. "The pay is $4.76 an hour":** Author interview with Patrick Donahoe.

240   As he put it, he was "trying to get things organized in a world that's not terribly organized": Ibid.

240   "You had mail going all over the place for years!" Donahoe says: Ibid.

241   If we do no nothing, we face a future without the valuable services that the postal service provides," Carper said: Leonard, "The End of Mail."

242   "UPS and FedEx are doing just fine," he joked: Helene Cooper, "Obama Offers Reassurance on Plan to Overhaul Health Care," *New York Times*, August 11, 2009.

242   Now Obama remained silent, even though the White House quietly inserted language in its federal budget proposal absolving the USPS of all but $1.5 billion of that mandatory 2011 payment: Leonard, "The End of Mail."

243   "This morning, there were 10 inches of new snow," said Tanya Yerdon, the town supervisor: Author interview with Yerdon.

243   "We are adamantly opposed to it," said Dana Grubb, president of the local historical society: Charles Malinchak, "Residents Deliver Message to Postal Service: Don't Close Bethlehem Branch," *Morning Call*, October 14, 2011.

243   "We're not going to take this lying down," said Philip Lack: David Namanny, "Orchard Post Office May Be Closed," *Mitchell County Press News*, March 22, 2011.

244   "We ain't started carrying no picket signs or throwing rocks yet," he said. "Maybe in the future": Angela Greiling Keane, "Revolt in Virginia Hollow Complicates Postal Service Survival," *Bloomberg News*, October 13, 2011.

245   "Right now, 70% of Americans pay bills online," Donahoe said: Denise Jewel Gee, "Postal Chief Loudly Booed on Plan for 5-Day Delivery," *Buffalo News*, August 15, 2012.

245   He lamented that the USPS was "insolvent," that Congress was "deadlocked and dysfunctional . . . especially when it came to postal issues," and that the White House was "like a deer frozen in the headlights": Concluding Presentation of President Fredric V. Rolando on Behalf of the National Association of Letter Carriers, AFL-CIO, 2011 Negotiations.

245   "If we let nature take its course, we won't be fighting five-day delivery," Ronaldo warned: Ibid.

246   "The least-used delivery day is Tuesday, and mail builds up on Thursdays and Fridays," he said: Ibid.

246   "You are the ones [who] for 200 years have gone to every home in America six days a week tying this country together, building communities, making sure that everybody stays in touch, not skimming the cream off the top": Cheryl Makin, "Hundreds Rally to Keep 6 Days of Mail Delivery," *Asbury Park Press*, March 25, 2013.

246 **"Neither rain, nor snow, nor the postmaster general's misguided plan will stay these supporters from protecting six-day delivery":** Derek Quizon, "Postal Workers Picket, Rally Near Capitol Against 5-Day Delivery," *News and Observer*, March 24, 2013.

246 **"If they open the door here for eliminating one day, we're in trouble," he said:** Annie McCallum, "Postal Workers Protest End of Saturday Delivery," *Roanoke Times*, March 24, 2013.

247 **New Zealand announced it would move to three-day delivery in cities and five days in rural areas to avoid a financial crisis:** Nick Perry, "New Zealand Approves 3 Days a Week Mail Service," Associated Press, October 23, 2013.

247 **Canada said it would end home delivery in urban areas over the coming five years:** "Canada Post to Phase Out Urban Home Mail Delivery," *CBC News*, December 11, 2013.

247 **Australia Post asked its customers if they would be willing to pay the equivalent of $26 a year for five-day delivery:** "Australia Post Plan 'Harebrained': Union," *News 9*, January 21, 2014.

247 **"At the end of this year, we will only have 30 post offices left in Norway," said Norway Post's chief executive officer Dag Mejdell:** Author interview with Mejdell.

247 **Itella, the Finnish postal service, keeps a digital archive of its users' mail for seven years and helps them pay bills online securely:** Leonard, "The End of Mail."

248 **"Staples is open seven days a week, they're open nine o'clock at night," he said:** Author interview with Donahoe.

248 **"This is a direct assault on our jobs and on *public* postal services," he said:** Joe Davidson, "Staples' Selling Postal Products Without USPS Workers Stirs Fear of Privatization," *Washington Post*, January 17, 2014.

248 **"We talk to the White House people," he said:** Author interview with Donahoe.

249 **"There's a little saying that we have," Donahoe said:** Ibid.

249 **"We did this with the idea that we were going to have some non-traditional deliveries—evening deliveries, Sunday deliveries," says Jim Sauber, the NALC's chief of staff:** Author interview with Sauber.

249 **"We did get a rush of packages at the end, and our people came through," Donahoe said:** Laura Stevens, "The Secret Weapon at Christmas at the Post Office: Sundays," *Wall Street Journal*, February 7, 2014.

250 **David Vernon, an analyst at Bernstein Research who tracks the shipping industry, estimates that in 2014, the USPS handled 40 percent of Amazon's**

packages—almost 150 million—more than either UPS or FedEx: Devin Leonard, "It's Amazon's World. The USPS Just Delivers in It," *Bloomberg Businessweek*, July 30, 2015, http://www.bloomberg.com/news/articles/2015-07-30/it-s-amazon-s-world-the-usps-just-delivers-in-it.

250 "I never thought I would order groceries and have them delivered to my house, but people do it," Donahoe says. "It's amazing": Author interview with Donahoe.

251 "Nobody is really delivering letters anymore," Sapp says: Author interview with Shante Sapp.

251 Amazon warehouse employees in some cases make only $12 an hour: Robert Channick, "Amazon Hiring for Holidays; Online Retailer Adding 100,000 Temps, Including Hundreds at Its Joliet Factory," *Chicago Tribune*, October 21, 2015.

251 "Amazon will drop us in a heartbeat if they find a better way," says the NALC's Sauber: Author interview with Sauber.

253 "Who is he?" a senator asked: Author interview with U.S. Senator Thomas Carper.

254 "Today," she said, "Dr. Angelou receives the Postal Service's highest honor": "Postmaster General/CEO Megan Brennan, 'Maya Angelou' First-Day-of-Issue Ceremony," April 7, 2015, https://about.usps.com/news/speeches/2015/pr15_pmg0407.htm.

255 "The strength of the postal service": Bernie Sanders speech to APWU conference, October 14, 2015. http://www.apwu.org/news/web-news-article/bernie-sanders-addresses-apwu-conference

255 "The goals are laudable": Lisa Rein, "Bernie Sanders's Passion for the Prosaic—or Why the Post Office Is Part of What Makes America Great," *Washington Post*, November 9, 2015.

255 "Do I have to watch these?'" he asked her: Author interview with Megan Brennan.

Index